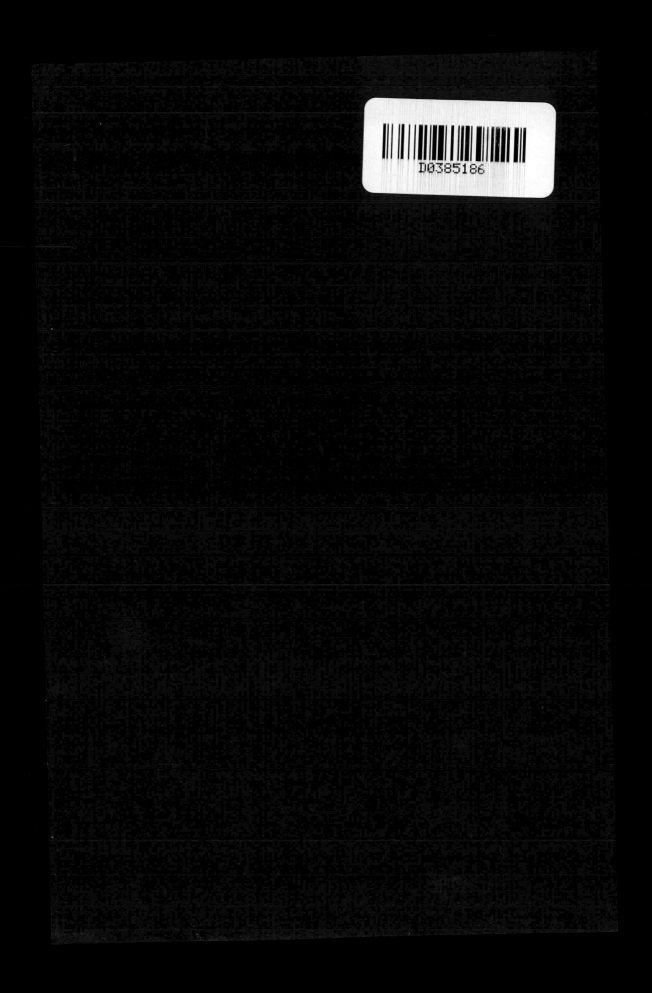

REVIEWS OF THIS BOOK

Unchained Eagle is the most exact blow-by-blow account yet written about events which changed our world and touched the lives of us all – the ending of the Cold War and the settlement of the 'German question' which has bedevilled Europe for centuries. *Unchained Eagle* gives us a ringside seat at the greatest drama of recent history.

Tom Heneghan is a consummate professional, a reporter's reporter. He writes lucidly and with forensic accuracy, lighting a path through the minefield of contradictions and prejudices that greeted the Germans' bid to re-unite as a nation and its stormy aftermath. He shows us how the building blocks of post-Cold War Europe were forged and pieced together – with a mixture of luck, judgement and the extraordinary zeitgeist of 1989.

He writes without fear or favour about the fate of nations, and the series of chances that helped the builders of the new Europe – Kohl and Gorbachev, Bush and Shevhardnadze, to achieve a historic and monumental change. Tom Heneghan unerringly portrays the German proteus, which changes with time and circumstance – from the diffident "late nation" in the shadow of its Hitlerian past to the provincial arriviste on the world stage, and the new would-be leader of a united Europe. He gives us an unbiased, clear-headed view of what at the time were all smoke, turmoil and uncertainty.

Unchained Eagle is both an accomplished piece of detective work, and a gripping account of the greatest story of our time.

William Horsley, BBC TV and Radio journalist

"Tom Heneghan has written a highly informative and very readable chapter in the history of contemporary Europe. He is uniquely qualified for the task, bringing to his subject just the right balance between familiarity and distance, sympathy and critical judgment. His excellent book is an unrivalled account of Germany in the 1990s."

Michael Mertes, Deputy Editor-in-chief, *Rheinischer Merkur*

"A fine book rich in information and solid judgment. Tom Heneghan's description and analysis reflect the reality of post-reunification Germany. The 'Berlin Republic' is a normal state, with its strengths and its scandals. This book challenges non-German readers to put aside their suspicions and see the country as it is."

Alfred Grosser, French political science professor, author of *Germany in Our Time: Deutschland in Europa*

"The keys to understanding some of the most important challenges ahead for Germany and Europe can be found in the decade and in the events Heneghan describes so well from the perspective of a passionate and well-informed journalist.

Heneghan's uncompromising analysis of reunificaiton's effect on eastern Germany gives a very valuable tool to understand the risks and problems involved in the enlargement of the European Union into Eastern Europe. The author provides readers with the historical, political and social framework needed to understand what is happening now and what will happen in the next few years. He goes well beyond that. With his own lively point of view shaping his perspective on events, he avoids falling into cliches.

As a correspondent reporting on Germany, I have found very useful information in this book. I regret not having been able to read a book like this before, because it would have helped me to be more accurate in my analysis of today's Germany. The issues treated in this book are by no means simply local events, since German politics affect all Europeans as well as the relationship of the continent with the world.

By sharing his experience and knowledge of Germany, Heneghan takes a stand against selective memory and against the tendency to transform this crucial period of history in lifeless cliches. He does not overwhelm the reader with a heavy dose of facts and figures. His views blend smoothly with the historical facts, figures and events needed to support his theses. Heneghan combines all this with human touches in a very readable manner."

Pilar Bonet, Berlin Correspondent, *El Pais*, author of *Figures in a Red Landscape*

"Tom Heneghan has a journalist's eye for detail and voice for telling a story. This history book by someone who lived the history is a pleasure to read."

Marjorie Miller, *Los Angeles Times*

"Putting the challenge of Germany's reunification into historical perspective is a daunting task. With his remarkable study *Unchained Eagle*, Tom Heneghan has succeeded in giving a fair and thorough analysis of an epochal change that has led to a new perception of Germany's role in the decade since the fall of the Berlin Wall. His first-hand account and brilliant interpretation of events up to Helmut Kohl's temporary fall from grace contribute to a better understanding of what makes Germany tick today."

Christian Müller, *Neue Zürcher Zeitung*

"What an opportunity Tom Heneghan had to observe and analyse at first hand the far-reaching changes that occurred in the heart of Europe between the fall of the Berlin Wall and the Kosovo war! How exciting they were, the years that *Unchained Eagle* describes!

The author has accomplished two feats: a chronicle of the news in the best traditions of agency journalism and a perceptive interpretation of daily events it describes.

Tom Heneghan brings an open mind to the complex and often enigmatic country called Germany. His confident curiosity guides him along the way. Heneghan's book stands out for its clarity, both in the details it chooses to highlight and the broad trends it identifies. For English-speaking readers, there is no better guide to the politics of Germany in the 1990s."

Joachim Fritz-Vannahme, Europe Correspondent, Die Zeit

"For anyone who wants to understand Europe's key country at the beginning of the 21st century, this is the book to read. Tom Heneghan avoids the cliches. He is sensible and fair in tracing the rise and fall of Helmut Kohl – and the new rise of Chancellor Gerhard Schroeder. He understands how Germany became normal – and he shows just why this achievement is so precious for a haunted land."

Elizabeth Pond, author of The Rebirth of Europe and Beyond the Wall

"As Head of the Reuters bureau from 1989 to 1997, Tom Heneghan covered day by day the major events and junctures that created the new unified Germany. This book encapsulates that experience, combining accurate and often little known detail garnered from his professional life with his personal ability to stand back and see the whole. It is written with clarity and humour. As such it is a must-read for those dealing with the new Germany in any professional capacity, and also for those wishing to understand Germany's role in the new Europe.

Tom Heneghan is that rare foreign journalist who managed to immerse himself in the details of political and social German life but yet write about it with admirable and critical distance."

Matt Marshall, San Jose Mercury News, author of *The Bank*, the *Birth of Europe's Central Bank* and the *Rebirth of Europe's Power*

"In his clear, direct style of the foreign journalist/observer, Heneghan demonstrates a differentiated, perceptive view of divided, united and disunited Germany as well as compassion for the emergence of the new Germany – from its 'brooding past' to a normal country."

Angelika Volle, Executive Editor, *Internationale Politik*

"This is an important book. Few people know Germany and Europe better than Tom Heneghan. The author uses his skills as reporter and analyst to guide the reader deep into the interior of the new Berlin Republic. I highly recommend this insightful report."

Lucas Delattre, Le Monde, co-author (with Guy Herzlich) of *Daniel Cohn-Bendit: Une Envie de Politique*

UNCHAINED EAGLE

UNCHAINED EAGLE

GERMANY AFTER THE WALL

TOM HENEGHAN

REUTERS

Published by **Pearson Education**
London/New York/San Francisco/Toronto/Sydney/Tokyo/Singapore
Hong Kong/Cape Town/Madrid/Paris/Milan/Munich/Amsterdam

PEARSON EDUCATION LIMITED

Head Office:
Edinburgh Gate
Harlow CM20 2JE
Tel: +44 (0)1279 623623
Fax: +44 (0)1279 431059

London Office:
128 Long Acre
London WC2E 9AN
Tel: +44 (0)20 7447 2000
Fax: +44 (0)20 7240 5771
Website: www.business-minds.com

....

First published in Great Britain in 2000

© Tom Heneghan 2000

The right of Tom Heneghan to be identified as Author
of this work has been asserted by him in accordance
with the Copyright, Designs and Patents Act 1988.

ISBN 0 273 65012 2

British Library Cataloguing in Publication Data
A CIP catalogue record for this book can be obtained from the British Library

10 9 8 7 6 5 4 3 2

Typeset by Pantek Arts, Maidstone, Kent
Printed and bound in Great Britain by Biddles Ltd, Guildford and King's Lynn.

The Publishers' policy is to use paper manufactured from sustained forests.

For Elisabeth, Patrick, Mark and Christopher

ABOUT THE AUTHOR

Tom Heneghan took up his posting as Reuters Chief Correspondent for Germany in the spring of 1989 and was on the spot when the Berlin Wall fell that autumn. Over the next eight years, he travelled around the country covering the events and issues that make this book and followed Helmut Kohl on foreign trips as far afield as Moscow, Tokyo and Denver. At the end of the NATO bombing campaign in 1999, he entered Kosovo with the Bundeswehr to report on the first German combat troops deployed abroad since World War Two.

Born in New York in 1951, Heneghan studied languages and international relations in New York, Boston and Göttingen, West Germany. Since joining Reuters as a trainee in 1977, he has held postings in London, Vienna, Geneva, Islamabad, Bangkok, Hong Kong, Bonn and Paris. Apart from his reporting for Reuters, he previously published work includes contributions to *Eastern Europe's Uncertain Future* (New York: Prager, 1977) and *EMU Explained* (London: Kogan Page, 1997) and articles in *The World Today*, *Europa-Archiv* and *Commonweal* and other US and German publications.

Heneghan is currently Senior Correspondent for France and lives in Paris with his wife, French journalist Elisabeth Auvillain, and their three sons.

CONTENTS

FOREWORD

THE DIVISION OF GERMANY HAS FASCINATED ME ever since I first saw the Berlin Wall in the summer of 1968. My high school study tour had just arrived from New York and the Wall was the first place we visited. The crude cinder-block barrier and barbed wire were a grim sight. Standing on an observation platform looking over into East Berlin, I tried in vain to imagine what it would be like to have a wall like that running through Times Square.

Three years later, when I was a student at Göttingen university in West Germany, the Iron Curtain was only a short drive away. It was a jagged gash splitting what would have otherwise been just pleasant rolling countryside. In the very few open talks I had on infrequent visits to the other side, I found East Germans to be friendly, well-informed and curious about the West. By contrast, West German students I knew ignored the East, revealing a mental border as interesting as the actual frontier itself.

My career with Reuters gradually took me across Europe and Asia, but I always wanted to return to Germany someday to see it with a correspondent's eye. The opportunity came in early 1989, when I was a news editor in exotic Hong Kong and West Germany seemed singularly boring by comparison. But there was a general election coming up in 1990 and Helmut Kohl's grip on power looked shaky. That might liven things up a bit, I thought as we settled into sleepy Bonn.

A few months later, I was in East Berlin and the Wall was wide open. As I fired off story after story throughout that night, I was overwhelmed by the feeling that anything could happen. The end of communism, the reunification of Germany, the dissolution of the Warsaw Pact and NATO – in a flash, it all seemed possible. The fact that all but the last option actually did come about shows how much depended on the ugly Wall that fell that night. Another by-product of the Wall's fall – the emergence of Helmut Kohl as Europe's leading statesman – seemed so unlikely that nobody thought of it then.

In the months and years that followed, there was much talk about all the other developments now possible. Germany could become more assertive, Germany might dominate Europe, German nationalism could revive, Germany might turn to the East – there were any number of theories based on the country's behaviour in the past. From a front row seat in Bonn, however, the picture looked quite different. If anything, the West Germans seemed to want as little change as possible. They were doing very nicely in their prosperous, pro-European, post-nationalist Federal Republic and didn't really want to rock the boat. On countless issues during and after reunification, what struck me most was their deep conservatism and reluctance to stand out again.

Helmut Kohl's party financing scandal has shown the world the local politician we journalists often saw in Bonn. Europe's towering statesman could look quite different at home as he dithered on important issues or calculated his options through the prism of petty rivalries and local election schedules. Although his slush funds were not known about at the time, they fitted into the pattern of the machine politician determined to keep a tight grip on his power base.

During my eight years in Germany, spanning episodes from Mikhail Gorbachev's triumphant visit to Theo Waigel's failed bid to snatch Bundesbank gold, I covered most of the main events and issues dealt with in this book. This included travelling all around the country and reporting on Kohl in Bonn, at party congresses, on the campaign trail and on foreign trips as far away as Moscow, Tokyo and Denver. After moving to Paris in 1997, I returned for Gerhard Schröder's election the following year. In June 1999, when the NATO bombing of Yugoslavia had ended, I rode into Prizren with the German army to report on the liberation of Kosovo. That mission was a fitting way for Germany to crown a confused decade as it struggled to adjust to its new role in the world.

Most uncredited material in this book is based on my reporting or Reuters dispatches available in our vast database now known as Factiva. Full texts of many speeches can be downloaded from Web sites run by the Bundestag (**www.bundestag.de**) or the government (**www.bundesregierung.de**). I have tried to limit footnotes to essential sources or material of my own not fully used in Reuters copy.

A final note on two terms used in this book. *Ossi* and *Wessi* are such common and useful shorthand for east and west Germans that it is hard to do without them. Some Germans say they are derogatory, others find them simply the best way to express the continuing differences between easterners and westerners. I use them with affection for both.

ACKNOWLEDGEMENTS

SINCE SO MUCH OF NEWS AGENCY WORK IS TEAMWORK, this list of thanks must start with a word of appreciation for the whole Reuters team in Germany during my time there and the London desks and outside staffers who helped us out. We could not have covered this story so thoroughly without the high professional standards and commitment they brought to the job.

Special thanks for their support go to my various editors and deputies in Germany during that time: editors for Germany Annette von Broecker and Wolfgang Wähner-Schmidt, Frankfurt bureau chiefs Anthony Williams and Janet Northcote and Bonn deputies Richard Murphy and Michael Shields. Also thanks to the German service editor Peter Rall and his deputies Peter Ehrlich and Christian Burckhardt and, in East Berlin, Martin Nesirky and Erdmute Greis-Behrendt.

It is impossible to mention every person who helped with interviews, criticisms, suggestions and arguments that helped deepen my understanding of Germany. There were many diplomats and officials who asked to remain anonymous then and will remain so now. But I would like to thank by name: Deborah Cole, Udo Cordts, Hans-Joachim Falenski, Wolfgang Gibowski, Alfred Grosser, Susanne Höll, Josef Joffe, Chong-Sook Kang, Thomas Kielinger, Ewald König, Karl Lamers, Matt Marshall, Marianne Möck and Gerd Schmidt-Möck, Dominique Moïsi, Christian Müller, Herbert Müller, Loraine Nesirky, Cem Özdemir, William Pfaff, Norbert Prill, Jens Reich, Rolf Reissig, Axel Sauder, Reinhard Schwarzer, Fritz Stern, Wolfgang Templin, Eugene Tuttle, Bettina Vestring, Angelika Volle and Monika Zimmermann. Special thanks go to Michael Mertes for his tireless energy in explaining policies and offering ideas.

I am very grateful to friends who read parts of the manuscript: Crispian Balmer, Alex Ferguson, Mark Heinrich, Erik Kirschbaum, Richard

Murphy and Paul Taylor. Here I owe a special debt of gratitude to Don Larrimore for supporting the project from the start and editing the manuscript through its various stages. They all offered useful insights and suggestions that have greatly helped the finished book; any mistakes are my own responsibility.

The biggest thanks of all go to my wife Elisabeth, who supported this project when it seemed it might never come to an end and offered the best editorial guidance throughout. I could not have written it without her.

Tom Heneghan
Paris
July 2000

1

TO THE BERLIN REPUBLIC

AT THE END OF A TUMULTUOUS TWENTIETH CENTURY, the German government moved back to the city that symbolised the nation's greatest triumphs and defeats: Berlin. The name of the chaotic metropolis echoed with all the contrasts the troubled country had seen over the past hundred years. The kaisers and Prussian militarism ... the Roaring Twenties ... Hitler and his Nazi marches ... the Holocaust ... the total defeat of 1945 ... the divided island in the communist sea ... the Wall and its fall. Even the frenetic building boom of the 1990s could not erase the memory of what had gone before. Like no other city, Berlin recalled the last time Germany was a big power. With the country reunited and a major power once again, the government had abandoned the modest western capital Bonn in the summer of 1999 for the brash Prussian city in the east. It was a step full of hope and uncertainty.

> ❝ It was Berlin's dynamism that appealed so much to the city's supporters. The new and more self-assured Germany, they felt, needed a capital worthy of its size and influence ❞

Like Berlin itself, reactions to the move were schizophrenic. The city's critics feared a return to the centralisation and power that had brought the country to ruin in two world wars. With 3.5 million inhabitants, twice as large as its nearest rival Hamburg, Berlin was unlike any other city in Germany. It was in the same league as London, New York, Paris and Tokyo – an ominous thought for Germans who wanted their country to keep a low profile. But it was Berlin's dynamism that appealed so much to the city's supporters. The new and more self-assured Germany, they felt, needed a capital worthy of its size and influence. Only in Berlin could Germany find the daily clashes – between past and present, between east and west, between tradition and innovation – that would drive it forward in the new century. Located midway between Paris and Moscow, Berlin stood to become the metropolis at the heart of the new united Europe.

The architecture of the new capital seemed to send out conflicting signals. At Potsdamer Platz, once the bustling heart of Berlin, sleek corporate towers gave the impression that Europe's leading economy was erecting a futuristic Manhattan on the Spree. Just down the road, the Finance Ministry settled into the foreboding building built in the 1930s for Hermann Göring's Aviation Ministry. The Foreign Ministry moved into a cold squat building with endless corridors and a double past: first it was the Reichsbank, the Third Reich central bank that stored plundered gold in its vaults, and then it housed the central committee of the East German communist party. In a city weighed down by symbols, the Reichstag was the most ambiguous of them all. The massive exterior exuded the pomp of the imperial age. In place of the old cupola destroyed in the war, an incongruous glass dome now rose over the roof. The city seemed to be forgetting its past, then remembering it and then trying to blur the difference. Would Germany do the same?

> 66 Located midway between Paris and Moscow, Berlin stood to become the metropolis at the heart of the new united Europe 99

The move coincided with a change of generation in politics. The "Berlin Republic", as they called this new Germany, represented a new start for the most influential nation-state in the middle of Europe. The Third Reich and World War II, the defining events for the "Bonn Republic" in the west, were starting to recede into history. Chancellor Gerhard Schröder and Foreign Minister Joschka Fischer were the Federal Republic's first leaders with no personal memory of the war. The starting point for their political awareness was the protest wave of 1968, not the defeat of 1945. The Social Democratic chancellor was a former student leader who had worked his way up the political ladder to become the pro-business state premier in Lower Saxony. His deputy was an erstwhile radical who had fought the police in Frankfurt, used to drive a taxi to pay the rent and who had eventually emerged as the leading voice in the ecologist Greens party. Now in their fifties, these leaders had the self-assurance of a generation that had known only the prosperity of West Germany. They could make a new start. Germany was reunited and sovereign, the veteran Chancellor Helmut Kohl had been voted out and sleepy Bonn was behind them. Would the German eagle start to soar now that it was completely unchained?

KOHL'S LEGACY

Schröder tackled the question when he addressed the opening session of the renovated Reichstag in April, even before the government had arrived. "The move to Berlin is certainly a return to German history, to the place where two German dictatorships ruled and brought great suffering to people in Germany and Europe," he said in the plenary hall, as daylight poured in through the vaulted skylight above. "But making 'Reichstag' the equivalent of 'Reich' would be as foolish as mixing up Berlin with Prussian glory or German centralism ... We're not going from Bonn to Berlin because we failed in Bonn. The successful Bonn democracy, the policy of seeking agreement with our neighbours, Germany's firm anchoring in Europe and the Atlantic Alliance and the attraction of a life in freedom have all made it possible to have a 'Berlin Republic' in united Germany. Regardless of how one interprets this concept, we will naturally remain the Federal Republic of Germany in Berlin."

The crisp northern accent and straightforward style were unmistakably Schröder. The Reichstag and the vast building site surrounding it were the very symbols of renewal and change. Yet the chancellor's words sounded reassuringly familiar. They had the ring of something the deputies had heard hundreds of times before. They sounded like ... Helmut Kohl. The Berlin Republic (a term Kohl never liked) would bear his unmistakable mark. More than anyone else, he had been the architect behind the reunification, closer integration with Europe, the refurbished Reichstag and even the sense of normality that surrounded it. Regardless of the changes in style, the Berlin Republic would be the institutional sequel to Bonn.

Bonn's longest-serving chancellor also helped shape the Berlin Republic in a way he never intended. The party financing scandal that erupted late in 1999, ending his career in disgrace, also cracked a central pillar of the old Bonn Republic. The political machine that he had built up through a tangle of favours, jobs and slush funds reached deep into the ranks of his Christian Democratic Union (CDU). This network was a relic of the Cold

War, when business bankrolled centre-right parties to keep the left at bay, and it long afforded the CDU a crucial advantage over the fractious Social Democrats (SPD). By doggedly refusing to admit he broke party financing laws, Kohl discredited a generation of CDU leaders that he himself had promoted, and badly weakened the conservative bloc that had dominated the Bonn Republic. Politics in the Berlin Republic would be more transparent and media-oriented, more along the lines of the American-style "television democracy" that Schröder operated in so well. The political geography could shift, with centrists looking beyond the CDU, and right-wingers flirting with the extremist fringe. In a country so wary of change, Kohl accelerated the transition to the Berlin Republic by showing the shadier sides of politics in Bonn.

> 66 For all his shortcomings when it came to the details of politics, Kohl got the big issues right 99

For all his shortcomings when it came to the details of politics, however, Kohl – to his lasting credit – got the big issues right. His rush to unity solved the "German question" dividing Europe, thereby avoiding the instability in the heart of the continent that a lingering eastern state would have caused. He kept Germany firmly rooted in the European Union and NATO, two institutions that anchored his country in the successful democratic west. And he agreed to blunt Germany's potentially dangerous dominance by integrating it more deeply into a Europe with a single currency. His wheeling and dealing in local politics had given him an instinctive appreciation of the crucial role a support network could play. His CDU system, built on people and money, collapsed when its central figure stumbled, but the network Kohl spun for the Berlin Republic was built on institutions that would survive long after he had left the scene.

FEARS FOR REUNIFICATION

It was not obvious, back when the whole adventure began, that reunited Germany would turn out this way. Nobody knew whether German nationalism would resurge once the country was fully sovereign again. Bonn had close ties with Moscow – would it cave in to a Soviet demand for neutrality in exchange for reunification? The 80-million-strong reunited state threatened to upset the delicate balance in the European Union, where, before 1990, the main states – Britain, France, Italy and West Germany – had roughly the same population of 50 million to 60 million. Furthermore, the man destined to lead the new state was not exactly a statesman or diplomat. Kohl was better known as an amiable provincial politician prone to gaffes and little scandals. Could he be trusted to lead the way through the biggest upheaval in Germany since the war?

Consider, for example, some of the horrendous visions that thankfully did not become reality. Conor Cruise O'Brien, a former editor of *The Observer*, published a shrill warning entitled "Beware, the Reich is Reviving" two weeks before the Wall fell. "We are on the road to the Fourth Reich: a pan-Germanic entity, commanding the full allegiance of German nationalists," he wrote. "Reunification will be celebrated with an explosion of nationalist enthusiasm, and a rejection of everything thought to have been imposed in Germany: the Democratic Republic along with West Germany; NATO along with the Warsaw Pact."

O'Brien saw nationalist thinkers cleansing the Third Reich's image. "I can see some of the consequences: expulsion of Jews, breaking off of relations with Israel, a military mission to the PLO; a statue of Hitler in every town … I fear that the Fourth Reich, if it comes, will have a natural tendency to resemble its predecessor."[1] O'Brien soon regretted rushing into print with such an apocalyptic vision.

In the United States, *New York Times* columnist William Safire saw the reunited state quickly making up for lost time in the military sphere. "Germany, tired of apologetics, will stare down its own Greens and become a nuclear power with Star Wars rocketry making it an Überpower before the turn of the millennium," he wrote four days after the Wall fell. On another front, he predicted, "Economic crisis will be transferred to Turkey as West Germany absorbs its Eastern German unskilled workers and sends back the legions of Turkish workers."[2]

Only two days after telling journalists in Bonn that he was not afraid of reunification, French President François Mitterrand remarked in private, "A reunited Germany would represent a double danger for Europe. By its power. And because it would create pressure for alliance between Britain, France and the Soviet Union. That would mean certain war in the 21st century. We must create Europe very quickly to defuse German reunification."[3]

In a calmer but equally gloomy analysis, *Washington Post* columnist Charles Krauthammer wrote in March 1990 that the pending merger would stop Europe's advance towards further integration. "German reunification challenges the idea and derails the process … It will reverse one of the most salutary European developments of the last fifty years: the decline of sovereignty … It derails a process by which Europe was hoping to make itself safe from itself. We return instead to the old Europe, balance of power Europe, the Europe that produces more history than it can consume."[4]

Also in March, British Prime Minister Margaret Thatcher invited six leading British and American experts on Germany to her country residence, Chequers, for an off-the-record discussion about the reuniting nation. A memorandum on the meeting listed some unflattering traits the group identified as "an abiding part of the German character: in alphabetical order, *Angst*, aggressiveness, assertiveness, bullying, egotism, inferiority complex, sentimentality". The experts had no serious misgivings about Kohl's leadership. "But what about ten, fifteen or twenty years from now?" the memorandum asked. "Could some of the unhappy characteristics of the past re-emerge with just as destructive consequences?"[5]

Life is lived forwards but understood backwards. In 1989 and 1990, when the pages of history were turning faster every week, politicians, diplomats, academics and journalists naturally consulted earlier chapters to find patterns to explain it all. Twentieth-century Germany presented them with, as Krauthammer might say, "more historical parallels than they could consume". But for a correspondent living in Bonn at the time, several popular parallels that looked back to before 1945 hardly seemed to apply any more. The Bonn Republic was the most democratic, prosperous and peaceful state that ever existed on German soil. The number of eastern Europeans and other would-be immigrants clamouring to get in – what British historian Timothy Garton Ash called the "Statue of Liberty" factor – was running into the hundreds of thousands a year. East Germans were mustering the rare virtue of civic courage to challenge their communist leaders. Four decades after the war, the two countries had developed separate political cultures that defined their options better than traditions from the earlier united past. Their head-over-heels merger needed to be handled carefully, but the trends pointed in the right direction.

> 66 Many Germans feared that reunification would revive an aggressive streak they had suppressed for so long 99

The underlying assumption of the worried analyses was that Germany would forget its recent successes and repeat its earlier mistakes; that, divorced from time and space, a supposed national character would drive it into actions dangerous for Germany's neighbours. Sceptical foreigners were not the only ones to think this. Many Germans feared that reunification would revive an aggressive streak they had suppressed for so long.

This apparently understandable caution overlooked how much Europe had changed since 1945. The Federal Republic was the West's model post-war success story. In its twilight years, it was so well-off and contented that sociologists used terms such as "post-nationalist" and "post-modern" to describe it. Would Bonn, where *Stabilität über alles* (stability over all) was the watchword, really gamble this away? Reunification presented an opportunity that Bonn would seize, but it would change as little of its own system as possible.

"ALL POLITICS IS LOCAL"

In trying to understand Germany's motives, one also had to weigh Bonn's options as a whole. "I often hear foreigners say what they would do if they had Germany's wealth, its size or its population," a senior German diplomat once remarked to me. "I never hear them say what they would do if they had Germany's past." The Bonn Republic was founded as a conscious rejection of that past. Reunited Germany"s leadership class, including the easterners, came of age politically through learning about the mistakes made in those years. There were critics of some aspects of Bonn's firmly pro-Western policies – the easterners were notably uneasy about joining NATO – but the overwhelming majority of voters wanted them to continue. Only a tiny minority – the three per cent or so hard core that voted for the extreme right – rejected outright the pro-Western and pro-European policies that all Bonn governments had followed.

When analysing decision-making in Kohl's Bonn, one of the most useful guides is the motto of the late US House of Representatives speaker Tip O'Neill: "All politics is local." Ideals and interests exist cheek-by-jowl in any political system, especially in a democracy. A federation such as Germany, where frequent state and local elections act like a running referendum on the national parties, can amplify the pressures on a national government. In Kohl's political world, where even small pressure groups had to be cultivated if the whole machine was to work smoothly, local interests sometimes had to take precedence over national or even international considerations. There was always another election coming up somewhere, always another vested interest he did not want to alienate. All Helmut Schmidt's brilliant speeches, fluent English and international reputation could not save his chancellorship when he was abandoned, first by rebellious young Social Democrats and then by his own coalition partners. To avoid his predecessor's mistake, Kohl put his power base first and worried about his image later. It sometimes confounded his partners abroad, but it made sense at the grass roots. The fact that he maintained illegal slush funds long after his name had gone down in the history books spoke volumes about how local a politician Kohl could be.

Indeed, it is hard to understand Germany in the 1990s without taking a close look at the two faces of Helmut Kohl. His sure-footed leadership during reunification made the chancellor a monument to his own achievements. This towering reputation and his political skills then helped make him the leader of European unity. Behind the monument, though, Kohl's leadership was more often weak than strong. He spent his first seven years in office being ridiculed in the press as a bumbling provincial. He was so dogged by scandals, including an earlier party funding affair he just barely scraped out of, that CDU rivals almost staged a palace coup against him only months before the Wall fell. He often wavered or ducked a decision, but he never gave up. Whether at a regional CDU rally or a Group of Seven summit, he used his relaxed charm, loyalty, stubbornness and tactical cunning to spin a web of contacts and friendships. He was such a master back-slapper that journalists covering him never seriously thought he needed a slush fund to buy the support he enjoyed.

Kohl, who was 59 when the Wall fell, was a towering figure standing 1.93 m (6′ 4″) tall and weighing in at around 115 kg (254 lb). In a nation of worriers, his self-confidence was an inspiration to the CDU party faithful. He had a way of sitting out problems until they lost their sting. The chancellor came across badly where Germans saw him the most, on television, but could easily win over small groups with his hearty laugh, endless stories and insatiable appetite. Despite all his political skills, he had the body language of a spoiled child. His fleshy face flared red when he was angry and beamed when he got his

> ❝ Kohl was such a master back-slapper that journalists never seriously thought he needed a slush fund to buy support ❞

way. Challengers within the CDU were banished to the political wilderness, often ruthlessly. Abroad, where he could not choose the leaders he dealt with, he oscillated between showing respect to the likes of George Bush or François Mitterrand and offering paternalistic cooperation to Boris Yeltsin or the heads of smaller European Union countries. Someone like British Prime Minister Margaret Thatcher, who had a will to match his own and disagreed with him regularly, flustered and frustrated him.

Helmut Kohl's most fervent political wish was to make Germany a normal country again. It should not forget its past, but it should not be paralysed by it either. As a major power, it should be neither domineering nor dominated. After making enemies across Europe in the first half of the century, Germany would be "encircled by friends" at the end. Kohl's greatest achievements (and some of his worst gaffes) stemmed from this desire for Germany to be normal again. European unity, the most consistent goal throughout his career, was the best way to ensure that Germany found a secure place among its neighbours and stayed there. If a single European currency would further this cause, then even the mighty deutschemark could be sacrificed for it. Reunification was not so much an active goal of his career as a result of it, a normal step for a divided nation to take when the walls separating it fell down. Seasoned politician that he was, he left most other issues up to the daily course of legislative give-and-take.

For all his leadership skills, however, Kohl was remarkably indecisive when it came to other important issues facing the reunited state. From a front-row seat in Bonn, a marvellously open capital where the slush fund secret was one of the few that was kept under wraps for any length of time, journalists could see him duck the issues as often as he tackled them. Once reunification was achieved and the decade wore on, Europe was all that seemed to really interest him. By the time the 1998 election came around, Kohl had hardly anything but history to offer voters as his platform. He had succeeded on the biggest issues and run out of steam on the rest. It was time for another generation to take over.

NOTES

1 See *The Times*, 31 October 1989.

2 Quoted in *The Washington Post*, 7 November 1999.

3 Note dated 5 November 1989 in Attali, Jacques (1995) *Verbatim III 1988–1991*. Paris: Fayard, page 333.

4 See Krauthammer, Charles (1990) "The German Revival" *The New Republic*, 26 March.

5 See *Independent on Sunday*, 15 July 1990.

SHEDDING THE POST-WAR CHAINS

2

BEFORE THE FALL

THE RED CARPET WAS ROLLED OUT AT THE CHANCELLERY IN BONN. The honour guard stood at attention just as it did for the arrival of every other visiting head of state. Slight changes in protocol showed this was not a normal foreign visit, however. Foreign Minister Hans-Dietrich Genscher was absent. The escort had fewer motorcycle outriders than usual. All 16 flags carried the black, red and gold German stripes, but every other one also bore a hammer and compass emblem. Erich Honecker, the Saarland coal miner's son who built the Berlin Wall, was coming for his first visit to West Germany on 7 September 1987. After 16 years at the head of communist East Germany, he was finally being recognised as an equal. After this, he could expect to visit Paris, London and Washington, the capitals of the countries that guaranteed Bonn's security. What better way to show the world that Germany was irrevocably divided?

Honecker beamed in quiet triumph as he and an awkward-looking Chancellor Helmut Kohl stood for their national anthems. When photographers begged them to shake hands for the cameras, Kohl brushed them off and whisked his guest into the chancellery. A "grip and grin" photo could make him look too friendly towards the communist, especially in the eyes of right-wingers in his party.

Although Honecker's visit would further cement the division of Germany, few dissenting voices were heard. A handful of demonstrators turned up outside the chancellery gates carrying a banner reading *"Deutschland, einig Vaterland"*, ("Germany, united fatherland").[1] But the slogan sounded hollow, seemingly as empty as Ronald Reagan's challenge in Berlin that year for Moscow to "tear down this Wall". This was the era of detente. Europe was divided into two blocs and practical politics dictated peaceful coexistence, not the settling of old accounts. Nobody understood this better than the West Germans, especially after Willy Brandt launched his *Ostpolitik* on becoming chancellor in 1969. Tensions with the Soviet bloc eased, new markets for West German industry opened and contacts between East and West Germans increased. This was so successful that Kohl continued it almost unchanged after he took office in 1982.

> 66 The two Germanys have come to accept the status quo … a divided Germany has become part of the furniture 99

This was the West Germans' dilemma. It was harder and harder to pay lip service to what critics called the *Lebenslüge* (living lie) of reunification. Bonn's constitution set unity as a national goal. But the longer the division lasted, the further away this end seemed to be. Wolfgang Schäuble, Kohl's main aide dealing with East Germany, put it bluntly just before the visit, "Reunification is completely beyond reality."

Bonn's partners watched the visit closely, but without much concern. The *New York Times* noted that Honecker's trip would have been unthinkable a few years earlier. "Now the visit, while historic, seems perfectly natural," it wrote. "After decades of political conflict the two Germanys have come to accept the status quo … a divided Germany, like the Atlantic Alliance, has become part of the furniture."[2] *Part of the furniture? Perfectly natural?* Phrases like these cause post-unity readers to do a double take. But this was the conventional wisdom of the time.

THE DISUNITED PAST

Disunity was the natural state of affairs for Germans until fairly recently in their history. From 962 to 1806, the centre of Europe belonged to an unwieldy construct nostalgically called the Holy Roman Empire of the German Nation. This empire, which encompassed up to 300 kingdoms and principalities, from the Netherlands to Croatia and from Burgundy to Poland, was seriously weakened by the Thirty Years War. From 1648 on, Prussia and Austria jockeyed for influence. Smaller kingdoms such as Bavaria or Saxony became regional power centres. This proliferation of small states held sway while European nations such as Britain, France and Spain consolidated their centrally ruled states and expanded abroad.

The Germans had to wait for their nation-state until 1871, when Prussia's Iron Chancellor Otto von Bismarck forged the first Reich. This militaristic "delayed nation" gave way at the end of World War I to the Weimar Republic, the first full democracy in Germany. But that disappeared in 1933 when Adolf Hitler became chancellor and founded his Nazi dictatorship. By the time the Third Reich collapsed in 1945, Germans had grown quite used to living in a large united state. From that point on, many also concluded this was not the best way to ensure democracy.

The wartime allies – the United States, Soviet Union, Britain and France – split defeated Germany into four occupation zones after the war. The Cold War soon divided the allies in an East–West stand-off. When Washington, London and Paris proposed setting up a separate western state as a bulwark against the Soviets, western politicians such as Konrad Adenauer made the pragmatic choice to seize this opportunity rather than hold out for a pan-German solution.

> Adenauer had no problem with turning his back on the east

Adenauer, who became chancellor when the Federal Republic of Germany was founded in May 1949, had no problem with turning his back on the east. With his Rhinelander's suspicion of the Prussians, he was convinced the Germans needed a tight cocoon of western links to keep to the democratic path. The Basic Law, or constitution, left the unity issue open by saying only that "all Germans are called upon to complete the unity and freedom of Germany in free self-determination." Radically departing from past thinking, the constitution also said the federal government could surrender part of its sovereignty to international organisations.

Adenauer spent his 14 years in office tightening those western links. West Germany joined the Council of Europe, the European Coal and Steel Community, NATO and the Western European Union. It was a founding member of the European Economic Community in 1957. Adenauer and Charles de Gaulle signed the Franco-German treaty in 1963 to bury the hatchet between the two neighbours after three wars in less than 70 years.

East Germany – officially named the German Democratic Republic – spent the first two decades of its existence tightening its ties to Moscow. Founded in October 1949, its constitution also set reunification as a goal, but under communist colours. East Berlin joined Comecon, the Warsaw Pact and the whole panoply of other communist organisations. But it could not establish the same popular support for its separate state as Bonn did. When the state imposed higher work norms and prices in June 1953, workers took to the streets in protests that Moscow promptly crushed with its tanks. For the rest of the 1950s, disillusioned East Germans streamed over the open sector borders in Berlin. The exodus reached crisis proportions in 1961. By August of that year, the total number of refugees since the war had reached 3.4 million. East Germany took the ultimate step on 13 August by building the Wall through the former capital.

THE ICE THAWS

With the *Ostpolitik* under Willy Brandt, who became chancellor in 1969, Bonn accepted that division had become a fact of life. As he put it, Germany was "two states in one nation". Brandt almost lost his job trying to make this official policy. The CDU bitterly accused him of giving away the eastern lands ceded to Poland in 1945. It fought tooth and nail against the treaties with Moscow, Warsaw and East Berlin that recognised the post-war reality. Once Brandt had established diplomatic relations with East Berlin, East Germany was on its way to becoming something like Austria – German-speaking but not West German.

While Germans in east and west approved of reunification in the abstract, the number of them doubting they would ever see it rose steadily. In the west, the doubters rose from 41 per cent in 1951 to 97 per cent by 1987. At the same time, West Germans became increasingly used to simply calling their own country *Deutschland* and using the initials *DDR* for their communist neighbour. This was especially the case among younger Westerners, half of whom considered the authoritarian society next door a foreign state.[3] The few opinion surveys conducted behind the Wall showed the number of East Germans expecting to see reunification falling from 14 per cent in 1970 to almost zero in 1984.[4]

The *Ostpolitik* allowed Bonn to pursue a constructive policy towards the east without being nationalist, arrogant or old-fashioned. After agreeing to disagree on reunification, Bonn and East Berlin expanded contacts steadily even as superpower relations chilled in the early 1980s. East Berlin also established diplomatic links with western countries that had previously stayed aloof, especially NATO states. International acceptance also cleared the way for western bank credits to boost the performance of East Berlin's centrally planned economy.

But the opening to the west proved to be a mixed blessing. East Berlin had to start being more liberal with its most precious privilege – permission to visit or emigrate to West Germany. Legal emigration picked up in the 1980s while visits by working-age East Germans (rather than just by pensioners East Berlin hoped would stay abroad) jumped from around 64,000 in 1983 to 1.5 million by 1988. The more visas were granted, the less those denied them were ready to accept their fate. The credits were another double-edged sword. As early as 1978, the state planning commission concluded that East Germany was dependent on western funds to remain solvent. Bonn demanded humanitarian concessions in return for loans. In 1984, after two large West German credits, East Germany dismantled guns along the border that automatically shot down would-be refugees when they hit a trip wire. It also let a record 34,982 East Germans emigrate to the West that year.

> **The more visas were granted, the less those denied them were ready to accept their fate**

But small concessions could not bring in enough money to keep the economy going. A small group of officials began thinking the unthinkable. "To save what could be saved, we drew up a plan to open the borders during Honecker's visit if West Germany would in exchange recognise there were two German states and help East Germany with its financial problems," Foreign Trade Minister Gerhard Beil later revealed. "Bonn had already agreed to the idea in principle, but it failed because of Honecker's stubbornness."[5] Honecker refused to believe the economy was doing so badly.

STABILITÄT ÜBER ALLES

On both sides, the watchword was "Stabilität über alles." Bonn was deeply concerned about upsetting the East–West balance. Just how distant the idea of reunification was for West Germans became clear in 1986 when some CDU deputies suggested that progress in US–Soviet nuclear arms talks had opened the way towards reconsidering the unity issue. Tension in Europe could be reduced if one of its main sources, the division of Germany, were overcome, they argued. When one of these deputies brought this up at a CDU leadership meeting in November 1986, Kohl refused to consider it. When the deputy persisted, saying he saw signs of new thinking about this in Moscow, Kohl bellowed back that this was "incredible rubbish".[6]

Most influential Germans agreed. An informal survey of politicians and businessmen, published in June 1989, showed that none of them sensed this to be the twilight stage of Germany's division. Stuttgart Mayor Manfred Rommel, son of the famous World War II general, said, "The idea of reunification is completely hopeless." Former chancellor Helmut Schmidt hoped that East and West Germans would be able to live under a common roof at some stage in the coming hundred years. "I express myself ambiguously," he stressed. "I have not used the word 'reunification' for thirty years."[7]

After the collapse of the Soviet Union, former Soviet Foreign Minister Eduard Shevardnadze revealed that he and his aides had begun reconsidering German unity as early as 1986. In 1991, Honecker recalled hearing that Shevardnadze had called Germany's division unnatural as early as 1984. "Our ambassador in Moscow reported in 1987 that Soviet personalities were putting forward with increasing openness the demand to end the division of Germany," he added. "I spoke with Gorbachev about this ... he told me those were personal opinions."[8]

The Government had no monopoly on caution. Some Social Democrats wanted Bonn to recognise East German citizenship. The SPD worked out a joint position paper with the SED agreeing to disagree on ideology but work together for peace. So supporters of this SPD *Ostpolitik*, even those in opposition, had little time for the democracy movements bubbling up from below during the 1980s. Poland's trade union Solidarity met with barely disguised hostility in West Germany. In 1989, when a few East Germans wanted to found a social democratic party, they got a distinctly frosty reception at SPD headquarters in Bonn.

> ❝ Vernon Walters, US ambassador, met with polite silence when he told German officials he thought reunification was coming soon ❞

Vernon Walters, who took up his post as US ambassador in Bonn in April 1989, met with polite silence when he told German officials he thought reunification was coming soon. The polyglot general saw Soviet power crumbling after the retreat from Afghanistan and predicted that East European states would try to break away from Moscow. Foreign Minister Hans-Dietrich Genscher "smiled indulgently, even a bit condescendingly ... (he said) it was simply not within the realm of the possible for the foreseeable future. The Soviets were not yet ready to put up with such a development and Germany's neighbours in Europe could not live with it either."[9] Kohl and his crown prince, Interior Minister Wolfgang Schäuble, were the only ones who did not rule out unity when Walters mentioned it. But they also could not imagine it coming soon. "We were so caught up in our status quo thinking that we overlooked this," Schäuble said later when he presented Walters' book in Bonn.[10]

When West Germany marked its 40th anniversary in May 1989, it celebrated its triumph independently of the east. Speakers at the official anniversary celebration patted themselves on the back for their successful democracy and made only fleeting references to division or the Wall. That same month, just across the border, the SED assembled 750,000 youths in East Berlin for the annual rally of the Free German Youth (*Freie Deutsche Jugend*). Row upon row of blue-shirted teenagers marched down the Karl-Marx-Allee past a beaming Honecker and his Politburo. The official media presented it as a convincing sign of the party's link with the younger generation. Things looked shakier under the surface. At preparatory meetings, FDJ members objected to such old-fashioned marches. Some criticised the hard-line SED's opposition to Gorbachev's *glasnost* and *perestroika* reforms.

One problem went directly to Honecker. The FDJ orchestra refused to give its traditional concert if it had to wear the movement's trademark blue shirts. Honecker, who founded the FDJ, had never seen such insubordination. After a moment of uncomprehending silence, the leader of the Warsaw Pact's front-line state caved in to a few restless teenagers. "Well, then, they can just forget it," he said, and cancelled the concert altogether.[11]

NOTES

1   The line came from the East German national anthem *Auferstanden aus Ruinen* (Arisen from the Ruins).

2   *The New York Times*, 7 September 1987.

3   For these and more polls tracking the changing West German view of the divsion, see Jansen, Silke (1989) "Zwei deutsche Staaten – zwei deutsche Nationen?" *Deutschland Archiv*, October, pages 1132–43.

4   *Materialien der Enquete-Kommission "Aufarbeitung von Geschichte und Folgen der SED-Diktatur in Deutschland,"* published by the German Bundestag. Baden-Baden: Nomos, 1995, V/1, pages 687–8. This 18-volume series is a gold mine of information about East Germany based on two years of parliamentary hearings after reunification. Hereafter referred to as *Enquete-Kommission*.

5   Mathiopoulos, Margarita (1994) *Rendezvous mit der DDR*. Düsseldorf: Econ, page 66. For more on East Germany's economic problems at this time, see Hertle, Hans-Hermann (1996) *Chronik des Mauerfalls*. Thans-Hermann Berlin: Ch.Links Verlag, pages 43–4.

6   The deputy, Berhard Friedmann, wrote a book about this discussion entitled *Einheit statt Raketen*. Herford: BusseSeewald, 1987.

7   Marsh, David (1989) *The Germans – Rich, Bothered and Divided*. London: Century, pages 271–4.

8   Shevardnadze, Eduard (1991) *The Future Belongs to Freedom*. New York: The Free Press, page 131. Honecker's interview was broadcast by ARD television on 10 November 1991.

9   Walters, Vernon (1994) *Die Vereinigung war voraussehbar*. Berlin: Siedler, page 36. Although written in English, the book has only appeared in German translation.

10 On 2 March 1994.

11 Schabowski, Günter (1991) *Der Absturz*. Berlin: Rowohlt Berlin, pages 177–9.

3

THE IRON CURTAIN CRUMBLES

MIKHAIL GORBACHEV CAME, SAW, CONQUERED AND TEASED. On his first visit to West Germany in June 1989, the dynamic Soviet President added a new word to the political vocabulary – "Gorbymania". Cheering crowds met him wherever he went. The fresh breeze that Gorbachev's *perestroika* and *glasnost* had brought to Soviet politics seemed to promise a new era of peace and cooperation in Europe. He and his attractive wife Raisa were worlds away from the *apparatchiks* who used to reign in the Kremlin. "Gorby" ended his triumphal tour with a tantalising little hint. Asked at a news conference about the Berlin Wall, he said, "The Wall could disappear once the conditions that created the need for it disappear." A follow-up question about reunification brought the Delphic answer: "Everything is possible ... time will decide."[1]

Perestroika was already bringing changes throughout the Soviet bloc. Only a month before Gorbachev's visit to Bonn, Hungarian border guards began dismantling the Iron Curtain along the Austrian frontier and handing out bits of the barbed wire as souvenirs. A free election in Poland in June brought in the Soviet bloc's first non-communist government to office. In July, Gorbachev announced the end of the Brezhnev doctrine of limited sovereignty in Eastern Europe. The mood of change and hope sweeping the communist world

> 66 Gorbachev and his attractive wife Raisa were worlds away from the *apparatchiks* who used to reign in the Kremlin 99

was so strong that even the bloody Tienanmen Square massacre in June, which crushed China's democracy movement, could not dampen it.

But where was democracy in the German Democratic Republic? The old hard-liners in the Politburo refused to drop their ideological guard. The leadership feigned indifference to the new trends coming from Moscow. As the party ideologist Kurt Hager put it, "If your neighbour put up new wallpaper in his apartment, would you feel you had to paper your apartment over again as well?" When East Germans began reading about reform in the rejuvenated Soviet press, censors banned the popular weekly *Sputnik*.

Parallel to this, the number of East Germans applying to leave for the west rose dramatically. East Berlin let 10 to 20 thousand people leave every year in the 1980s. Those applying to leave were usually fired from their jobs and shunned by colleagues. Many sought help from the Protestant churches, which formed support groups and provided some work while they waited – sometimes for years – to be allowed out. They also started organising protests. In March 1989, when foreign businessmen flocked to the Leipzig Spring Fair, several hundred people marched through the city chanting "We want out."

It was one of the great banalities of life in the communist world that provided the final spark. On 7 May 1989, East Germany held local elections, and official candidates officially chalked up a 98.85 per cent "yes" vote. The dissidents, in an unprecedented move, filed official complaints about vote-rigging. Attendance at Leipzig's Monday peace prayers, a late afternoon service started by the Nikolai Church in 1982, swelled from 500 in early May to around 2,500 by late June. "Worshippers" (many of whom had never seen the inside of a church before) had to file past plain-clothes men from the hated Stasi security police to get in. On their way out, they would shout, "Stasi pig" and "Stasi out." For them, free elections and the right to travel would be a little piece of heaven on earth.

When summer vacation time came, thousands of East Germans flocked to Hungary hoping to cross the border into Austria. They could get West German passports at Bonn's embassy in Budapest, but Hungarian border guards often refused to let them out. Desperate, the East Germans returned to the embassy in the hope that it would help them emigrate. By the beginning of August, about 130 East Germans were holed up in the embassy in Budapest and hundreds more camped out elsewhere. At the same time, another 80 had fled into the West German permanent mission in East Berlin and a further 20 were in the embassy in Prague. The crowds grew steadily during the month.

THE FLOODGATES BURST OPEN

Throwing in its lot with the West, Hungary flung open its border at the stroke of midnight on 10 September. Long lines of Trabis, Wartburgs and Ladas poured out and raced through the night across Austria. When the first cars reached the West German border, relief agencies were ready with free petrol, drinks and food. Local businessmen searched for skilled labourers. Television reports of the enthusiastic reception prompted another wave of East Germans to pull up stakes and leave. The new arrivals were overwhelmingly young and mostly male. Most had been trained in a traditional German apprenticeship, making them the kind of skilled workers the communist state was supposed to favour. These were people with the most comfortable life the Soviet bloc could afford, yet they were ready to bolt from home at the first opportunity. Three-quarters said the lack of free speech or the right to travel drove them to quit the country.

Even while so many were leaving, over 16 million others stayed put. In many cases, that decision was just as challenging to the government. Those who did not go west wanted a better east. It made no difference whether they stayed behind out of political conviction, for family reasons or simply because they didn't want to move. Each departure tore holes in the cosy private networks of family, friends and colleagues, the "niches" that made life in East Germany liveable.

As the departures mounted, official East Berlin wavered between speechlessness and denial. The controlled press ignored the exodus. Honecker spent the summer recovering from a gall bladder operation. In his absence, the Politburo rigidly ignored the rising discontent. When Krenz suggested staying in East Berlin because of the tension, Honecker was so annoyed at the suggestion that things were not under control that he ordered him to take four weeks' vacation. The crown prince obeyed.

The denial could not endure. East Germany's fortieth anniversary was coming up on 7 October and the malcontents would not be allowed to steal the show. By coincidence, the fortieth anniversary of China's communist state was due one week earlier. This led to an outpouring of solidarity messages from East Berlin to Beijing, a name now synonymous with the Tienanmen massacre. The ailing Honecker made his first major public appearance of the season at a ceremony in East Berlin's State Opera House to mark China's anniversary. The message

> 66 These were people with the most comfortable life the Soviet bloc could afford, yet they were ready to bolt from home 99

was not lost on loyal communists. On 6 October, a workers' militia unit in Leipzig threatened a "Chinese solution" to end the swelling weekly demonstrations after the Monday peace prayers. "We are ready and able to defend our achievements effectively to stop these counter-revolutionary actions once and for all. If needed with weapons in our hands," it said in a statement in the local newspaper.

It was in this overheated atmosphere that the opposition began to form. Just after Hungary opened its border, 30 activists met outside East Berlin to found New Forum as a nation-wide platform for public dialogue on reform. Its leading figures were living examples of how East Germany had gone wrong. Bärbel Bohley, an East Berlin artist who became the group's spokeswoman, was a feminist and peace campaigner. She and two other dissidents were expelled to Britain in early 1988 after demonstrating for free speech at a ceremony honouring the legendary Communist Rosa Luxemburg. They returned six months later. Another founder, Jens Reich, was a soft-spoken molecular biologist. For about 20 years, he and other East Berlin intellectuals had met privately for weekly talks on politics, philosophy, history and any other taboo topic. When the time came, many became charter members of the New Forum.

In the weeks that followed, other groups launched political parties to rival the SED. Many were led by Protestant pastors, a reflection of the relatively independent role enjoyed by their church under communism and their activism in sheltering dissidents during the 1980s. Some of the most active pastors formed Democratic Awakening on 2 October as a reform socialist opposition. Others founded the Social Democratic Party on 7 October.

Within weeks, 200,000 people had signed the New Forum manifesto. Bohley started a media blitz with a unique German–German twist. Her calls for reform went out over crackling telephone lines to radio stations in West Berlin, Cologne and Hamburg, which beamed them back to East Germans astonished by her courage. A new breakfast show on West Berlin's RIAS-TV gave East Germans a daily round-up of the previous night's protests, and tips about what to expect next.

Honecker returned to work in late September determined to clear up the exodus mess. On 29 September, he agreed to allow the 5,490 East Germans occupying Bonn's embassy in Prague to leave for West Germany. But they had to travel in East German trains through the GDR and be stripped of their citizenship en route. Another 809 refugees in the West German embassy in Warsaw would cross their homeland in another train. Two days after the Prague embassy was emptied, 4,500 new arrivals had crowded into the building waiting to emigrate. Desperate, East Berlin suspended visa-free travel to Czechoslovakia at 5 pm on 3 October. In a secret report to the Politburo on 4 October, Erich Mielke, the head of the Stasi, said that even communists were threatening to quit the party and apply for an exit visa.[2]

The embattled government rounded up more "freedom trains" to ferry another 7,600 refugees from Prague and 600 others from Warsaw. In Dresden, some 3,000 youths chanting "We want out" and "Gorby! Gorby!" stormed the railroad station hoping to hop on to a passing train. Blocked by riot police, they fought a three-hour battle in vain. About 400 blocked the tracks further down the line. In the confusion, one man had both legs cut off by a passing train and many others were injured.

> 66 Teenage girls in blue FDJ shirts and jeans squealed 'Gorby! Gorby!' 99

When Gorbachev arrived in East Berlin on 6 October for the anniversary, he found the same Brezhnev-style stagnation he was battling against back home. That evening, the Soviet bloc's old guard lined up along Unter den Linden to watch an FDJ torchlight parade. Honecker pumped the night air with his traditional clenched fist salute. Poland's Wojciech Jaruselski stood at ramrod attention. Romanian dictator Nicolae Ceauşescu grumpily tried to ignore the boos wafting up from the crowd when he was introduced. As every FDJ group passed the reviewing stand, the parade slowed down. Teenage girls in blue FDJ shirts and jeans squealed "Gorby! Gorby!" Other youths echoed dissident slogans. Poland's former Prime Minister Mieczysław Rakowski leaned over and asked, "Mikhail Sergeievich, do you understand what they're saying?" Gorbachev nodded, but Rakowski translated the slogans anyway. "They're saying 'Gorbachev, save us.' This is the end."[3]

A Politburo meeting after the military parade on anniversary day got nowhere. Gorbachev addressed the group first, spelling out his policies and hinting that East Berlin should do likewise. Unruffled, Honecker sang his country's praises in communist clichés. When he finished, Gorbachev looked up in amazement, then got up and left the room without saying a word.[4]

At their final reception that evening in the East German parliament, the communist elite had a front-row seat on the spreading unrest. Just outside, across a canal, about 3,000 protesters in Marx Engels Park were shouting "Gorby, come out!" and "Freedom! Freedom!" One of the guests watching the scene from inside recalled, "It was spooky. The mood was depressed, there was a touch of *Götterdämmerung* about … It was like being on the Titanic."[5] Police and Stasi men tried to haul away the ringleaders, prompting scuffles with the young crowd. Once riot police had dispersed the crowd, it snaked instead through the dark streets of East Berlin, swelling as it progressed. Phalanxes of truncheon-wielding police, some with attack dogs, swept along the main boulevards while smaller units chased demonstrators down side streets where they were beaten and arrested.

The spectre of a "Chinese solution" hung over Leipzig as the Monday Peace Prayers neared on 9 October. Local army units and special mobile police joined the city police, workers' militia and Stasi units in a security force of at least 8,000 men. Extra blood supplies were distributed to hospitals. Workers in the city were let off early and parents were told to pick up their children from school by 3 pm. SED members were warned of a looming counter-revolution. In the early afternoon, riot police took up position near the four churches in central Leipzig that were holding peace prayers at 5 pm.

Up to 9,000 people turned up for the prayer sessions, far more than could fit into the churches. One participant, Susanne Rummel, later recalled seeing her church ringed by police and Stasi. "None of us wanted to say the words civil war or bloodletting aloud, but it seemed tangibly near to everyone."[6] After the services, at least 20,000 people gathered on Karl Marx Square. As they advanced around the Ring Road in a sea of flickering candles, the crowd swelled to 70,000. "For me, the greatest moment came when I marched in that crowd and started calling, first softly and then louder and louder, 'We are the people! We are the People!'" said 58-year-old housewife Eva Günther. "I saw police, but I was not afraid. I felt strong and I threw my arms into the air and screamed my heart out."

> 66 Extra blood supplies were distributed to hospitals. Workers in the city were let off early 99

Most marchers had never dreamed of protesting in public before. They were bitter over the exodus that put relatives and friends beyond a border they might never be able to cross. The sight of so many frustrated neighbours shouting out political demands that normally brought instant arrest broke down the wall of fear and taboo that was crucial to keeping East Germany under control.

Another invisible pillar of the state, the threat of violent repression, also crumbled that night. No tanks rumbled over the cobblestones to replay the bloody suppression of the 1953 workers' uprising. There were no beatings or arrests. In fact, the riot police withdrew during the evening. "We had a plan of operation for everything," parliament speaker Horst Sindermann said later. "We just weren't prepared for candles and prayers." Both Krenz and Honecker subsequently tried to claim credit for averting a bloodbath, but it seemed that Leipzig security authorities had no clear guidelines from East Berlin as to whether to shoot or not.

> 66 We had a plan of operation for everything. We just weren't prepared for candles and prayers 99

The victory in the churches and on the streets of Leipzig that night marked the decisive turning point in the grass-roots struggle for democracy. It forced the once omnipotent SED into a retreat that seemed less dramatic than it was only because the protesters were so disciplined. It began the first successful and peaceful revolution in Germany.

LIFE PUNISHES THOSE WHO COME TOO LATE

During his East Berlin visit, Gorbachev coined the phrase of the year when he said, "Life punishes those who come too late."[7] It was a warning to Honecker, but he failed to get the message. Others understood it, however. Fearing they might go down with Honecker's sinking ship, Krenz and the East Berlin SED chief Günter Schabowski began plotting to oust him. They lined up about half of the 26-member Politburo behind them. Gorbachev was informed in advance and sent his best wishes for the conspiracy's success. When Honecker opened the Politburo session on 17 October, Prime Minister Willi Stoph promptly broke in and proposed that he be fired. Honecker looked stunned but agreed to allow a discussion. One by one, his colleagues all turned against him. In the end, Honecker joined in the unanimous vote to relieve him of his duties. His protégé Krenz was named to replace him. When it was announced the next day, the news of Honecker's resignation caused as much surprise as the appointment of his hard-line deputy did consternation.

Krenz did his clumsy best to keep up with the pace of change. The new party leader proclaimed a policy of "*Wende*" ("turnaround"), coining the name East Germans came to use for the tumultuous autumn of 1989. He visited factories to hear workers' complaints. He met Protestant church leaders and announced an amnesty for those who had fled to the west. He let the dull grey media come to life. By early November, Krenz was frantically jettisoning almost every piece of unpopular ballast he could. He fired targets of public wrath such as Margot Honecker, the former leader's wife and hard-line education minister, and later sacked five elderly leaders including Mielke and chief ideologist Kurt Hager. He promised a new travel law, a constitutional court and alternative service for conscientious objectors. "Trust our policy of renewal," he begged in a televised address. "Your place is here. We need you."

By now, who was listening? The news that Prague had opened its border to West Germany that evening drowned out Krenz's speech. East Germans were soon racing through Czechoslovakia into Bavaria at the rate of two to three hundred an hour. When half a million protesters massed at East Berlin's Alexanderplatz on 4 November, the SED was the target of public ridicule. Posters full of wit and satire bobbed up and down in a sea of banners calling for free elections and democracy. "Put Asterix in the Politburo" one demanded. One of the best depicted Krenz as the Big Bad Wolf over the words, "Grandmother, why do you have such big teeth?"[8]

> 66 The Leipzigers had shown that the emperor had no clothes. The Berliners were now laughing at his nakedness 99

Forty years of fear were forgotten. Chinese solutions and Soviet invasions were history. If Leipzig won the decisive battle for democracy, East Berlin got to stage the victory parade. The Leipzigers had shown that the emperor had no clothes. The Berliners were now laughing at his nakedness. Reform-minded communists were booed when they joined dissidents to address the crowd. The legendary former spymaster Markus Wolf, who secretly pictured himself as the great hope for *perestroika* in East Germany, saw his dreams collapse within minutes of starting to speak. Chants of *"Aufhören!"* ("Stop!") gave way to scattered calls of *"Aufhängen!"* ("Hang him!"). "People's power" was on the verge of victory. Anything could happen.

From then on, each day seemed to bring the highpoint of the drama, only to be surpassed by events the next day. On the Monday, the press published the draft of a new travel law that granted East Germans 30 days in the West annually but made no provision for hard currency. This was as good as telling the unemployed they were allowed to window-shop for a Mercedes. The government of Willi Stoph, prime minister since 1976, resigned on Tuesday. The Politburo was the next to fall at a special session of the Central Committee on Wednesday. Trying to put a convincing face on its plans for reform, the SED nominated Dresden party boss Hans Modrow – another supposed "East German Gorbachev" – as the next prime minister.

9 NOVEMBER 1989

On the morning of Thursday, 9 November, four senior officials met at the Interior Ministry to draft a new law to legalise emigration. About 225,000 people had left so far that year and there was no end in sight if East Berlin didn't act decisively. These officials were no closet liberals. Two were from the Ministry of State Security (MfS), the other two were "unofficial collaborators" (IMs) of the Stasi. But they sensed there would be trouble if they legalised emigration without also permitting day trips to the west. So they decided to tackle the problem head-on by allowing private travel without any conditions or delay. None of them thought things would change quickly, since travellers would still need to apply for passports and visas.

That afternoon, Krenz interrupted a Central Committee session on economic reform to mention the travel law. "Whatever we do in this situation, we're bound to make a mistake," he said. "But this is the only solution that spares us the problem of dealing with this through third countries, which harms the international image of the GDR." Only three officials had any comments, all of them minor. When Schabowski, who was due to meet journalists later, turned up to be briefed, Krenz handed him the short text of the draft law and said, "Announce this. It will be a bombshell." Without even reading it, Schabowski decided to announce it at the end of his news conference.[9]

The day's excitement seemed to be drawing to an end when Schabowski met the media at 6 pm. After an hour of wandering questions and answers about the Central Committee, he announced in passing that a new law would allow East Germans to travel abroad or emigrate freely. "When does that go into force?" a voice called out from the hall. Looking baffled, Schabowski thumbed through his papers and said, "As far as I know, right away … immediately." Suddenly all ears, reporters asked if this applied to trips to West Berlin. Schabowski frowned, shrugged his shoulders and wondered in silence whether the Soviets had been

> **66 Krenz handed him the short text of the draft law and said, 'Announce this. It will be a bombshell' 99**

informed of all this. But he found the relevant passage and read it aloud: "Permanent emigration can take place at all GDR border crossing points to the Federal Republic and West Berlin." On his way out, RIAS-TV cornered Schabowski and asked if he expected an exodus. "I hope it doesn't come to that," he remarked.[10]

NOTES

1   Kohl says he told Gorbachev during the visit that Germany's division harmed their relations and that reunification was inevitable someday. At one point, the president stopped contradicting him. See Helmut Kohl with Kai Diekmann and Ralf Georg Reuth, *Ich wollte Deutschlands Einheit*. Berlin: Propyläen, 1996, pages 43–4.

2   For this and other Stasi reports during 1989, see "Ich liebe euch doch alle!" *Befehle und Lageberichte des MfS*. Berlin: BasisDruck, 1990, pages 192–4.

3   *Der Spiegel*, 4 October 1999.

4   *Der Absturz*, pages 241–2.

5   Carl-Heinz Janson, a member of the Politburo's Economic Commission, quoted in Reuth, Ralf Georg and Bönte, Andreas (1993) *Das Komplott: Wie es wirklich zur deutschen Einheit kam*. Munich: Piper, page 109.

6   Quoted in Pond, Elizabeth (1993) *Beyond The Wall: Germany's Road to Unification*. Washington DC: The Brookings Institution, page 116.

7   It seems the original Russian was less punchy, but the interpreter's quick translation – *Wer zu spät kommt, den bestraft das Leben* – has become a popular political quote in German.

8   The sight of these and other posters lampooning the communists was so striking that several Bonn-based foreign correspondents who saw television reports at home (myself included) rushed to East Berlin over the next few days – just in time to be there when the Wall opened.

9   Hertler, Hans-Hermann (1996) *Chronik des Mauerfalls*. Berlin: Ch.Links Verlag, pages 118–36.

10 *Chronik des Mauerfalls* has the full transcript of Schabowski's answers on pages 142–7.

4

THE WALL FALLS

ONLY MINUTES AFTER SCHABOWSKI'S HESITANT ANSWER, the first East Berliners appeared along the Wall at the Bornholmer Strasse border crossing, asking to be let through. A few people turned up at Leipzig train station to buy tickets to West Germany. Soon the East Berlin police headquarters received a call from a man complaining that he had been refused a visa at his local police station. At Checkpoint Charlie, a café waiter from the western side brought champagne over to the eastern guards to toast the border opening. But these loyal officials had no instructions. They waved him away.

Schabowski went home unaware of the uproar he had left behind. The SED's security czar Wolfgang Herger suspected something when he drove home and passed a long line of west-bound cars. Colleagues found Egon Krenz wandering alone in the corridors of the Central Committee building at around 11 pm. "What should I do now?" he moaned. "We can't close the border now. We have to get this under control."[1]

But it was the people out on the streets who were in control. The crowds streaming westwards trampled over the bureaucratic hurdles meant to keep them in line. Only military force could stop them now, but that would have triggered a disaster. So, for the first time in its history, East Germany found itself riding the fickle waves of public opinion. The people felt the rush of empowerment after decades of being muzzled.

Now they, and not the Politburo or other self-appointed leaders, would decide which way the country would go.

"WE CAN'T HOLD UP ANY MORE"

The border crossing at Bornholmer Strasse was the first to burst under the pressure of the crowds. Shabby tenements stretched right up the Wall there. It took only minutes for residents to bundle up against the cold and stroll down to the checkpoint. Border guards tried to convince the swelling crowd to wait until the next day. They refused. The 8 pm ARD television evening news from West Germany reported that the border was open. By 9 pm, border guards let a few of the most boisterous East Berliners through, hoping to ease the pressure on the border point. As the first lucky few ran across to West Berlin, the crowds left behind chanted, "Open the gates! Open the gates!" Pushing ahead, they knocked down a metal fence separating them from the checkpoint proper. Passport officer Harald Jäger called his Stasi superiors at 10.30 pm and barked down the line, "We can't hold up any more ... I'm shutting down the controls and letting the people out."[2]

> 66 It was as if a cork had popped and champagne sprayed out. Total strangers hugged and kissed like long-lost relatives 99

"The gates in the Wall are wide open," ARD announced at 10.42 pm, even though the checkpoint where its correspondent was reporting live was still closed. But all eight border crossings were bursting at the seams. By midnight all were open. It was as if a cork had popped and champagne sprayed out. Total strangers hugged and kissed like long-lost relatives. West Berliners lit fireworks and handed out drinks to the new arrivals. Stunned East Berliners whooped with joy or burst into tears as they reached the west. Some had left home so quickly they had only their pyjamas under their coats. Very few carried suitcases or looked like they were emigrating. At the Brandenburg Gate, youths danced on top of the barrier where a day earlier they could have been cut down by gun fire. Some took hammers to the concrete and chipped away their own souvenirs.

As the night wore on, the revellers trickled back, returning to normal lives in a completely changed world. "Going to West Berlin was as good as going to Australia for me," one woman enthused as she crossed back. "It was just as far away. But now I've been there and back while my children were home in bed." People came back to the drab east because it was home. They were elated; they had won the right to travel and nobody could take it away now.

The news reached Helmut Kohl in Warsaw, just before he was to dine with Prime Minister Tadeusz Mazowiecki. Wary of insulting the Poles on this sensitive visit, he decided to stay the night. But he left early the next day, eager to get back to address a rally planned for the late afternoon in West Berlin.

As Kohl stood at the Berlin rally that evening waiting to speak, an urgent call came in from the Soviet ambassador in Bonn. Gorbachev wanted to ask Kohl if enraged citizens were attacking Soviet bases in East Germany. "Only later did I find out that Gorbachev had been fed false information on purpose," Kohl later wrote. "Opponents of reform in the KGB and the Stasi wanted to provoke a military intervention by Soviet troops stationed in East Germany, I have no doubt about that. But I was stuck on the balcony of Schöneberg city hall and couldn't call Gorbachev myself … I sent a message to Gorbachev that he had my word – these fears were not true."[3]

Gorbachev believed Kohl, but he had good reason to worry. Krenz was slow to inform Moscow of what was happening and his messages were more alibi than information. The situation was far more tense than the joyous atmosphere at the Wall suggested. At noon that day, East Berlin put a crack motorised rifle division and a paratroop regiment on combat alert. Even two days after the checkpoints had opened, Defence Minister Heinz Kessler still considered sending in troops to stop crowds from tearing down the Wall. The alarm was lifted later that day.[4]

After the wall that protected it had fallen, the SED was speechless. When the Central Committee resumed the next morning, Krenz opened the session without even mentioning the previous night's events. A bleak economic report seemed to interest the delegates more than Krenz's later comments on "the situation". It was not until that evening that Krenz and other SED leaders spoke in public about the Wall's opening. At a pro-Communist rally in the centre of East Berlin, Schabowski portrayed his botched announcement as "the most daring step" in the SED's "policy of renewal".[5]

KOHL SEIZES THE INITIATIVE

Kohl got a shaky start to what would be his greatest year. The chancellor was instinctively cautious at first. He fell back on well-worn phrases about Germans wanting "unity in freedom" and avoided mentioning reunification. Others were careful, too, but they expressed the public mood better. Willy Brandt, 76, blossomed into a grandfather figure for both Germanys.

His simple phrases like "What belongs together is now growing together" expressed a widespread feeling. As a native of the Eastern city of Halle, the popular Hans-Dietrich Genscher, his Free Democratic Party (FDP) coalition partner, personified unity far more than Kohl.

In the east, new faces were starting to jockey for position before the free elections, due sometime in 1990. Prime Minister Hans Modrow made a strong start in his maiden speech on 17 November, proposing a "community of treaties" to broaden German–German cooperation considerably while still staying as two separate states. After shaking off his spymaster's reticence, Markus Wolf presented himself as an East German Gorbachev. Leipzig's Monday protest marches continued to grow, as did the numbers of East Germans leaving for the west.

In West Germany, the welcome for the *Ossis* – as the easterners quickly became known – wore out within weeks. Lines of sputtering "Trabi" cars blocked the streets in West Berlin and along the border every weekend. Customers could hardly enter their banks because long lines of East Germans clogged them waiting to get their "welcome money". Staff in shops and supermarkets groaned as wave after wave of East Germans cleared their shelves as quickly as they could be stocked. Remarks like "*Ossi* go home" or "I want the Wall back" started making the rounds. Saarland state premier Oskar Lafontaine, the SPD's challenger to Kohl for the 1990 elections, was beating the drum against a headlong rush towards a merger that would end up costing huge sums.

When it came, Kohl's response was framed within the political activity he knew most about, the election campaign. Lafontaine was already stumping for a combination of employment plans and ecology he was sure would be the wave of the future. Dramatic gains by the far-right Republicans Party in local and European Parliament elections during the year threatened to steal "patriotic" votes on Kohl's right

> 66 Staff in shops and supermarkets groaned as wave after wave of East Germans cleared their shelves 99

if he did not show some leadership. With free elections in East Germany now only a matter of time, Kohl also had to keep an eye on what Modrow had up his sleeve.

Kohl called his closest advisors together for a campaign strategy session on 20 November. They told Kohl he had to seize the initiative on unification or watch the SPD or the FDP beat him to it. Nikolai Portugalov, one of Moscow's leading German experts, had just told Kohl's foreign policy adviser Horst Teltschik that the Kremlin was ready to "think the unthinkable" and consider a German confederation. He also disclosed that Moscow did not expect Krenz to survive in power for very long. Krenz had let Bonn know he would hold free elections by early 1991 and open the Brandenburg Gate to pedestrians if the West Germans would put up two billion marks for a "travel fund" to help finance East Germans' trips. Kohl thought these urgent issues could be tackled right away. But he still needed a longer-term perspective, something going beyond Modrow's plan that would put him in the vanguard of the movement.

The chancellor made that leap forward on 28 November with his Ten Point Programme. Addressing the Bundestag, Kohl announced for the first time that Bonn now wanted to reunite the two Germanys. Bonn would provide extensive economic aid if East Berlin held free elections and dismantled central planning. "We do not want to stabilise conditions that have become untenable," he declared. Unification (which he privately thought could take five years, although he did not say this) should be prepared through "confederative structures" that would bring the two states increasingly closer. "Nobody knows at the present time what a reunited Germany will look like," he said. "I am sure, however, that unity will come if the German people want it ... Reunification – that is, the regaining of Germany's unity as a state – remains the government's political goal."[6]

Kohl the politician was so fixed on seizing the initiative that he ignored protocol and kept the plan secret from even his closest allies. George Bush was the only foreign leader tipped off in advance. This diplomatic insult, out of character for the telephone addict who usually consulted his partners tirelessly, prompted questions abroad as to whether Germany still cared about what its neighbours thought. But his conspiratorial behaviour had more to do with rivalries in "spaceship Bonn", as the political hothouse on the Rhine was known. The Ten Points had to be Kohl's plan alone if he wanted to present himself to the voters as a decisive leader. If news of the plan had reached Genscher, even from his counterparts abroad, Bonn's craftiest soundbite specialist could have turned to the first available microphone and announced it as his own.[7] "If I had discussed the Ten Points within the coalition or even with our allies, they would have been torn apart," Kohl later argued. "This was not the time for doubting Thomases. It was the moment when the German chancellor could not let the initiative towards German unity be taken from his hand."[8]

MISTRUST ABROAD

November 1989 was a schizophrenic time for foreigners watching Germany. It was hard not to cheer when the Wall fell. At the same time, the scenes conjured up worrying visions of a reunited and reassertive Germany. If a country could shake off communism with such apparent ease, would it try to break free of all the other chains that had held it down since the war? Could Germany's future be a repeat of its past?

The chilliest official response came from Britain. Margaret Thatcher hailed the fall of the Wall as a great day for freedom. But she chided a journalist who asked about unification, "You're going much too fast … The task now is to build a genuine democracy in East Germany." She thought Germany was "by its very nature a destabilising rather than a stabilising force in Europe". Hoping to "check the German juggernaut", she carried in her handbag a map to show other European leaders "the various configurations of Germany in the past, which were not altogether reassuring about the future." [9] When Mitterrand first heard the Ten Points, he exploded, "But he didn't tell me anything. Nothing! I will never forget this!" But in the end he kept his options open. "Gorbachev will be furious," he told his aide Jacques Attali. "He won't let it happen, it's impossible. I don't have to oppose it – the Soviets will do it for me." [10]

In early December, Mitterrand held a quick meeting with Gorbachev in Kiev. The two should visit East Berlin together, he suggested, for what would have been a dramatic sign of Franco-Soviet support for Modrow against Kohl. Gorbachev was apparently too surprised to reply. [11] Mitterrand declined Kohl's invitation to join him at the opening of the Brandenburg Gate before Christmas and visited East Germany instead. "Other countries, starting with mine and the European Community, are ready to contribute to efforts to speed your development," he told his East German hosts at the official banquet on 20 December. [12]

> 66 Mitterrand exploded, 'But he didn't tell me anything. Nothing! I will never forget this!' 99

The Soviets also lost their *sang froid* after Kohl's ten-point surprise. Genscher got an angry blast from Gorbachev when he visited Moscow in early December. "You're supposed to present a document like this only after consulting with your partners," he said. "Doesn't the chancellor have to anymore? He seems to think he's setting the tone now." Gorbachev said that Kohl had assured him in mid-November that Bonn did not want to destabilise East Germany. "But the Chancellor's actions do not match his words. He is giving ultimatums." [13]

Of the four World War II victors, the United States was the only one to back reunification from the start. As the German question heated up that autumn, President George Bush pre-empted the debate by declaring he had no qualms about any merger. "I don't share the concern that some European countries have about a reunified Germany," he told the *New York Times* on 25 October. "There's a lot written on the fear of reunification that I personally don't share." Bush sensed the merger was inevitable and that any further "two Germanys" policy would backfire. He also knew he could not gloat over a communist defeat if he wanted to keep US–Soviet relations on an even keel in other areas such as arms control. So in public, Bush was strikingly low key. When reporters pressed him on why he was not overjoyed, he said, "I'm not going to dance on the Wall."

> 66 Thatcher was dismayed by Washington's calm and kept trying in vain to get Bush to distrust the Germans 99

Thatcher was dismayed by Washington's calm and kept trying in vain to get Bush to distrust the Germans more. On 22 February, she warned the president by phone that Germany "will be the Japan of Europe, but worse than Japan". She said Mitterrand shared her worry that "the Germans will get in peace what Hitler couldn't get in the war" and that he was talking with her about a "closer Entente Cordiale". But her suggestion that Soviet troops stay indefinitely in eastern Germany after unity was something Bush could not support.

SPD ON THE SPOT

The Social Democrats tried to kick the domestic political football of reunification in two different directions at once. Since going into opposition in 1982, the SPD had moved to the left as Willy Brandt and Helmut Schmidt made way for younger leaders. In domestic politics, the party focused on ecology and women's rights while expanding West Germany"s welfare state. Its foreign policy bordered on pacifism. With Kohl's popularity ratings low, the 1990 election seemed to be the occasion for the younger leaders known as "Brandt's grandchildren" to rise to national power.

The fall of the Wall upset this game plan by reviving an issue the SPD had long left dormant. Older Social Democrats such as Brandt instinctively supported unity as the crowning achievement of their *Ostpolitik*.

The younger generation had almost no link to the east and basically accepted Germany's division as a reality. When they toured the region with Brandt, they saw a dangerous nationalism reviving.[14] To them, reunification was a right-wing issue. Some saw the division as the political atonement for Auschwitz and a guarantee that the aggressive fatherland would not be reborn.[15]

Lafontaine was a classic product of this generation. His cocky style and taste for the good life made him a charter member of the so-called "Tuscany faction" of ambitious politicians in their 40s, including Schleswig-Holstein premier Björn Engholm and state opposition leader Gerhard Schröder from Lower Saxony. They had grown up in *West* Germany and knew France, Italy and Britain better than Thuringia or Saxony. Feeling at home in Western Europe was the sign of the cosmopolitan *Bundesbürger*, or "federal citizen", as West Germans called themselves in decidedly post-nationalist fashion. Concern about the east was too stubbornly German for them.

66 **To the younger Social Democrats, reunification was a right-wing issue** 99

Lafontaine tried to avoid the unity issue whenever possible and redefine it in tormented "yes, but ..." arguments when he couldn't. A passionate speaker, he delighted in provoking his audiences. Wouldn't the public funds spent on tent cities and soup kitchens for arriving *Ossis* be better used helping people in East Germany itself? He dropped hints that East Germans should not have the automatic right to a West German passport, but the SPD would not buy that idea.

By the time the party held its annual congress on 19 December, Lafontaine had honed his argument into one of social justice. Instead of sounding like beer-hall populism, it now came packaged as a higher ideal. "People in East and West Germany care above all whether they have medical care, whether they are warm in winter, whether they have enough to eat, whether they have work and a home," he said. "This interests them much more than whatever legal arrangements they may live under." Social Democrats must not let patriotic pathos divert them from global issues such as pollution, Third World poverty and the nuclear threat. Lafontaine missed the point. Germany had entered a turbulent period in which the main question was whether and how its two parts would be united. Voters would want a leader with a vision worthy of the challenge.

MEANWHILE IN THE EAST

Without the Wall to stabilise it, the East German political scene plunged into a chaotic blur of events. Emigration continued unabated. Fearless citizens barged into once off-limit places such as the Politburo's walled compound at Wandlitz. Stasi offices around the country were stormed. State television revealed shocking cases of ecological destruction. The East German mark dropped to a fraction of its official value on the West Berlin black market.

Leipzig's Monday evening protest march saw its first cautious pro-unity banners on 20 November. Small groups switched from chanting "We are the people" to "We are *one* people." Some called out "Germany, United Fatherland". But most marchers were more concerned with reforming East Germany than handing it over to Bonn.

Intellectuals began a campaign to preserve an independent East Germany. Their manifesto "For Our Country," drawn up by leftist writers and artists including Christa Wolf and Stefan Heym, declared, "We *still* have the chance to develop a socialist alternative to West Germany ..." it said. "We *still* can turn back to those anti-fascist and humanist ideals we started with ..."

Taking a cue from Poland, where communism had collapsed several months earlier, opposition groups pressed for "Round Table" talks. These meetings would effectively be an all-party crisis cabinet running the country. Starting in early December, they set a free democratic election for 6 May, decided to dissolve the Stasi and write a democratic constitution. Its chaotic sessions played a crucial role in stabilising the country until a new democratic government could be elected. While it sat, cabinet ministers came to consult on draft laws that would then be passed by the Volkskammer parliament, which was still dominated by the SED. Even years later, many eastern leaders looked back at the Round Table as the most exciting political experience of their careers.

THE RUSH TO UNITY

Even with these new forms of government emerging, the real momentum was still out on the streets. Kohl flew to Dresden on 19 December 1989 for a first round of talks with Modrow on expanding bilateral cooperation. What he saw on arrival made his thoughts race far ahead of his plans. Onlookers crowded the arrival building and scrambled on to the roof to wave to him. "We had hardly landed when it hit me like a flash – this regime is finished. Unity is coming!" Kohl later recalled. "A sea of black, red and gold flags fluttered in the cold December air … After the plane taxied to a halt, I was on the last step of the stairway and Modrow was waiting on the tarmac only ten metres away with a stony face. I turned around to (Chancellery Minister) Rudi Seiters and said, 'It's all over'."[16]

The potholed road into the city was lined with clapping young people, workers in blue overalls and classes of school children with their teachers. In town, the crowds kept shouting "Helmut! Helmut!" long after Kohl and Modrow had begun their talks inside a luxury hotel. The two agreed a long list of steps towards a "contractual community", including a spring 1990 target deadline for a formal cooperation treaty, a DM 3.5 billion West German credit, visa-free travel between East and West and the opening of the Brandenburg Gate just before Christmas.

Kohl had not planned to address the crowds but the rapturous reception changed his mind. That evening, about 40,000 Dresdeners jammed into a square to hear him speak. After an appeal for calm, he gradually worked his way into a speech sprinkled with phrases such as *"liebe Landsleute"* ("dear fellow countrymen") and "God bless our German fatherland." It took a while before he got to his main message: "My goal, when the hour of history allows it, remains the unity of our nation." The atmosphere was so charged that Kohl made sure a choirmaster was on hand to start singing the old church hymn *"Nun danket alle Gott"* ("Now thank we all our God") just in case the crowd should break into a round of *"Deutschland, Deutschland über alles."* But nationalism was not the mood that night. The crowds were full of hope for a free and prosperous future. Standing before the blackened ruins of the *Frauenkirche* church, the bombed-out symbol of the war whose burdens they still bore, the chancellor seemed like a saviour.

> 66 Apart from freedom itself, East Germany's first Western 'imports' were all the negative ones 99

By early January, the heady days of autumn had given way to a worrying new everyday life in the east. Apart from freedom itself, East Germany's first western "imports" were all the negative ones. Crime, neo-Nazis, traffic jams, overloaded telephone lines and black market speculation upset the quiet life easterners once knew. Their fledgling democracy also seemed under threat. The communists were also resorting to their old tricks. The SED, which added PDS (Party of Democratic Socialism) to its name in December, still had 1.3 million members and held sway over much of the media and the economy. As discontent with daily problems grew, it began trying to reassert control. It started with a propaganda exercise in early January, a big "anti-fascist rally" to protest against anti-Soviet slogans that had been mysteriously painted on the Soviet War Memorial in East Berlin. Then Modrow tried to establish a new security police force to replace the hated Stasi. The prime minister promised the Round Table that he was not reviving the Stasi, but the opposition feared that any new force could intimidate non-communist parties before the election.

Fear that the Stasi could roll back their new freedoms spread to the streets. Construction workers called a wildcat strike to demand an end to all security police and a swift reunification with West Germany. Demonstrators formed a human chain around the parliament, rattling keys, tearing down East German flags and scuffling with passers-by. On 15 January, the Round Table heard an astonishing report that the Stasi previously had 85,000 employees and 109,000 "informal collaborators", far more than anyone had thought. That afternoon, several thousand protesters stormed the sprawling Stasi headquarters in East Berlin. They overturned furniture and dumped blizzards of file papers down stairwells and out of windows. Spray-painters adorned the walls with slogans like "Stasi – Gestapo – KGB – Securitatae" or "I want my dossier!" It turned out that the Stasi had steered the protesters to harmless areas such as the canteen, bookstore, barber shop and travel agency. Top secret departments dealing with the domestic opposition or spying abroad were never in danger. This soon became known, heightening the suspicion that the communists were up to no good.

> 66 East Germans began to see reunification as the only way to defend the feedoms they had marched to achieve 99

With this, Modrow lost his remaining moral credit. East Germans began to see reunification as the only way to defend the freedoms they had marched to achieve. They lost interest in "third ways" and socialist experiments. On 28 January, the Round Table brought the elections forward, from 6 May to 18 March. Modrow told parliament the next day that the situation was dangerously out of control, and proposed a "government of national responsibility" with the opposition.

THE FRANTIC FORTNIGHT

Modrow demonstrated how far events had spun out of his control on 1 February, when he threw in the towel and came out in favour of reunification himself. "The unification of the two German states is now on the agenda," he declared. His "Germany, United Fatherland" plan sounded much like Kohl's Ten Points, the main difference being a call for the reunited state to be militarily neutral. Like the chancellor, he drew it up in secret and informed only his superpower ally in advance. With Moscow telling him it was ready to ride the tiger of change, East Germany's final line of defence had crumbled. His sudden conversion opened up a "frantic fortnight" that paved the way for unity.

Naturally, Bonn rejected Modrow's condition of neutrality. In the next two weeks, the separate state's foundations crumbled. With the monthly total of East German refugees reaching over 58,000 in January, Bonn was now convinced the communist state was falling apart. Expecting an uncontrollable human flood by summertime, Bonn began to take charge of the future of the 17 million East Germans.

The shift in thinking dominated the meeting between Kohl and Modrow on 3 February at the World Economic Forum in the Swiss resort of Davos. Tanned and well fed, the chancellor was the very picture of West German prosperity. Addressing the Forum, he proclaimed victory for capitalism in the East–West struggle and warned that any attempt to block unification now would spark off a crisis. He made only a passing and scornful reference to Modrow, saying his neutrality plan was dreamed up by someone "who understands nothing about history or geography". When the East German arrived later for talks with Kohl, his thin frame and grim face reflected his country's condition. Modrow asked for a 15 billion mark credit to help pay East Berlin's bills until the election. Kohl refused. After the meeting, Modrow dodged behind some potted plants to slip away, while Kohl went straight for the cameras to hold court. The caution Kohl had originally shown was now completely gone. "What worries me especially is the enormous loss of the state's authority. The collapse of the economic substance is proceeding apace," he told journalists. "There was a complete change in the atmosphere after New Year. People have for the most part lost hope that things will get better."

Kohl did not wait long to act. On 6 February, he announced his plans to start talks soon with East Berlin on forming an economic and monetary union. This would put the East German economy under the strict control of the powerful Bundesbank (central bank) in Frankfurt. His announcement came so suddenly that Bundesbank president Karl Otto Pöhl, in East Berlin to meet his counterpart Horst Kaminski, had no warning. Just before Kohl was about to propose the idea in Bonn, Pöhl told journalists, "We both believe it would be premature to consider such a far-reaching step at this stage ... It is an illusion to imagine that even one of the problems in East Germany would be solved by the introduc-tion of the West German mark in East Germany." When he heard what had happened in Bonn, Pöhl was so frustrated at being overruled and humiliated that he briefly considered resigning.

Once again, the rivalries in Kohl's complex political world were influenc-ing tactics and timing. An East–West currency union was shaping up as the only political option, no matter how much or how little economic sense it made. As the Leipzig marchers were saying, "If the deutsche-mark doesn't come to us, we'll go to it." By late January, Willy Brandt was stumping through East Germany telling enthusiastic crowds that the deutschemark had to come to them soon. At the Finance Ministry, senior officials concluded in late January that Bonn should push for a quick reunification. It would soon have to extend massive aid to East Germany anyway, they argued, but that could be wasted if a western market econ-omy were not introduced. Since a currency union would lead inexorably to reunification, Bonn should push for a merger as quickly as possible. Finance Minister Theo Waigel threw his weight behind the plan on 2 February.[17] That same day, Kohl's closest aides urged him to seize the political initiative again, as he had done with the Ten Points Programme. On 6 February, Kohl learned that Lothar Späth, the popular Baden-Würt-temberg state premier who had led a failed bid to topple him as CDU chairman only six months before, also planned to join the chorus. Annoyed that Späth should strike out on his own again, the chancellor pre-empted him by announcing his own plan that afternoon.[18]

Amid all this activity, Bonn also had to convince its neighbours that a united Germany would not be a threat to peace. The four victorious powers of World War II – the United States, the Soviet Union, Britain and France – still had residual rights over Germany and could theoretically block any merger. Aware of the concern abroad, Kohl and Genscher agreed that unity must be achieved in harmony with Germany's allies and neighbours. The highest hurdle along that road was the Soviet Union. The two West Germans flew off to Moscow on 10 February hoping for a green light from Gorbachev.

Kohl and Gorbachev met as equals, each the only man who could solve the other's problem. After some introductory remarks, Kohl's notetaker Teltschik recalled, "Gorbachev leaned over the table and spoke the decisive sentences. There were no differences of opinion between the Soviet Union, the Federal Republic and the GDR about unity and the people's right to seek it ... Germans in east and west had already proven that they had learned the lessons of history and no more wars would start on German soil."[19] Gorbachev set only one condition – that current borders were inviolable – before bringing up his main concern. What would happen to Soviet trade with East Germany, one of Moscow's main suppliers of industrial goods? Kohl quickly pledged to take over the contracts and help in any way he could.

After a relaxed dinner, Kohl called a news conference to announce the breakthrough directly to German television viewers. "This evening, I have a single message for all Germans," he announced. "General Secretary Gorbachev told me unmistakably that the Soviet Union will respect the decision of the Germans to live in one state and that it is up to the Germans to decide themselves the time and the way to unite." On the flight back to Bonn, Kohl ordered champagne for all and proposed a toast – "to Germany."

The last piece of the puzzle fell into place on 13 February at a meeting in Ottawa of foreign ministers from NATO and the Warsaw Pact. Behind the scenes, the US, Soviet Union, Britain, France and West Germany worked out the framework for talks on the external aspects of German unification. They emerged with plans for a multidimensional balancing act to allow the two Germanys and the Four Powers to find an agreement to replace the World War II peace treaty that was never signed. The talks were to be called "Two Plus Four" negotiations, in reference to the two Germanys and the Four Powers. The participants agreed on a schedule of monthly meetings, with the intention that all foreign policy aspects of unification should be solved by November.[20]

> 66 Kohl and Gorbachev met as equals, each the only man who could solve the other's problem 99

That same day, when Modrow arrived for his first visit to Bonn, the chilly reception told him that Kohl no longer took him seriously. The chancellor had not even officially informed him of the currency union proposal, which would naturally be on the agenda. Modrow hoped in vain for a "solidarity contribution" of up to 15 billion marks in immediate aid. Kohl refused and told Modrow that the gradual three-phase plan for unity he had unveiled in November – with a network of treaties, then confederative structures and finally a unified federal state – had been overtaken by events. "Now we are, so to speak, jumping with a single leap into the third phase," he said.

Looking back over the hectic fortnight on 15 February, Kohl told the Bundestag that the Germans had never been so close to unity. West Germany was also never better prepared to take on the economic challenge. "The tasks before us will not put the economic efficiency, stability or social security of our Federal Republic of Germany in jeopardy," he reassured his listeners. "No pensioner and no patient, no unemployed person, no war victim and nobody on welfare has to fear that his or her benefits will be cut. To the contrary, the dynamic economic growth will continue to benefit our social security system in the future."

EAST GERMANY VOTES

East Germany's first free elections on 18 March were hardly its own. West Germans were everywhere but on the electoral rolls. Behind the East German campaigns were Western parties plotting strategy, paying salaries and providing experienced staff. Even though reunification still seemed a year or more away, parties from both sides campaigned as if the border had already disappeared. Ibrahim Böhme, the eastern SPD's main candidate, was already being tipped as the next prime minister. Opinion polls predicted a 54 per cent result for the SPD and the party looked forward to regaining its pre-Nazi era popularity, especially in old strongholds such as "Red Saxony".

The SPD's head start alarmed the western CDU, but the party balked at linking up with its eastern counterpart. The *Ost-CDU* had 40 years of collaboration with the SED behind it. It was a classic front organisation, seen by the public as a forum for opportunists. Its new leader, Lothar de Maizière, was a respected lawyer who, for western tastes, was too slow to shake off the habit of praising socialism. But the eastern CDU had about 140,000 members and an intact network of party offices, newspapers and bank accounts – the perfect infrastructure for a successful campaign.

Kohl's party came up with the idea of an "Alliance for Germany", a coalition of the CDU and two new opposition parties. To the left of the CDU was Democratic Awakening. Its leader, Wolfgang Schnur, was a Rostock lawyer who had defended conscientious objectors during the communist period. His deputy, a well-known activist, pastor and peace campaigner from East Berlin named Rainer Eppelmann, had been a

thorn in the communists' side for most of the 1980s. The party claimed
to have about 55,000 members. The German Social Union (DSU), the
second party that Kohl brought in, was a tiny conservative group based
in Leipzig. It had been adopted by Bavaria's CSU, which wanted a partner in the East to expand its influence in a united Germany.

Bonn's constitution foresaw two contrasting legal paths to reunification
and choosing the right one would make all the difference. The fast track
was spelled out in Article 23, which allowed states simply to declare they
wanted to join the Federal Republic and Bonn would take them in. This
was the way the Saarland acceded to West Germany in 1957 after France
agreed to give up its post-war administration there. Although some leaders in the CDU, DA and DSU disliked this option, since it gave Bonn the
upper hand in deciding the conditions of accession, all came around to
this position by the time the "Alliance for Germany" was formed. Most
other parties, including the Eastern SPD, preferred to reunite according
to Article 146. This would require a constitutional convention, which
could take months if not years of unpredictable haggling to produce a
result. The SPD would also have an advantage here thanks to its strong
position in the federal states. Once Kohl had allies in the east, who also
wanted a fast merger that kept the SPD at bay, he agreed to hold six campaign rallies in East Germany.

The more the SPD strode towards victory, the more it tripped itself up.
Böhme, a former SED member, irritated his colleagues by calling himself
an "alternative Marxist". Lafontaine spent the crucial first half of February on vacation in Spain after his landslide re-election in Saarland state
on 28 January. Convinced his warnings about the huge cost of unification would stave off a pro-unity wave, he was irritated to hear that fellow
Social Democrats were jumping on the unity train. Once back home,
Lafontaine tried in vain to slam on the brakes. Out on the stump, he
lambasted Kohl as a liar and a fool for thinking he could reunite the two
Germanys in a few months. Lafontaine's pronounced post-national men-
tality was as appealing to his western supporters as it was irritating to
voters in the east.

Over in Kohl's camp, campaign strategists skilfully twinned the message of prosperity and freedom. Slick posters appeared even in remote
villages, with the clear messages "We are one people", "Prosperity for
all", and "Freedom, not socialism". Thousands of pamphlets, clearly
western products on high quality paper, denounced the Social Democrats as ideological cousins of the communists. The decisive factor,

though, was the chancellor himself. *"Ohne Kohl keine Kohle"* ("Without Kohl, no cash") was the word going around East Germany. More than 150,000 turned out in Erfurt on 20 February to cheer him through his first of six campaign appearances in East Germany. The crowds got bigger with each rally. And Kohl knew how to please them. One of the average East German's biggest worries at the time was whether his wages and savings in eastern marks would be swapped for deutschemarks at the rate of one-to-one, devalued by half with a two-to-one exchange rate or cut even more by *Wessi* technocrats at the Bundesbank. Five days before the election, the chancellor told a rally in Cottbus what all *Ossis* were waiting to hear. "We want savers to know that when the change in currency comes, it will be at one-to-one for them," he told the cheering crowd.

> 66 The crowds got bigger with each rally. And Kohl knew how to please them 99

NOTES

1 *Chronik des Mauerfalls*, pages 204–6.

2 *Chronik des Mauerfalls*, pages 163–6.

3 *Ich wollte Deutschlands Einheit*, pages 131–2.

4 *Chronik des Mauerfalls*, pages 218–19 and 258–61.

5 *Chronik des Mauerfalls*, pages 247–9.

6 For an English-language text, see James, Harold and Stone, Marla (1992) *When the Wall came down: reactions to German unification*. New York: Routledge, Chapman and Hall, pages 33–41.

7 Genscher saw it as domestic rivalry as well, writing in his memoirs that Kohl intended the speech to counterbalance his popularity in the East. See Genscher, Hans-Dietrich (1995) *Erinnerungen*. Berlin: Siedler Verlag, pages 669–74.

8 *Ich wollte Deutschlands Einheit*, page 167.

9 Thatcher, Margaret (1993) *The Downing Street Years*. New York: HarperCollins, pages 790–9. As Kohl put it, "The reservations in Number 10 Downing Street were the strongest ... (Thatcher) just could not comprehend that Germany, at the end of a century in which it had been defeated in two world wars, could emerge as the big winner," See *Ich wollte Deutschlands Einheit*, page 196.

10 *Verbatim II, 1988–1991*, page 350. A keen student of history, Mitterrand also had a pet theory that seemed to reassure him in the early days after the Wall fell. "Even if reunification takes place one day, Prussia – that is to say, the GDR – would never accept to pass into the control of Bavaria, i.e. the FRG," he said on 22 November (page 347).

11 This comes from the Soviet notes of the meeting, as cited in Zelilcon, Philip and Rice, Condoleezza (1995) *Germany Unified and Europe Transformed.* Cambridge: Harvard University Press, page 137.

12 Until his death in January 1996, Mitterrand tried to recast his policy in a more favourable light to counter charges that he had initially bet on the wrong horse. His book *De L'Allemagne, de la France* (Paris: Editions Odile Jacob, 1996) skims over the reluctance and ambiguity that all his interlocutors from those hectic weeks all reported. *Le Monde* described it as "an unfortunate rewriting of German reunification".

13 Gorbachev, Mikhail (1995) *Erinnerungen.* Berlin: Siedler, pages 715–16 and Genscher, Hans-Dietrich (1995) *Erinnerungen.* Berlin: Siedler, pages 682–7.

14 Gerhard Schröder, then SPD candidate for premier of Lower Saxony state, told the party paper *Vorwärts* (February 1990) that hearing the cheers of *Deutschland, Deutschland!* at a Brandt rally in Magdeburg gave him "fits of fear and rejection of such a strong erupting nationalism".

15 Fichter, Tilman. (1993) *Die SPD und die Nation.* Berlin: Ullstein.

16 *Ich wollte Deutschlands Einheit*, pages 213–14.

17 The details of the currency union debate as seen from the Bonn Finance Ministry are discussed in articles by Waigel's aides in Waigel Theo and Schell, Manfred (1994) *Tage, die Deutschland und die Welt veränderten.* Munich: Edition Ferenczy bei Bruckmann.

18 *329 Tage*, pages 129–30.

19 *329 Tage*, page 140.

20 The cycle of six meetings started in May in Bonn and was due to end in November (no session was planned for August).

5

FROM TREATIES TO UNITY

LOTHAR DE MAIZIÈRE WINCED AS THE TV CAMERAS NARROWED IN.
The Alliance for Germany had just won a landslide victory. Around him,
jubilant CDU supporters tried out an un-
familiar new chant – *"Lothar! Lothar!"* The
shy man with the trim grey beard froze. He
mumbled. He looked away. He paused for
little eternities. "This is an unexpectedly
good result which makes us very proud," he
finally stammered. The future prime minister eventually regained
enough composure to reveal the secret of his success: "We said from the
beginning that we wanted German unity without any ifs, ands or buts."

> 66 The West German
> electorate never got a chance
> to vote on the biggest issue it
> ever faced 99

That clear message won the Alliance a stunning 48.1 per cent of the vote.
The eastern CDU itself won 40.9 per cent, a result due more to Helmut
Kohl than anyone else. The SPD won only 21.8 per cent with its calls for
a slower merger. The Alliance's near-majority amounted to a massive
plebiscite for a rapid merger. That settled the question; the West German
electorate never got a chance to vote on the biggest issue it ever faced.
The other surprise of the evening was the PDS, which held on to 16.3 per
cent of the vote. That might have constituted the hardest of its hard core
– old SED functionaries, ex-Stasi men and incorrigible GDR nostalgics –
but it was enough for Gregor Gysi to build on. Alliance 90, a coalition of
New Forum and other grass-roots groups that had started the democracy

marches, mustered a mere 2.9 per cent of the vote. Adept at challenging communist power, the reformers were far less skilled at seeking democratic power themselves.

Now the road was clear to move ahead; but how fast? Kohl bubbled with optimistic predictions. "The country will be flourishing in about five years," he announced. The next day, he predicted that his centre-right would win the first election in a united Germany. He doubted Bonn's general election in December would be expanded into an all-German vote. De Maizière also seemed uncertain as to whether unity could come fast. When the new prime minister made his maiden speech to the Volkskammer on 19 April, he said, "Together with West Germany, we should work towards sending an all-German team to the 1992 Olympics in Barcelona."

TURNING THE ECONOMY AROUND

Once the new East German government was formed, both sides got down to the business of organising their merger. The issues fell into four categories, each of which would need a treaty to settle it. The State Treaty would introduce the deutschemark as legal tender in East Germany and put monetary policy under the control of the Bundesbank. The Unity Treaty would set down common legal ground on everything from health care systems and farm subsidies to abortion. The Election Treaty would spell out the new voting system and set a date for the first all-German polls. The final task would be the Two Plus Four Treaty to abolish the wartime Allies' remaining rights over Germany. The nearly simultaneous work on all four treaties dominated German politics for the next six months. Campaigning for the looming all-German vote intruded daily. In the east, the amateur politicians made the Volkskammer look like a student parliament. De Maizière brought the SPD into a grand coalition to ensure that East Berlin had a broad majority behind its unity policies.

After being overruled by Kohl, the Bundesbank kept criticising the monetary union he wanted to introduce. In late March, a confidential Bundesbank proposal leaked to the press showed that the bank wanted to swap the *Ostmark* at a two-to-one rate to the deutschemark. East Germans cried, "Stop the thief!" With a passion not seen since the autumn, demonstrators around the country marched for a one-to-one exchange rate. "We're not half-Germans," they shouted. With all the confidence he lacked on election evening, de Maizière said in his first speech as prime minister,

"One-to-one should be the basic rate. We must agree on terms that ensure East German citizens do not feel they are becoming second-class citizens." Kohl, whose prospects were now tied to the success of the new prime minister, stuck to the one-to-one rate despite the Bundesbank's reservations.

The final deal was announced on 2 May, only four days before local elections in East Germany. Wages and pensions would be converted at a one-to-one rate; anything else would have been an open invitation to move west. Some savings would be exchanged at par, others at two-to-one. Bonn also offered to boost pensions from half the average industrial wage in East Germany to the 70 per cent level common in West Germany. Not surprisingly, the local polls confirmed the CDU landslide seen in March. The generous exchange rate was one of the few victories the easterners scored against the west. In the negotiations, the eastern side failed to get its way on full debt relief, a moratorium on land sales to *Wessis* and continued industrial subsidies to avoid mass layoffs. These were all incompatible with a free market, the westerners explained.[1]

In the end, the State Treaty turned the eastern economy into a near carbon copy of the West German model. East Berlin agreed to take over Bonn's "social market economy". Economic policy would be harmonised with European guidelines, with free movement for workers, capital, goods and services. West German guidelines on banking, insurance, legal services and other businesses were extended to what the text called "the monetary area". The east would also introduce western-style labour laws and the complex web of health, unemployment and pension benefits that cushioned the West German system. Bonn's environmental laws would also be imposed. What East Berlin had boasted was the world's tenth-strongest industrial economy was going to be swallowed up at breakneck speed.

> 66 The generous exchange rate was one of the few victories the easterners scored against the west 99

"D-mark Day" came on Sunday, 1 July. When *Ossis* went shopping on Monday morning, they found scenes reminiscent of the 1948 currency reform that introduced the deutschemark in West Germany. Shelves that had emptied in the dying days of the old communist economy were suddenly full of brightly-packed yoghurt, fresh fruit and appetising cuts of meat. Store windows now displayed West German appliances, Japanese cameras and the latest ready-to-wear Italian fashions. With subsidies gone, prices for bread rolls jumped from 5 to 25 pfennigs. A 5 kg bag of potatoes now cost 5 marks, not 1 mark.

The western system also brought an unwanted western scourge – unemployment. By the end of the first month of monetary union, joblessness had almost doubled, to 250,000. Companies and state farms were shedding workers because they could not pay wages or buy materials. Company debts, little more than ledger entries in the unreal communist economy, drove many firms to shut down because they could not repay them in real deutschemarks.

THE UNITY AND ELECTION TREATIES

The next step forward was the Unity Treaty. This marriage contract between the two states aimed to introduce West Germany's complex political and legal system in the east. As a guiding principle, Bonn's laws would apply fully. Exceptions would be allowed only when needed to ease the radical transition the east had to make.

Concerned about the psychological impact of reunification, de Maizière focused on symbols to help his compatriots identify with the new state. At the first formal round of negotiations in East Berlin on 6 July, he caught Bonn's main negotiator Wolfgang Schäuble off guard with detailed questions and suggestions. The new state could be called *Deutsche Bundesrepublik* (German Federal Republic) to distinguish it from West Germany's *Bundesrepublik Deutschland*. The talks should also consider designing a new flag, a surprising idea since both states used nearly identical black, red and gold banners.

> ❝ De Maizière's suggestion was typical of East German ideas at the time – original, intriguing and doomed to failure ❞

A professional viola player before he entered politics, de Maizière then baffled Schäuble with a proposal for a new national anthem. It could keep the tune of Bonn's hymn, the Haydn melody known around the world as *Deutschland, Deutschland über alles*, but take its verse from the old eastern and western anthems. It took a musician to realise that the Communist text fitted Haydn's music perfectly. The East German text also contained the line *Deutschland, einig Vaterland*, the motto of the 1989 protests.

De Maizière's suggestion was like so many of those made by the East Germans in those days – original, intriguing and doomed to failure. Schäuble took these suggestions "with varying degrees of seriousness" and told de Maizière he saw no reason to change anything. He reminded the East Germans that their state was falling apart, not his. "My standard speech was – dear friends, this is a case of East Germany joining West Germany, not the other way around," he recalled. "You are heartily welcome. But this is not the unification of two equal states."[2]

The most important symbol of all was Berlin. De Maizière insisted the treaty must declare the city Germany's new capital. Moving the government would show Bonn's commitment to integrating the eastern states into the larger Germany. Schäuble agreed but knew the Bundestag would never approve any treaty that dictated where it should sit. In the end, he came up with a compromise: to name Berlin as the new capital, but ask the all-German parliament to decide after the election where it wanted to meet.

Abortion was just as divisive. East Germany allowed abortion on demand within the first three months of pregnancy. Even conservative eastern parties refused to give up this "socialist achievement", which perplexed many Christian Democrats in West Germany. Abortion there was outlawed in principle as a violation of the right to life, defended by Bonn's constitution in a conscious contrast to the Nazis' contempt for life. Doctors were allowed to make exceptions in the first three months of pregnancy. The emotions stirred up by this debate clouded over an aspect of the abortion issue that transcended the details of the laws involved. "At least according to the statistics, the protection of unborn life is neither more nor less guaranteed in East Germany than it is in West Germany," Schäuble found, to his surprise. "The number of abortions per capita is about equally high in both parts of Germany."[3] Since the Volkskammer would oppose a treaty that imposed the western law, this had to be left to the all-German parliament as well. In the meantime, abortion would stay legal in the east and restricted in the west.

The struggle over property rights was another legal nightmare. Around 4.4 million people had quit East German territory for the West since the end of World War II. Many left behind homes, shops and land. The fall of the Wall meant the possibility of reclaiming them. For the lucky Westerners involved, windfall wealth beckoned. Fear spread like wildfire among East German tenants and owners of houses that had once belonged to refugees. Soon after the Wall opened, *Wessis* started driving up in BMWs and Mercedes to barge in and inspect run-down houses they claimed as their own. There were frequent cases of disputed ownership, due to the confusing way the communists had nationalised property over the years. In some cases, property confiscated from Jews under Hitler went first to Nazi officials and was then expropriated by the communists. Thus one house could have three "legal" claimants – the original Jewish owner, the Nazi who took it in the 1930s and the communist who got it after the war.

Under heavy pressure from the west, the negotiators agreed that property should in principle be returned to its original owners. The easterners wanted to pay compensation instead, saying returning property to strangers was unfair to the East Germans who had lived in it or cared for it for decades. Using its leverage as Kohl's coalition partner, the pro-business FDP threatened to torpedo the monetary union unless former owners got their property back. Businesses would not invest in eastern Germany if such elementary issues as property rights were not settled, it argued. The negotiators agreed that, apart from land redistributed in the 1946 land reform implemented by Soviet authorities, most property should be returned. This turned out to be a major stumbling block for economic revival in the east, because drawn-out legal battles over ownership held up many investment plans.

Then there was the problem of east–west espionage. Schäuble and East Berlin negotiator Günther Krause wanted to include an amnesty for all spies, both to be fair to East German agents (since West German agents naturally would not be jailed) and to avoid driving former Stasi spies into the arms of other espionage networks such as the KGB. But popular opposition to a "Stasi amnesty" quickly killed this plan. The two negotiators also wanted very tight controls over the Stasi archives. "The Stasi left behind ... huge mountains of files. The incredibly intensive tapping of West German telephone calls is also recorded in these dossiers," Schäuble wrote. "Sometimes I wondered whether we couldn't destroy all of them without reading them."[1] But this time, the East Germans, who feared the Stasi files would be hidden away in the West German archives in Koblenz, stood their ground. "I want my dossier!" was a motto of the 1989 protests. The *Ossis* refused to let *Wessis* take away their past. After the Volkskammer passed a law ensuring fairly open access to the files, Schäuble and Krause reluctantly wrote similar guidelines into the Unity Treaty.

> 66 This being Germany, picking a date for Unity Day was a minefield 99

The Election Treaty had to lay down when and how the reunited country would hold the first all-German poll since 1932. West Germany was scheduled to hold a general election on 2 December. Kohl initially doubted the merger would be finished in time, but it would be absurd to elect a West German parliament only to dissolve it soon afterwards to hold all-German elections. Leaving the Volkskammer working any longer than necessary ran the risk of establishing it as a kind of regional assembly. The legislators, as Kohl once complained, would get to like "playing GDR" and not want to give up their seats. So when it became clear, by mid-1990, that the merger could come by autumn, Bonn and East Berlin agreed to make 2 December the date for the first all-German poll.

This being Germany, picking a date for Unity Day was another minefield. The obvious date for this was 9 November, the day the Wall fell, but it turned out to be too symbolic. The ill-fated Weimar Republic was founded on 9 November 1918. On the same day five years later, Adolf Hitler staged his "beer-hall putsch" in Munich. In 1938, 9 November brought the *Reichskristallnacht*, the "Crystal Night" Nazi pogrom that started the Holocaust. In the end, the Germans picked the earliest date available. The last hurdle was a CSCE foreign ministers' meeting in New York on 1 October to pronounce a final blessing on the Two Plus Four Treaty. Given the fact that Genscher would have to dash back for the celebrations, 3 October was the first possible date. In their haste, officials unfortunately overlooked the option of waiting another week for 9 October, the date of the crucial 1989 Leipzig protest. It would have linked Unity Day to the historic evening when Germans defied their dictators and won.

THE TWO PLUS FOUR TREATY

The trickiest treaty was the Two Plus Four agreement. The World War II allies still held some residual rights over Germany and had to work out a replacement for the peace treaty that never was. The hardest part was getting Moscow to give up its proudest war trophy, East Germany, without making this look like Moscow's own Versailles Treaty. As it turned out, the talks were a *tour de force* of the new Germany's diplomacy. Kohl deftly staked out Bonn's goals and tirelessly wooed Gorbachev, Bush, Mitterrand and Thatcher to reach them. After years of juggling German and foreign interests across the East–West divide, Genscher stood at the crowning point of his career as he negotiated the details. The timing was a stroke of luck for Bonn. Gorbachev was at the beginning of his end and needed western help to hang on.[5]

In a first show of their new determination, the Germans insisted they would not sit on the sidelines while the wartime allies discussed their fate. Bonn made sure it was an equal partner and boasted it had ensured the negotiations were called Two (Germanys) plus Four (allies) and not the other way around. Miffed, the French insisted on saying "Quatre plus deux" while British foreign secretary Douglas Hurd quipped that he preferred "Zero plus four."

Before the talks started, Kohl's allies insisted he clear up the issue of Poland's western border, which cut off one-third of pre-war Germany. Bonn had never officially recognised the Oder–Neisse line because, as a supreme court ruling had laid down, a rump German state could not give up part of the former united Germany. Only an all-German parliament could do that. Although it no longer claimed the territory, Bonn's insistence on this legalism sounded suspicious to its partners. There was still a small minority of voters expelled from the eastern lands who hoped to get them back. Wary of alienating them at a time when the far right was advancing at the ballot box, Kohl stubbornly ignored all appeals to give his approval to the post-war border. Britain and France openly pressured him, and Polish Prime Minister Tadeusz Mazowiecki suggested he would not let Soviet troops leave his country until the issue was solved.

> 66 Kohl deftly staked out Bonn's goals and tirelessly wooed Gorbachev, Bush, Mitterrand and Thatcher to reach them 99

Kohl's partners could hardly have believed he harboured plans to get that territory back, especially since he assured them in private that he did not. His strategy was to deal with the issue later in the reunification process, at which point the expellees would be told they could not hold up the merger with a demand nobody else supported. Appearing to the interests of this small group over those of the Poles placed Kohl's most stubborn and local side on full display. Kohl tried to calm emotions with a Bundestag resolution on 8 March declaring the border inviolable. But he came off looking mean and small-minded by linking this to a call for Warsaw to renounce all rights to reparations for World War II.[6]

THE MEETINGS

When the talks opened in Bonn on 5 May, Soviet Foreign Minister Eduard Shevardnadze said the Kremlin accepted reunification but was absolutely opposed to NATO membership for the reunited nation. At the second meeting in East Berlin in June, he presented a full draft treaty saying Two Plus Four would be only a temporary deal to be reviewed in 1992, in the light of Germany's behaviour after unity. "The western half of the merged country should stay in NATO while the eastern half should stay in the Warsaw Pact, for at least five years." There would be a demilitarised zone along the old frontier. During Shevardnadze's presentation, Baker wrote "What does this mean?" on a slip of paper and passed it to Genscher. "Window dressing," he scribbled back.[7]

Shevardnadze was bluffing. A crucial Soviet Communist Party congress was coming up in early July and Gorbachev had to score points with the military, which was deeply suspicious of the new friendly West. The Western partners in this lopsided poker game had no interest in calling his hand. The reassurances he sought came with the olive branch offered by NATO's London summit in early July. To prove the Cold War was really over, NATO leaders were ready to soften their nuclear strategy of "flexible response" and make atomic arms the "weapons of last resort". The US would withdraw all its nuclear artillery shells from Europe if the Soviet Union did the same. Faster troops cuts, especially in Germany, could be agreed at the Conventional Forces in Europe (CFE) talks in Vienna. On the political front, NATO pledged to support new institutions that would make the CSCE a more effective forum for preventing conflict.

The final breakthrough came outside the Two Plus Four framework. Kohl flew to Moscow on 14 July to iron out the issue of Germany's NATO membership. Having survived the stormy party congress, Gorbachev told Kohl in a closed-door meeting that he was ready to make a deal. Germany could remain in NATO provided the alliance's authority did not extend to eastern Germany while Soviet troops were still there. Moscow was also ready to end Four Power rights over Germany as soon as the Two Plus Four talks were finished. Just to make sure he had heard correctly, Kohl made Gorbachev confirm his concession one more time over lunch with the other delegation members. "As far as we know, reunification will come by the end of this year," the chancellor reported. "This is an enormous event. It will be different from 1871," he said, stressing that Bonn and Moscow would sign a non-aggression pact. Gorbachev listened and then said in German, "*Gut.*"[8]

The deal was announced on 16 July at the Zheleznovodsk mountain spa in the Caucasus region, where Gorbachev had started his political career. In a crowded auditorium, Kohl slowly read out their eight-point agreement. Germany could unite and choose its military alliance, he told journalists who had flown with him from Moscow. This clearly meant NATO, since he then said the alliance's authority would not extend eastwards for the first four years after unity, while the 360,000 Soviet troops there were withdrawn. Units of the Bundeswehr could be stationed in eastern Germany immediately. Kohl pledged to cut Germany's overall troop strength from almost 600,000 down to 370,000. Reunited Germany would consist of the Federal Republic, the GDR and Berlin – an implicit recognition of the Oder–Neisse line. As Kohl read out the details, a journalist in the hushed hall let out a long low whistle of amazement. This was it. The Cold War was finally over. The division of Germany, the cornerstone of the bipolar post-war world, was ending with the Kremlin's approval. Kohl had gambled and won across the board.

The Two Plus Four talks were heading for their final session in Moscow when the Kremlin pulled out its trump card. The Soviet military would need far more help than anticipated to meet the troop withdrawal target, Gorbachev said in late August. On 5 September, it presented the bill – 36 billion marks, or eight times the sum Bonn's experts had calculated. Kohl, who at the same time had Washington pressing him to help pay for the Desert Shield operation against Iraq, called Moscow to offer 8 billion marks. After several days of haggling, they agreed on 15 billion marks. "We knew all too well that Gorbachev held the trump card," Kohl recalled. "He could make the last round of the Two Plus Four talks collapse and create enormous problems for us just a few metres before the finish line."[9] The signing took place in Moscow. "We have drawn a line under World War II and started keeping the time of a new era," Shevardnadze said. "We are now dealing with a new Germany that has learned its lesson from history."

> 66 This was it. The Cold War was finally over ... Kohl had gambled and won across the board 99

UNITY AT LAST

Reunited Germany was officially born at the stroke of midnight on 3 October 1990, only 11 months after the Wall had fallen. The organisers of the unity celebrations tried to recapture the joy and togetherness of that landmark day. But the exhausted nation had been through too much to party with abandon now. Problems that were unthinkable in November 1989 were now part of everyday life. The reunion of *Ossis* (easterners) and *Wessis* (westerners) had proven far more difficult than anyone had imagined. With the euphoria gone, Unity Day seemed to come at the wrong time.

There were also many other mergers at that time. Kohl's CDU took the eastern Christian Democrats into its fold and made de Maizière their deputy chairman. The Social Democrats merged in late September, naming eastern SPD leader Wolfgang Thierse as one of their deputy chairmen. East German branch trade unions joined up with their west German counterparts, the western Protestant and Catholic churches linked up with their congregations in the east and new all-German sports leagues sprouted all over.

The only major group to miss the boat were the Greens. The western Greens opposed the Unity Treaty in the Bundestag and denounced the merger as the biggest land grab by Germans since the Nazis. The affluent *Wessis* focused more on pacifism and ecology while Alliance 90, their natural partners in the east, cared more about mass unemployment. The two sides agreed to merge after the December election.

It was the bittersweet end of two eras for the *Ossis* both of their country and of its short-lived experiment in independent government. The state most *Ossis* had grown up in and learned to live with, for better or for worse, was about to disappear. The Volkskammer, where the new democratic élite did its political apprenticeship, was closing down. When they gathered on the steps of the Reichstag at midnight, Kohl and de Maizière

> 66 The exhausted nation had been through too much to party with abandon now 99

stood side by side waving to the crowds together. The chancellor looked misty-eyed as they all sang the *Deutschlandlied*, the western and now all-German anthem. After the short ceremony, Kohl and his new deputy retired for a chat inside the Reichstag. But the crowds kept chanting "Helmut, Helmut!" Time and again, Kohl got up to wave to the crowds. He motioned to de Maizière to join him, but the former prime minister quietly refused. He was exhausted. He had done his duty. His time in the spotlight was over, he thought.

THE CAMPAIGN FINISHES

After a year like that, the general election on 2 December was an anticlimax. There was never any doubt that Kohl would win. The chancellor appeared positively presidential, ignoring his challenger, Lafontaine, and focusing on the larger issues. When Gorbachev appealed for food shipments to overcome menacing winter shortages, the chancellor leaped to his aid and mobilised public and private donations worth over 800 million marks. It was a popular gesture of thanks to Gorbachev and a way to reassure the world that the reunited Germans were good neighbours.

Lafontaine, who had considered quitting after being stabbed in the neck by a crazed attacker in April, fought on as if on autopilot. Even the SPD's setbacks in October, when it lost four of the five elections in the new eastern states, hardly dented his determination to prove Kohl was wrong. On the stump in western Germany, he started his speeches according to his pre-unity plan with warnings about the ozone layer, the death of the tropical forests or the fate of Arctic seals. Were these problems any less pressing, he would ask, just because a wall has fallen? Flag waving wouldn't solve any of Germany's economic or social problems, he roared at packed audiences. In the east, this "Napoleon from the Saar" told the *Ossis* they were fools to think Kohl would bring them prosperity. Helmut Schmidt spoke for more than just himself when he remarked shortly before the vote, "Lafontaine will lose, and he deserves to."

Kohl sailed through to the victory he richly deserved. The Christian Democrats won 43.8 per cent of the national vote. They scored over 40 per cent in both electorates. Kohl's bet had paid off; he won his re-election in the east. The FDP surged from 9.1 per cent in 1987 to 11 per cent in 1990 thanks to its "Genscher bonus". This strong result gave the coalition a solid overall score of 54.8 per cent and a crushing 134-seat majority in the Bundestag. The SPD ended up with only 33.5 per cent of the national vote, its worst result since 1957. It did especially badly in the east, winning only 23.4 per cent of the vote. Lafontaine capped the year's work on the day after the election by abruptly turning down the job of party chairman he was supposed to take and declining to take up his seat as opposition leader in the Bundestag. It was like a driver running away from his car after wrecking it in a crash.

The western Greens paid dearly for their reluctance to merge with Alliance 90 before the vote. They slumped to 4.7 per cent, crashing out of the Bundestag, while Alliance 90 scored 6.2 per cent in the east. If the two parties had united, the eastern votes would have produced a 5.1 per cent result nation-wide and helped the *Wessis* back into office. As it turned out, only eight Alliance 90 deputies entered the first all-German parliament. The PDS profited from the split electorate. Its national vote was 2.4 per cent, with a laughable 0.3 per cent in the west. But it racked up 9.9 per cent in the east, enough to win 17 seats in the new assembly and fend off what looked like its inevitable end.

> 66 Lafontaine was like a driver running from his car after wrecking it in a crash 99

After all the upheavals of 1990, the Germans wanted nothing more than peace and quiet. When asked in a survey what united Germany should be like in the year 2000, 75 per cent said that Germany should not play a larger role in world affairs. It should copy Europe's prosperous neutral states – 40 per cent wanted it to be like an oversized Switzerland, another 29 per cent named Sweden as their favourite model. No fewer than 85 per cent said Germany should be a world leader in environmental protection, 83 per cent wanted it to have open borders with all its neighbours and 81 per cent wanted Germany to be part of a much more integrated European Union. "The Germans have sketched out their ideal in this survey," Munich's *Süddeutsche Zeitung* wrote. "They want a state that makes environmental protection its top priority, keeps close ties to the Soviet Union, belongs to a European federation and is governed, if pos-sible, from Brussels by a woman prime minister from Luxembourg."[9]

NOTES

1 For more on the talks, see *Tage, die Deutschland und die Welt veränderten*, pages 201–25.

2 Schäuble, Wolfgang (1991) *Der Vertrag*. Stuttgart: Deutsche Verlags Anstalt, page 131.

3 *Der Vertrag*, page 232–4.

4 *Der Vertrag*, pages 272–3.

5 The best account of the Two Plus Four talks is *Germany Unified and Europe Transformed* (Cambridge: Harvard University Press, 1995) by Philip Zelikow and Condoleezza Rice, two members of the United States delegation. For a first-hand account in German, see *Ein runder Tisch mit scharfen Ecken* (Baden-Baden: Nomos, 1993) by Genscher's chief of staff Frank Elbe and journalist Richard Kiessler.

6 Although Bonn made various hefty payments after the war to the states Hitler fought, West Germany did not officially pay reparations to its former enemies because this issue was left open until a full peace treaty for all Germany could be signed. In 1953, Poland announced it sought no reparations from East Germany. But the reparations issue was techxnically open for Poland or any other country that fought against Germany in the war. The Two Plus Four Treaty, which was meant to replace the missing peace treaty, could have offered other countries the chance to demand such payments. Kohl's position here was one of the few times any West German leader publicly mentioned a key element in Bonn's strategy at the Two Plus Four talks – to bury the reparations issue quietly once and for all.

7 *Germany Unified and Europe Transformed*, page 298.

8 *Tage, die Deutschland und die Welt veränderten*, page 36.

9 *Ich wollte Deutschlands Einheit*, pages 466–8, *329 Tage*, pages 357–63 and document number 415 in *Deutsche Einheit, Sonderedition aus den Akten des Bundeskanzleramtes 1989/1990*. Munich: R. Oldenbourg Verlag, 1998, pages 1527–30.

10 *Süddeutsche Zeitung Magazin*, 4 January 1991, pages 8–15.

DISUNITED GERMANY

6

THE HELPLESS GIANT

THE GERMANS WERE STILL CONGRATULATING THEMSELVES for reuniting in peace when the Gulf War shattered their pleasant dream. Soon after the New Year's fireworks at the Brandenburg Gate, the television was suddenly broadcasting footage of bombing raids over Baghdad. It didn't make sense. With the East–West split gone and the nuclear threat fading, hadn't peace broken out all over? Hadn't reunification just proved the superiority of reason over force? Refusing to believe this new era was already over, the dormant peace movement sprang back to life. Protesters draped sheets saying *Nein*! from their bedroom windows. Over 200,000 turned out in Bonn for the largest anti-war gathering in Europe. Their rallying call: "Stop the Gulf War – We won't let the future be destroyed!"

Six months later, many of the same Germans fumed in frustration as they watched the Yugoslav war unfold on their television screens. Post-Cold War instability had reached Europe. Bombs and tanks were scarring landscapes familiar from summer vacations. Refugees were already arriving in Germany. In the republics of Slovenia and Croatia, Belgrade was trying to snuff out the drive for self-determination. Again, Germans demanded that the fighting should stop.

Stunned and disoriented by the rough new world outside, Bonn flip-flopped. Helmut Kohl and Hans-Dietrich Genscher scrambled for cover when the Gulf War broke out. They refused to send troops to join their allies fighting against Saddam Hussein. The best they could do was to write cheques to bankroll the allied effort. By contrast, when the Yugoslav war began, Bonn rushed to the front line of the crisis and it loudly championed independence for Slovenia and Croatia. Its allies doubted this would stop the war, but Bonn steamrollered ahead. After several months of arm-twisting by Kohl and Genscher, they reluctantly agreed to recognise the rebel republics.

Bonn's behaviour in 1991 wiped out much of the goodwill it had built up abroad the year before. The balanced diplomacy of the Two Plus Four talks seemed forgotten. Instead, after depending on its allies for defence for 40 years, Bonn was playing pick-and-choose on major security issues. Bonn's staunch support for Croatia, a Nazi-era ally now run by the authoritarian nationalist Franjo Tudjman, stirred some disturbing memories. The Helmut-in-a-spiked-helmet caricatures popped up again in the press at home and abroad.

66 Stunned and disoriented by the rough new world outside, Bonn flip-flopped 99

This was not an old Germany coming back but a new Germany over-whelmed by events. Neither the back seat it took in the Gulf crisis nor its high profile on Yugoslavia amounted to a new policy paradigm. The main constants in the two crises were the *Angst* and outrage that gripped public opinion. After all the changes of 1990, voters recoiled at the idea that Germany might soon go off to war again as well.

When the Bundestag met on 17 January to formally elect the chancellor, the deputies were in shock at the bombing of Iraq, which had broken out overnight. Kohl devoted most of his acceptance speech to the war. Germany stood by its allies, he announced, but would not send troops into action. After that, Bonn resolutely stuck its head in the sand. Kohl refused to discuss the hottest issue posed by the war – whether its NATO allies would call in Bonn's Cold War debts. Bonn had sent 18 Alpha ground-attack jets to Turkey in early January in a show of NATO support. If Iraq ever attacked Turkey, Ankara could invoke the alliance's mutual defence pledge. The SPD argued that Bonn should not help defend its ally.

Keen to avoid any commitment, the government resorted to hair-splitting. Since Iraq had not attacked Turkey, Kohl said, he would not "meditate in public about the issue". Even more remarkable was the silence from the foreign ministry. Hans-Dietrich Genscher, who some-times gave several broadcast interviews before breakfast, went off the air for days. When he resumed speaking in public, his statements of solidarity with the allies never clearly addressed the NATO issue. Genscher's few days off the air left a deep impression. The world was entering a new and unstable phase and Bonn's master tactician had no ready response.

Public opinion was just as unsure. Most Germans agreed that Iraq had to be driven out of Kuwait. There was also a solid majority against any German military involvement. At times, public opinion seemed most concerned about an ecological catastrophe from burning Kuwaiti oilfields.

After the war, Kohl said he had believed to the end that Saddam Hussein would back down. "On the basis of the information I had, I hoped the Iraqi dictator would show an understanding of the realities," he explained.[1] But what was his information based on? Kohl had just lost his long-time national security advisor Horst Teltschik, who went to work in the private sector. NATO members were sharing little information about their planning to partners who had not put up troops. So, despite Washington's preparations for war, Bonn bet on a last-minute compromise. "We were outside the loop," admitted Lutz Stavenhagen, Kohl's intelligence coordinator. Germany thought it would be enough to help Kuwait rebuild after the Iraqi withdrawal. As Stavenhagen ruefully put it, "We were going to be in the front line of the humanitarian aid effort."

PROTESTERS FILL THE GAP

The anti-war movement filled the gap the government had left unattended. Once the bombing started, protesters poured animal blood outside Luftwaffe bases and taunted troops with posters of recruits saying "I'm happy to die for cheap oil." A human chain blocked the doors to the Frankfurt stock market one day and fought a pitched battle with police and "war profiteers" (i.e. brokers and staff) trying to get to work. Cities in the Rhineland scrapped their pre-Lenten Carnival parades and fancy balls, something they did not even do during World War II.

To add to their shame and guilt, it turned out that German firms had helped build up Iraq's military machine in the 1980s. Investigators suspected that German technology had helped boost the range of Iraq's Soviet-built Scud-B missiles. Armed with mustard gas from German-built chemical factories, these were the biggest threat to Israel in years. Among the hundred or so German firms investigated for illegal arms exports to Iraq was one that built a luxury underground bunker for Saddam Hussein. Buried under the royal palace in Baghdad, this vast *Führerbunker* had thick walls of hardened concrete to withstand a nuclear attack and a reinforced canopy over Saddam's bed should any concrete fall from the ceiling.[2] As one war protester's sign put it: "Everybody opposes Iraq's war machine – we built it."

The widespread protests reflected how strongly many Germans had internalised their post-war lesson of "no more war" instead of their allies' lesson of standing up to aggression. The gesture of open refusal, even if it was only a bedsheet screaming *Nein!*, was important in moral terms, even if it was ineffective. "If the world won't follow Germany's example, they can at least demonstrate that nobody can beat the Germans for their peacefulness, compassion and caution," commentator Wolfgang Herles wrote sarcastically of the protesters. "And if the world unfortunately refuses to see this, these better Germans can at least demonstrate it to themselves. For them fear, trumpeted out as loudly as possible, passes as proof of the moral and intellectual superiority of the lambs over the lions."[3]

> ❝ Everybody opposes Iraq's war machine – we built it ❞

The reaction abroad was withering. None of its allies had really expected Germany to send troops to the Gulf. The US suggested it privately, but accepted Kohl's argument that the constitution banned this.[4] But they did think they deserved more public support. Turkish President Turgut Özal said in public what many of Bonn's allies muttered in private. "Germany has become so rich that it has completely lost its fighting spirit," Özal told ARD television on 24 January. He accused Bonn of trying to wheedle its way out of the same NATO commitment that it had expected from its allies for 40 years. "Why does Germany forget all this?" he asked. Bonn would be to blame if Saddam Hussein attacked Turkey with biological or chemical weapons. "Who gave them to him?" he taunted his viewers. "You are responsible. You should come and help us and shoulder your responsibility."

"The Germans are behind us ... way behind us," wrote the *New York Times* columnist William Safire. Washington worried that it could not depend on Bonn to help establish Bush's "new world order". Alliance strategists, concerned that the post-Cold War NATO had to go "out of area or out of a job", wondered how they could do this if the second-largest member refused. The European Community faced the prospect that its plans for a common security policy could be stymied from the start.

CHEQUEBOOK DIPLOMACY

The first fatal Scud attack on Israel finally hit a raw nerve in Germany. Late on 22 January, an Iraqi missile slammed into a middle-class Tel Aviv suburb. Three Israelis died, 96 were injured and about twenty houses were destroyed in the blast. The Jewish state's legendary defences were suddenly useless – and German technology had helped make them come tumbling down. The following morning, Kohl went on the offensive. "This is a clear attack on Israel's integrity and right to exist, for which we Germans have a special responsibility," he said after a cabinet meeting. In concrete terms, that meant an immediate payment of 250 million marks in humanitarian aid. Bonn would send Israel Patriot rockets, two submarines and equipment against chemical warfare including the *Fuchs* "sniffer tanks" that could help it detect poison gas. It also stepped up military aid to the United States, Britain, France and Turkey to help them wage the war.

When Genscher flew to Israel to distribute Bonn's aid in person, he went equipped with his own gas mask and a protective rubber suit. What he really needed, though, was a thick skin. On arrival, his first stop was the Tel Aviv suburb hit by Scud missiles. "I don't want to see any Germans here," a sobbing woman moaned as his delegation surveyed the damage. "The Germans killed my parents and now they're helping Saddam Hussein. I hate the Germans." Demonstrators heckled Genscher when he visited the Yad Vashem Holocaust memorial the next morning. When he then turned up at a Jerusalem hotel for a meeting, an angry protester screamed in his face "Go home, Genscher, go home! We don't want your filthy guilt money!" Posters in the crowd read "Eichmann's successors are helping Iraq" and "Zyklon B – Mustard Gas – Nerve Gas – all made by Germans for Jews."

Genscher toured Israel's Arab neighbours in mid-February in a second round of "chequebook diplomacy". There were handouts at every stop – 150 million marks and eight sniffer tanks for Egypt, 150 million marks for Jordan and 100 million marks for Syria. Once the floodgates were open, Bonn had to salute almost any ally that came looking for help. Within a week, it had to shell out once again. First it was $5.5 billion more for the USA. The next day, there was an 800 million mark cheque for Britain, then another 300 million marks for Paris. Turkey was promised anti-aircraft missiles and another 600 German airmen to beef up its defences. The bill for Israel was worth up to a billion marks, including funds to buy Patriot missiles from Washington. Bonn drew heavily on its munitions stocks to help equip its allies, and acted as the main shipping agent for Germany-based US and UK troops and equipment sent to the Gulf. "We told the Germans we needed goods worth $12 billion and they paid up without saying a word," US Ambassador Vernon Walters recalled with satisfaction.[5]

The final bill was staggering. By the start of war, Bonn had pledged 5.3 billion marks to the allied war effort. When the finance ministry drew up a final list of its Gulf War contributions in April, the total came to at least 17.2 billion marks. This amounted to about one-third of Germany's entire defence budget for that year. Bonn had ended up providing the allied forces with everything from ammunition to sunscreen cream. In the end, the ministry calculated, Germany paid about 16 per cent of the total cost of the war.[6]

Hypersensitive about domestic reaction, Bonn did not dare advertise how much it had actually supported the allies. Bonn even turned down a request from the British defence ministry for details of its aid to counter biting criticism of the supposedly disloyal Germans in the British press.[7] So Germany ended up paying huge sums to the Gulf alliance without having any influence or getting any credit for it. If Germany's partners expected it to play a bigger role, chequebook diplomacy would not be enough. Bonn would have to define a new role and build a domestic consensus to support it.

> 66 Bonn had ended up providing the allied forces with everything from ammunition to sunscreen cream 99

But what defence role should a reformed militarist nation choose? The only point of agreement was that Germany should not act unilaterally. This lowest common denominator appears in Articles 24 and 26 of the constitution, which allowed Germany to join a system of collective security and barred it from waging an offensive war. The articles did not ban "out of area" missions, but for years the government had interpreted them as a ban on sending German troops outside the NATO area. When Kohl signalled, after the war, that he wanted to let troops join multilateral peace-keeping missions, he triggered two years of hair-splitting debate. The SPD and Greens asked what kind of mandate German troops needed to deploy abroad. Should they be armed, unarmed or equipped only with light arms for self-defence? Could they impose a cease-fire by force or only maintain an existing one by their presence?

Faced with political blockade, Bonn took a detour and began to raise Germany's humanitarian aid profile in international military missions. Seven minesweepers combed the waters of the Gulf after the war, clearing away the Iraqis' floating bombs. This would help to de-escalate regional tensions, avert an ecological catastrophe – and set a precedent for sending German forces far afield. The Bundeswehr also joined an international effort to feed and protect Iraqi Kurds. A year later, German medics joined the United Nations peace-keeping mission in Cambodia. The new approach was slow and cautious. But this was the path of consensus, the traditional way of getting things done in Bonn.

THE HOME FRONT

The first half of 1991 was hardly the time for calm debates about Germany's new role abroad. Domestic politics was in an uproar. Factory closures in the east were in full swing. The region was sinking steadily into mass unemployment. The official jobless rate had reached 9.2 per cent by March, triple its level in July 1990. Tens of thousands of Leipzigers were demonstrating again, this time not for Kohl but against him. "Rather rid of Kohl than out of a job" read one of their posters.

When, in late February, the government unveiled a tax hike Kohl called a "solidarity surcharge," *Bild* ridiculed him as "The Flip-Flop Man". The 7.5 per cent tax surcharge was the bill for reunification that he had said Germans would not have to pay. He tried to explain that unexpected events such as the war, or the sudden slump in Germany's trade with Comecon, had upset his calculations. But the damage was done. Kohl's and the CDU's popularity plummeted.

66 With egg dripping down his face and jacket, the infuriated chancellor lunged at the group ... He was looking for a fight 99

After wooing the *Ossis* so assiduously during his campaign, Kohl avoided the region for months. When he visited the east in May, demonstrators shouted "Liar!" wherever he went. During a walk-about in Halle, a young man hit him with an egg. Kohl cracked. With egg dripping down his face and jacket, the infuriated chancellor lunged at the group of jeering young protesters. He was looking for a fight. He was fuming. Television cameras caught the scene as Kohl lost control under the pressure of recent months.

That was hardly the only embarrassment. On 13 March, the Soviet military in eastern Germany flew Erich Honecker out to Moscow. Stricken with liver cancer, Honecker had been using his hospital stay as a shield against a Berlin court's arrest warrant for his former shoot-to-kill orders along the border. The Soviets embarrassed Kohl by informing him of Honecker's departure just before his plane took off, leaving him no time to block the flight. Freedom came none too soon for Honecker. Two days later, Moscow's ambassador made the restoration of Germany's full sovereignty official by handing over the ratification documents for the Two Plus Four Treaty.

Germany strained under the weight of change. Popular anger at the "solidarity surcharge" ran so high that the SPD took power in Kohl's home state of Rhineland-Palatinate in April for the first time since the war. Winning this state election gave the SPD a majority in the Bundesrat, the upper house of parliament, and with it a potential veto over Kohl's legislation. On 20 June, the Bundestag voted to move to Berlin. Germany was taking on the trappings of a big power, the last thing many Germans wanted it to do.

When east Germans looked back on 1 July, the first anniversary of the German monetary union, few found much to cheer about. The official unemployment rate in the region was 9.5 per cent, with the unofficial rate roughly twice as high. Another 1.9 million were caught in a limbo of make-work schemes with little job security from month to month. By contrast, the post-unity boom in western Germany had led to unemployment of only 5.9 per cent – the lowest rate in ten years.

YUGOSLAVIA IMPLODES

Most Germans were too concerned with the Gulf War and the uproar in the east to notice Yugoslavia's gradual disintegration in early 1991. When Slovenia and Croatia seceded from the Yugoslav federation in June, average Germans woke up to the fact that instability had reached Europe. The Dalmatian coast, Dubrovnik's medieval walls and the mosques of Mostar were familiar sights to thousands of Germans who vacationed there every year. But their concern went beyond thinking about holiday havens. Unrest in Yugoslavia could trigger an exodus of refugees to Germany.

Sticking its head in the sand was not an option for Germany this time. When the crisis came, it reacted with leadership and vision. After a period of hesitation, Bonn decided that the Yugoslav federation had crumbled beyond repair. It set a clear goal of diplomatic recognition for Croatia and Slovenia and worked tirelessly to reach it. Both the political class and the electorate supported this strongly. But the exercise still backfired. Determined to lead, Kohl and Genscher twisted arms throughout the European Community until their reluctant partners fell into line. This blunt new approach fanned fears abroad of a renaissance of German hegemony. In the end, what diplomats politely called Bonn's "new assertiveness" turned out to be no better for the Germans' image than their low-key approach during the Gulf War.

The west's main interest in the crisis was to preserve a united Yugoslavia. A messy break-up could cause a civil war in Europe's traditional powder keg. Ethnic tensions could spill over to involve minorities living across the borders in Albania, Hungary or Romania. Even if no conflict arose, the redrawing of borders could set a dangerous precedent. What would that mean for the Soviet Union? A collapse of the USSR would present incalculable risks for the post-war international system.

By a coincidence of bureaucratic calendars, the Yugoslav crisis peaked at a time when Germany held the revolving chairmanship of both the Conference on Security and Cooperation in Europe (CSCE) and the Western European Union (WEU). The CSCE played a central role in Genscher's plans for a pan-European security system based on diplomacy and dialogue. He saw it as a kind of United Nations for Europe. As the EC moved towards a common foreign and defence policy, some countries saw the WEU evolving into the "military arm" of the trading bloc. It was time to try new ideas and Genscher was sitting at the controls.

> **❝ What diplomats politely called Bonn's 'new assertiveness' turned out to be no better for the German's image ❞**

However, Genscher was not the only one looking for new guidelines for reunited Germany's foreign policy. As early as February, the east German Greens deputy, Gerd Poppe, argued that Bonn should back a loose confederation of sovereign Yugoslav states "based on the principle of self-determination". Fresh from gaining their own freedom by demanding self-determination, east Germans naturally saw this as a guiding principle for other popular movements. How could a paradigm that had been so successful in Germany be denied to peoples elsewhere in

Europe? The fact that the republics were pitted against a communist nationalist, Yugoslav President Slobodan Milošević, made this point of view seem doubly apt.

Bavaria's staunchly Catholic and anti-communist CSU also clamoured for an independent Croatia. The CSU was close to President Franjo Tudjman and a wide array of German-speaking Croatian officials. About two-thirds of the 700,000 Yugoslavs living in Germany were Croatian Catholics whom the Church in Germany looked on favourably.

Bonn's pro-secessionist lobby took its biggest step forward, though, when the SPD shifted towards recognition for Croatia and Slovenia in May. After a fact-finding tour of Yugoslavia, SPD foreign affairs spokesman Norbert Gansel concluded that Bonn was indirectly abetting Serbian aggression by insisting that Yugoslavia remain united. "Recognition of the peoples' right to self-determination must take precedence over a supposed *Realpolitik* that is blindly and exclusively oriented on the still existing federal structure," he argued. Croatia would have to ensure full rights for its Serbian minority before foreign countries could sanction its secession. After winning diplomatic recognition, Gansel thought, the new states would need a security guarantee to protect them against the threat of Serbian aggression.[8]

> **How could a paradigm that had been so successful in Germany be denied to peoples elsewhere in Europe?**

Once Belgrade's army attacked Slovenia on 27 June, several SPD and Greens politicians upped the ante and demanded that Bonn grant immediate recognition to the breakaway republics. Volker Rühe, the ambitious CDU general secretary, joined the calls for a bold step. "We won our unity through the right to self-determination," he argued. "If we Germans think everything else in Europe can stay just as it was, if we follow a status quo policy and do not recognise the right to self-determination in Slovenia and Croatia, then we have no moral or political credibility." When the Bundestag foreign affairs committee began to pressure him, Genscher saw he was alone in supporting the Yugoslav federation against the republics. He made an about-turn and began pressing his European colleagues to recognise the republics.

One widespread impression abroad was that Bonn's support for Croatia was a CSU-inspired bid to restore ties with an old Catholic ally. While that did play a part, it is striking that the two leading champions of independence, Gansel and Rühe, were both Protestants from northern Germany. What they, and many other Germans, sought were new guidelines for Bonn's foreign policy as the Cold War division disappeared. With communism's hold loosening across eastern Europe, they saw self-determination as the best way to organise the new order there. Freedom for oppressed nations, especially when they were struggling against a communist central power, was a clear and compelling paradigm. In many ways, it recalled the idealism of US President Woodrow Wilson, whose campaign for self-determination after World War I helped carve new states such as Czechoslovakia and Yugoslavia out of the defeated Austro-Hungarian empire. Unfortunately, like Wilson, they too overlooked or played down the awkward fact that the ethnic patchwork in the Balkans was too complex for a one-size-fits-all solution.

In their haste to do something about Yugoslavia, the Germans overlooked the devastating impression it made on their allies. Editorial writers across Europe asked whether Bonn wanted to restore a German sphere of influence in the Balkans. German officials could not understand how their partners thought Bonn had any interest in creating Balkan allies that it would have to bankroll for years to come. "They are projecting old fears onto new problems," a Kohl aide explained. "Our worry is that a full-scale war will break out and we will be flooded with refugees."

GERMANY GETS ITS WAY

Once Bonn decided to back Slovenia's and Croatia's bid for recognition, the only question left was whether it would get its way. It had to convince its reluctant partners to jump on the bandwagon. But Bonn's arguments were not convincing. Recognition was no instrument of conflict management or strategy to end war. All it did was formally acknowledge a country's sovereignty. That might help Slovenia, which Belgrade gave up on after a few days of fighting. But one could hardly speak of Croatia's sovereignty when Serbian troops controlled one-third of its territory and were dangerously close to Zagreb itself. Croatia needed military aid, in the form of arms supplies or foreign troops, but neither Germany nor its partners were ready for that. Bonn's approach was only half a policy, but one it defended with full commitment.

The Europeans did not follow Genscher's logic. In Yugoslavia, granting self-determination in one case only led to it being ignored in another. If the Croats could have their own country, why couldn't Belgrade include the Serbian parts of Croatia and Bosnia-Herzegovina in a Greater Serbia? And what about Bosnia-Herzegovina, where Serb, Croat and Moslem populations were so mixed that any effort by one group to impose its will on another would lead to war? France briefly considered sending troops, but Britain, the other country needed to make a European force effective, was deeply suspicious of rushing into another conflict after two decades of unrest in Northern Ireland.

In August, the Moscow coup started exactly the process the EC wanted to avoid – the break-up of the Soviet Union. Genscher's persistence began to bear fruit in early October when EC foreign ministers agreed to consider "a political solution" for recognising breakaway republics. From here on, Bonn's warnings to Belgrade and pressure on Brussels escalated steadily. On 27 November, Kohl announced that he wanted a decision to recognise the republics before Christmas.

Only five days after the Maastricht Summit, EC foreign ministers were under heavy pressure to find an agreement when they met on 16 December. In a face-saving compromise, they agreed that all 12 states would recognize Croatia and Slovenia if they respected minority rights, existing borders and other guidelines laid down in the United Nations charter and the CSCE agreements. The EC could announce the recognition now, but delay the actual opening of embassies until 15 January. Genscher confirmed his partners' worst fears by announcing after the meeting that he would ignore the minority rights review if it came out against Croatia. The veneer of joint EC action was as thin as it could possibly be.[9] The others had no choice but to go along with Germany. "We're not talking about the recognition of Croatia," a Dutch official remarked after the meeting. "We're talking about the recognition of Germany as a superpower."

> 66 The spectre of a resurgent Germany throwing its weight around in the Balkans did not last very long 99

The spectre of a resurgent Germany throwing its weight around in the Balkans did not last very long. Bonn kept a lower profile as ethnic strife began tearing Bosnia-Herzegovina apart. Its warnings to Zagreb against expanding the war fell on deaf ears when Croatia decided to help Bosnian Croats seize part of the republic for themselves. With nobody to champion their cause, Bosnia's Moslems ended up under siege in Sarajevo or victims of ferocious "ethnic cleansing". The next step would have to be military, and Germany still hesitated to take it. So Bonn stepped back into line as the United Nations tried in vain to stop the bloodshed.

Slowly, Germany was learning some important lessons about the limits of its new power. Behind all the talk about a new Germany, old foreign policy guidelines such as multilateralism and military restraint still applied. But its new size and restored sovereignty meant it was now being drawn into crisis more often, beyond its normal horizon. So, Kohl insisted, it had to play a more active role whether it wanted to or not. "When peace comes (to Yugoslavia), we will soon be faced with the question of who will help to reconstruct it," he explained. "When it comes to paying, everybody says 'Germans to the front!' So when it comes to political responsibility, I think the Germans should also be standing up front."

The dust had hardly settled over the Croatian recognition issue when Rühe, the CDU general secretary, unexpectedly became defence minister. His predecessor, Gerhard Stoltenberg, was forced to resign in April in a scandal over unauthorised arms exports. Just three weeks later, on 27 April, Genscher surprised Bonn by announcing his retirement. Knowing Genscher's ruses, nobody in Bonn took at face value his claim to be leaving because 18 years in the same post were enough in a democracy. "He has realised he is at the peak of his power and popularity and it can only go downhill from here," the liberal *Frankfurter Rundschau* wrote. "Genscher has realised that much of what he has tried to talk into existence has little chance of becoming reality."[10]

NOTES

1   *Die Zeit*, 3 May 1991.

2   For more, see *Middle East Economic Digest*, 15 February 1991.

3   Herles, Wolfgang (1992) *Geteilte Freude*. Munich: Kindler, pages 181–2.

4   US Secretary of State James Baker told Kohl on 15 September 1990 it was regrettable no German troops would join the Gulf effort. "Baker pointed out that the Japanese were sending medical corpsmen to the Gulf ... People in America will say there are no Germans in the Gulf." See *Deutsche Einheit – Sonderedition aus den Akten des Bundeskanzleramtes 1989/1990*, memo number 423, pages 1542–4.

5   *Die Vereinigung war voraussehbar*, page 149.

6   Inacker, Michael J. (1991) *Unter Ausschluss der Öffentlichkeit?* Bonn: Bouvier Varlag, pages 94–106.

7   *Unter Ausschluss der Öffentlichkeit?*, pages 131–2.

8   *Frankfurter Allgemeine Zeitung*, 25 May 1991.

9   In the end, the review group said that only Slovenia and Macedonia met EC standards for respect for human rights and minorities. Croatia's minority rights guarantees were too weak to pass the test, it said. The findings were ignored.

10   *Frankfurter Rundschau*, 28 April 1992.

7

THE BONN–BERLIN DEBATE

THE BUNDESTAG USHERS WERE ALWAYS THE FIRST TO KNOW. These
solemn men with their black cutaway suits and broad Bonn accents had
years of experience with vote counts. They prided themselves on knowing a result even before it was announced. This skill was never more in
demand than on the evening of 20 June 1991. The deputies had strug
gled all day with the issue of moving the government to Berlin. With the
speeches over and the ballots cast, old hands in the press corps watched
the men in black as they glided around the floor. Suddenly, one usher's
face went blank. Sadness fell over another's as he struggled to keep a stiff
upper lip. Somebody in the hall called out *"Berlin!"* and an usher
responded with an almost imperceptible nod.

It was on that summer evening, at 9.47 pm, that the real shock of unification hit the west Germans. The east had been churning and changing
ever since the Wall fell. The introduction of the deutschemark a year
before had plunged the region into a depression that westerners could
not even imagine. The *Ossis* had no choice: to become like the *Wessis*,
they had to change. But western Germany? It didn't need to change
much at all, many westerners felt. And it especially didn't have to give
up something as important as its own capital.

The Bonn–Berlin debate raged for over a year and ended, for many, literally
in tears. The Bundestag was not only considering whether to change

address. Its vote would point to what kind of state the new united Germany would be. Would pulling up stakes mean uprooting the democratic culture Bonn had nurtured over the past four decades? Would moving to Berlin mean a return to pomp, glory and big power politics? It is a testimony to the bewildered state of the newly reunited Germany that its parliament ended up taking a split decision.

THE PERMANENT PROVISIONAL CAPITAL

If actions speak louder than words, all the construction work going on in Bonn in 1989 screamed out only one message – *We're here to stay*. The West German capital had settled down and was putting on fat. Construction cranes dotted the skyline. A new glass-and-steel parliament building was under construction. Near the chancellery, work was starting on the House of the History of the Federal Republic, a museum to celebrate four decades of democracy in West Germany. Further down the road, the ground was broken for two side-by-side art museums. Bonn was slowly betraying its 1949 pledge to be only a provisional capital.

The Germans didn't have a capital for most of their history. The early kaisers had residences dotted across the Holy Roman Empire, and moved from one to another to carry out their duties. The first elected national assembly met in Frankfurt in 1848–9. It was not until 1871, the time of Germany's first unification, that the Prussian capital Berlin became the centre for the new Reich. After World War II, Konrad Adenauer wanted a town so unassuming that it would never be more than a provisional capital. He chose Bonn and it won out against Frankfurt in a vote on 10 May 1949, two weeks before the Federal Republic was founded.

> 66 Would moving to Berlin mean a return to pomp, glory and big power politics? 99

In one of its first sittings in 1949, the Bundestag stated its determination to move to Berlin as soon as it could. "The leading organs of the federation will move their headquarters to the capital of Germany, Berlin, as soon as general, free, equal, secret and direct elections are held in all of Berlin and the Soviet occupation zone," it declared. In the meantime, the government got down to work in the sleepy town. There were no triumphal arches or victory columns, as there were in Berlin. Instead of memorials to kings and kaisers, it had a lone statue at the main post office depicting its favourite son, Beethoven. Many offices were set up in prefabricated barracks guaranteed to last 15 years, far longer than anyone thought Germany's division would last.

Bonn's glaring lack of pretension was a reassuring sign that a powerful Germany was not being resurrected. Two decades and one "economic miracle" later, West Germans began to wonder whether they were being too modest. Nothing in its architecture or style hinted this was the capital of what was becoming an important Western power. The novelist John le Carré, who was an intelligence officer at the British embassy in Bonn in the early 1960s, immortalised the capital in his 1964 thriller *A Small Town in Germany*. "The very choice of Bonn as the waiting house for Berlin has long been an anomaly," he sniffed. "It is now an abuse." The government worked out of "concrete tents ... discreetly temporary in deference to the dream, discreetly permanent in deference to reality."[1] With the *Ostpolitik* of the late 1960s, it became clear the government would remain in Bonn far longer than planned. A modest building boom started.

> 66 Two decades and one 'economic miracle' later, West Germans began to wonder whether they were being too modest 99

Ironically, Helmut Kohl made the biggest push to upgrade the capital. A great believer in political symbolism, it was he who commisioned the history and art museums that were under construction when the Wall fell. In 1987, the Bundestag voted to erect a new parliament building worthy of one of the world's economic powerhouses. Coming only months before Erich Honecker was due to visit Bonn, the subliminal message could not have been louder.

BERLIN! BERLIN?

Overnight 9 November 1989 changed all that. Soon there was excited talk about Berlin becoming the capital of a reunified Germany at the heart of a united Europe. The smart money got moving fast; real estate prices started climbing in Berlin and sliding in Bonn. But the government's official reaction was business as usual. On 13 December, Kohl signed a "Bonn treaty" assuring the city 1.3 billion marks in federal support until the year 2000.

Concern about upsetting the neighbours dominated the mood in those first few weeks after the Wall fell. After surprising his partners abroad with his Ten Point Programme, Kohl knew that coming out for Berlin now would be like putting on a spiked helmet and bellowing *"Achtung! Achtung!"* The symbolism of the "Bonn Treaty" did not go unnoticed. A reassured London *Times* editorialist confidently wrote, "So Herr Kohl's gesture in signing the new agreement to support the city through the 1990s is a significant indication that, for all his recent rhetoric, he at least does not realistically believe that German reunification is for this century."[2] Six days later, Kohl saw the cheering crowds in Dresden and knew that unity was not far off.

The public discussions about Bonn or Berlin took on the contours of a second national debate about reunification. Apart from the solidarity tax, unification at first brought only minor changes for most people in the west. But the capital debate was about more than thousands of bureaucrats just moving from one end of the country to the other. The familiar Bonn Republic was coming to an end.

Bonn supporters stylised the provisional capital into the anchor of post-war German democracy. They asked what foreigners might think if the government moved back to the city where the kaisers and Hitler had ruled. "In the world's eyes, Bonn stands for a democratic and peaceful post-war Germany," said an SPD deputy from Hamburg, Anke Fuchs, in a typical comment. "It's German in a nice and harmless way." Europe was brought into the equation. Bonn was so much closer to Brussels than Berlin. Would the greater distance make a difference?

Try as it might, the Bonn lobby could not truly identify the "Prussian faction" it saw lurking behind the Brandenburg Gate. Only a negligible minority of old-school nationalists stirred with emotion at the idea of reviving Berlin's former glory. Warnings about how Berlin would centralise everything rang hollow. Western state capitals such as Munich, Stuttgart and Düsseldorf were rich and self-confident power centres that would not bow to Berlin. By contrast, Berlin's supporters looked more to the future than the past. In a continent without borders, Berlin was the focal point, the place where Eastern and Western Europe met.

Even the historical arguments used by the Bonn lobby against Berlin turned in the city's favour. Berlin could not escape a past that neither Germany nor the rest of the world would ever forget. But if Germany was bound to play a bigger part in the world, wouldn't this memory be the best guarantee that it would not forget its past?

The Bonn Republic's credibility was at stake. Official West German policy had always insisted that Berlin was its once and future capital. With American support, it had weathered all the crises that Moscow had engineered to try to detach it from West Germany. Would the west Germans turn their backs on this now, just because they had invested so much in new buildings in Bonn? True to their western roots, West Berliners were often sceptical about whether the city could absorb the 100,000 or so politicians, bureaucrats, diplomats and journalists from Bonn. But the east Germans were almost unanimously for Berlin. Moving the government would be the clearest sign from the *Wessis* that a reunited Germany represented a new start. It would be a gesture of recognition towards the "peaceful revolution" and an economic shot-in-the-arm for the region.

THE SEARCH FOR CONSENSUS

If politics is the art of the possible, the work German legislators did over the next year belongs in the category of fantastic realism. Public opinion was split. Deciding this issue would require courage and conviction. But the political establishment searched feverishly for a way to avoid taking a clear decision. The longer it went on, the more this agonising quest for a consensus produced ever more absurd "solutions".

The idea of splitting the capital's functions came up in the spring of 1990. The Bonn lobby suggested that Berlin could host the Federal Assembly, the joint body of the upper and lower houses of parliament that meets only once every five years to elect the president, and the president himself. Everything else would stay along the Rhine. Berlin countered this with a plan to take the parliament, government and most of the bureaucracy. To underline Germany's continued loyalty to nearby NATO, the defence ministry would remain in Bonn. Several technical ministries such as science and research could also stay, to compensate Bonn for the loss of the parliament.

> 66 Moving the government would be the clearest sign from the *Wessis* that a reunited Germany represented a new start 99

The government that was so decisive during the rush to unity could not agree on how to approach the capital issue. Wolfgang Schäuble was for Berlin, while Theo Waigel thought that much of the government should stay in Bonn. Hans-Dietrich Genscher cautiously voiced his support for Berlin, but said the move didn't have to happen overnight. Kohl kept his cards close to his chest. Even after his re-election in December, he remained wary of alienating voters with a clear choice. The chancellor only came off the fence on 22 April 1991, one day after the CDU lost to the SPD in his home state of Rhineland-Palatinate. "I will vote for Berlin," he unexpectedly announced. But even then, he showed none of the conviction he had displayed in abundance the previous year. Kohl stressed he was speaking not in his capacity as chancellor – which would have given his words added weight – but as just another Bundestag deputy. He then faded out of the debate again.

As the deadline for the final vote neared, the efforts to split the spoils between the two cities became increasingly abstruse. The compromisers tried their best to prove that the 600 km gap between Bonn and Berlin was irrelevant in the age of faxes, video conferencing and high-speed trains. The human side of lawmaking – the chats in the halls of parliament, lunches with senior bureaucrats, chance meetings with journalists in a bar – was suddenly not so important any more. As late as the evening before the vote, an unworkable plan to send the parliament to Berlin but leave the government in Bonn seemed to have a fighting chance of winning. Faced with so many other urgent decisions, Schäuble and Kohl toyed with the idea of sending the president and the Bundesrat to Berlin immediately but delaying the final decision about the Bundestag for at least five years.

THE VOTE

When the deputies assembled for the capital debate, the Bonn lobby had a confident air. A poll broadcast the night before showed 53 per cent of Germans backed Bonn while only 43 per cent wanted Berlin. The westerners were overwhelmingly for Bonn, 60 per cent as opposed to 25 per cent for Berlin, and they far outnumbered the eastern deputies in the Bundestag. There were five resolutions to consider, but only two of them counted. The pro-Bonn motion was called "the federal solution" but turned out to be quite one-sided; only the president and the Bundesrat would move to Berlin. The pro-Berlin motion, on the other hand, wanted the parliament and core of the bureaucracy to move, but many lesser ministries to stay in Bonn. The Bundesrat would also stay in Bonn according to this motion, entitled "Completing German Unity." Bonn set up a huge video screen on its Market Square to broadcast the debate live and also the celebrations after the vote. In Berlin, so few believed their city would win that only a local television station bothered to prepare for a victory party.

> 66 In Berlin, so few believed their city would win that only a local television station bothered to prepare for a victory party 99

Kohl's jovial Labour Minister Norbert Blüm presented the pro-Bonn resolution at the start of the marathon debate. "States with a strong sense of their federalism must have had a reason why they didn't put their seat of government in their biggest city," he argued. "The Americans didn't put it in New York but in Washington, the Canadians didn't go to Montreal or Toronto but to Ottawa, the Swiss not to Zurich but to Bern. Shouldn't we learn a lesson from the wisdom and experience of other federal states? France and England show us what domineering centralised cities can mean for provinces and regions."[3]

East Berliner Wolfgang Thierse skilfully aimed at the guilt feelings among undecided *Wessis* in the hall. "What kind of ship of state is this if all the weight lies in the west?" he asked. "Frankfurt stays the financial capital, the Rhine and Ruhr are the business centre, Hamburg and Bremen are the trading centres, Stuttgart and Munich are the high-tech centres. What's left for eastern Germany? The problem region? The social case? No, here a consciously political decision has to push for a centre east of the Elbe."

The decisive swing came when Schäuble pulled up to the podium. It was only eight months since he had been paralysed by a would-be assassin's bullet. The deputies were still not used to seeing Kohl's iron-willed crown prince struggling around in a wheelchair. Once he began to speak, his direct words and dramatic pauses mesmerised them. "In the 40 years of our division, most of us would have not even understood the question if we were asked where the parliament and government should sit if we were reunited," he said. "We would have said: in Berlin, of course." Forty years of division could not be overcome simply by raising taxes and reshuffling chairs. West Germans would have to give up something for unity, too, and Bonn happened to be that price. Schäuble surveyed his silent audience and asked, "Would we really have been reunited without Berlin? I don't think so. A decision for Berlin is a decision for overcoming the division of Europe ... so I urge you to vote with me for Berlin." As Schäuble rolled away from the podium, applause rang out throughout the house.

Kohl placed Berlin at the heart of his dream for a future Europe. "This Europe has to be a Europe that is more than the Europe of the Twelve, the EC of today," he said. "If this Europe remained just what the EC is today ... that would not be our Europe. Northern Europe belongs to our Europe ... We want Czechoslovakia, Poland and Hungary to find their way to this Europe, too. Then Berlin will not be on the edge, but it will have a geopolitically important and central function. That is the reason why I think that Berlin will be a good location in the year 2000 or 2005, when the face of the new Europe is visible, and that's why I am voting for Berlin."

Many young western deputies identified strongly with Bonn. "My political fatherland is the Bonn democracy," declared Friedbert Pflüger (CDU), 36. "I would rather have our parliament in the Bundestag than in the Reichstag." Bonn's youngest deputy, 25-year-old Hans-Martin Bury (SPD), thought moving made little sense since capital cities would somehow go out of fashion in a more integrated Europe. "A Europe without borders, a Europe of the regions, does not need these old-fashioned power centres for nation-states," Bury argued. Willy Brandt chuckled at the thought that big cities would soon go out of style. "Let's reconsider that when the British have done away with London and the Spanish with Madrid," he advised his younger colleague.

The cosmopolitan vitality that Berlin is renowned for around the world received hardly a mention in the ten-hour session. It took someone free of Bonn's provincialism to portray the Prussian metropolis as the challenge it would be. "Berlin is the future, it is life, excitement and stress, it is restlessness and motion," declared Konrad Weiss, an eastern film-maker-turned-politician from Alliance 90. "Just imagine ... an American president saying 'I am a Bonner'," he laughed. "Bonn belongs to the old Federal Republic. It is and remains strange to those of us from the east." Bonn was a city "for people who have everything behind them."

There were cheers and tears when Süssmuth read out the final tally – 338 votes for Berlin, 320 for Bonn. Well-wishers crowded around Schäuble's wheelchair to thank him for the speech that carried the day. Slowly, the lawmakers filed out of the hall, to go and celebrate or commiserate respectively. All that was left behind were a handful of ushers, some of them openly weeping.

The final count showed that Bonn came out ahead in both the CDU/CSU and SPD factions. But the city's confident lobby had overlooked the small parties, where Berlin supporters dominated. Berlin's staunchest backers were in the PDS faction, which voted 15–1 for the city that had always been capital to them anyway. With their help, it would now be the capital of the state they never wanted.

THE FOOT-DRAGGING BEGINS

After finally making their decision, the politicians became afraid of their own courage. Their immediate concern was to try to ease the shock. The winning motion clearly stated that the Bundestag should meet in Berlin within four years, with everything else in place in 10 to 12 years. No sooner was this voted through, however, than deputies from both camps ruled out moving into temporary quarters in Berlin. Cabinet members flocked to Berlin to survey the east German ministries they were supposed to move into. All returned dismayed at their backward condition, saying they had to be replaced with brand new buildings. The remodelling of the Reichstag, construction of a new chancellery and ministries, refurbishing of existing office buildings had to be finished *before* anyone pulled up stakes in Bonn. Construction Minister Irmgard Adam-Schwaetzer (an outspoken Bonn supporter) declared that redoing the Reichstag alone would take eight years.

The scramble for a consolation prize for Bonn boosted the chances of the Bundesrat staying along the Rhine. The chamber met infrequently, gathering delegates from the states themselves, and employed about only 150 people in Bonn. But its location made it the next measure by which to gauge how far the west would have to change. Now that they had lost the lower chamber of parliament, the Bonn lobby rallied around the upper house as the latest crucial symbol of German democracy. A majority of states were ready to give Bonn a consolation prize, but only if the Bundesrat could review its decision and possibly move to Berlin later after all. This was enough to win a majority and the Bundesrat voted 38–30 on 5 July to stay – at least for a while – in Bonn.

> 66 With each month that passed, the planning became more ambitious, the financing more dubious and the timetable more shaky 99

With each month that passed, the planning became more ambitious, the financing more dubious and the timetable more shaky. Eastern Germans began to wonder if the decision would hold. Couldn't a new Bundestag, with more of those younger *Wessi* deputies so attached to Bonn, reverse the vote one day? So what was supposed to be a clear and strong signal to the east came across as blurred and weak. Yes, we'll have to change too, the comfortable *Wessis* seemed to be saying to easterners. *But we'll take our time about it* ...

NOTES

1 le Carre, John (1969) *A Small Town in Germany.* New York: Dell, pages 16–17.

2 *The Times*, 15 December 1989.

3 For texts of the day's speeches, see Herles, Helmut (ed.) (1991), *Die Hauptstadt-Debatte.* Bonn: Bouvier Verlag.

8

THE UGLY GERMANS

Here is German Radio with the news: Overnight, unknown assailants threw several firebombs into an asylum seekers' hostel. The hostel burned to the ground. Seven people, including two children, were hospitalised suffering from smoke inhalation. Damages were estimated at over a million marks. Police said they had no evidence of racist motives for the attack.

NEWS BULLETINS LIKE THIS WERE AS COMMON as the weather report on German radio and television in the summer and autumn of 1992. Three years after the joy of the Wall's collapse, Germans woke up almost every day to accounts of the latest hate crimes. The attacks on immigrants, the cries of *"Ausländer raus!"* ("foreigners out!"), the menacing young men roaming the streets – it all brought back agonising memories. Politicians wasted weeks blaming each other for the attacks. Police and judges showed racist bombthrowers more lenience than they ever showed leftist radicals. Some residents cheered the mob on, others expressed shock at the brutality and turned away confused.

At the ballot box, frustrated citizens abandoned mainstream parties for far-right groups once shunned as the lunatic fringe. Support for European unity, long taken as a reassuring sign that Bonn had left behind the nationalism of the past, began to fray at the edges. Neo-nationalists evoked a more assertive Germany on the opinion pages of well-known newspapers.

Despite the ugly attacks and screaming headlines, the vast majority of Germans supported democracy and deplored the violence. The hard core of support for far-right parties nationwide constituted only two or three per cent of the population, far less than similar movements in France or Italy. There was, however, a brush fire of frustration with the problems the new era had brought. With the end of the discipline imposed by the Cold War and the achievement of reunification, a sense of aftermath and letdown spread across the country. Everything seemed to be changing, and mostly for the worse. And just when the country needed leadership and vision, the politicians had no answers. The problems were manageable – but they had to be managed. Neither the government nor the opposition rose to the occasion. The elements of a workable response finally fell into place and the challenge was beaten back, but not before all the violence and indecision had written the worst chapter of the reunification story.

> 66 Everything seemed to be changing, and mostly for the worse 99

THE RETURN OF THE REPRESSED

History did not return suddenly after the fall of the Berlin Wall. The shared past had been creeping up on both west and east during much of the 1980s. An interest in rediscovering German identity and history grew in both states with a remarkable parallelism. On both sides of the Wall, a Freudian "return of the repressed" was making itself felt.

The west's new tendency to brood about the past was sparked in part by the US television series *Holocaust*. Broadcast on West German television in 1979, this Hollywood production brought the past to life by dramatising the fate of a fictionalised Jewish family. It was sentimental and shallow, but its message touched the younger generation far more than the heavy factual documentaries Germans tended to produce. Soon there was a wave of interest in what life was actually like during the Third Reich. The 1984 television series *Heimat* took a sepia-toned look at the century in an imaginary village in the Hunsrück hills south of Koblenz. Historians thought it was too soft on the Nazis, but average viewers saw a picture of everyday life that helped fill a 12-year gap in collective memory.

Upon taking office in 1982, Helmut Kohl tried to promote patriotism by stressing that the 12 years of the Third Reich could not overshadow all of German history. He was not out to whitewash the Nazi era as such. But he always tried to put it in a wider context where the post-war success story would shine. The chancellor did not always succeed. His bid to symbolise West Germany's post-war friendship with the United States by visiting Bitburg cemetery with President Ronald Reagan in 1985 back-fired. When 49 soldiers from Hitler's Waffen-SS were found to be among the dead at the military cemetery, Reagan tried to change the schedule. Thinking more about his right wing than about Washington, Kohl refused to budge and even claimed his government would fall if he did. The visit went ahead and was a disaster.[1]

The *Historikerstreit* (historians' dispute) represented a far more complex struggle with Germany's past. The conservative historian Ernst Nolte argued in 1986 that Stalin's mass killings and purges in the 1930s pro-voked the Nazis into the ruthless violence that climaxed in the Holocaust. The implication was that Stalin rather than Hitler was to blame for the century's unparal-leled brutality. The reaction from the left was swift and sharp. Philosopher Jürgen Haber-mas declared that Germany's guilt could not be relativised away. Admitting this was the starting point for West Germany's successful liberal democracy, and a way of ensuring that Germany did not slide back into its old ways. The debate faded after dozens of angry articles, with the liberal view represented by Habermas in the majority.

> 66 There is a continual struggle in Germany to understand what went wrong ... it is debated openly and seemingly endlessly 99

Although the term had not yet been invented, the debate was about political correctness. Since the 1970s, the liberal view of the past has dominated education and the media and served as the basis for the way Germans look at their state today. Reaching for a counterbalance, right-wing historians tend to de-emphasize the nation's guilt and compare German nationalism to nationalism in other countries. This dense and sometimes confusing debate is part of a continual struggle in Germany to understand what went wrong. Unlike in Japan, where the wartime past is still laden with taboos, the Germans debate the issues openly and seemingly endlessly. It is a reflection of the strength of democratic dis-course in Germany that such a lively discussion of the past takes place.

The past also seemed to come back at the ballot box. Franz Schönhuber, a former Bavarian television talk show host, roared to national promi-nence in 1989 when his Republicans party won over seven per cent in Berlin's city election and in the European Parliament poll. A former junior officer in Waffen-SS unit *Adolf Hitler* (the bodyguards of the *Führer*), he was at his best as a table-pounding spokesman for a hodgepodge of right-wing resentments. "I get the most applause when I announce that the re-education programme is over and humble pie has been taken off the menu," he liked to say. "When I say I'm proud to be a German – people have waited years to hear that."[2]

Schönhuber's standard speech included outbursts against criminals, sex offenders and "enemies of the German people". The few Jews left living in Germany were treated as undesirable aliens. He wanted traditional values restored at home, at work and in politics and censorship to rein in the liberal media. Schönhuber's programme was carefully worded to avoid coming too close to neo-Nazi views. But xenophobia lurked in the calls for stricter laws to prevent immigrants and asylum seekers from misusing the West German welfare system.

All this tapped a rich seam of resentment below the surface of West Germany's prosperity. The go-go 1980s were fine for the top two-thirds of society but tough on the lowest segment. Living costs rose so high in trendy boom towns like Munich that the post office had trouble finding recruits who would make ends meet on a typical postal worker's pay. The new Europe of open borders and a single market presented exciting new opportunities for university graduates, but what about workers, low-level civil servants and the unemployed? Their qualifications were steadily devalued. In a few years' time, even the poor people's pride – their identity as Germans – would mean little.

The far right thought its hour had finally come when East German communism collapsed. One day after the Wall fell, Schönhuber led a torch-light rally of about 30 Republicans in front of the Reichstag. But when they tried to march to the nearby Brandenburg Gate, a crowd of about 100 demonstrators shouting "Nazis out!" drove them away. Many of the western protest voters who had inflated the Republicans' results during 1989 lost sympathy for the "brothers and sisters in the east" when they realised how much they would cost them. Sure, they were Germans, but they were "welfare sponges" all the same. Rather than being ethnic nationalists, these voters were West German economic chauvinists. In their own way, they had internalised Germany's split just as much as the left-wing politicians and intellectuals they despised. Schönhuber's party only won 2.1 per cent in the 1990 election; the CDU was more successful in channelling the national issue into a constructive policy.

East Germany also went through a "back to the roots" phase from the beginning of the 1980s. In December 1980, a massive equestrian statue of Prussia's King Frederick the Great, long hidden away because he was a "reactionary", was returned to its pedestal in East Berlin. Erich Honecker allocated funds to restore two baroque masterpieces, Frederick's Sanssouci Palace in Potsdam and the Zwinger gallery built by Saxony's King August the Strong in Dresden. East Berlin pulled out all the stops in 1983 to organise joint east–west commemorations for Martin Luther, the founder of Protestantism whose Bible translation was as important for the modern German language as Shakespeare's plays were for English.

The east had its protest movements as well, although necessarily smaller because of the authoritarian state. Carefully watched by the Stasi, East Germany's Protestant churches began a decade of prayers for disarmament on 9 November 1980. Grass-roots peace groups and ecological movements such as East Berlin's Environmental Library sprouted around the country. By 1989, the Stasi counted about 160, almost all of them under the aegis of the Protestant church that played a central role in sweeping away the communists in 1989.[3] Police reported scattered incidents of Nazi graffiti or attacks on foreigners in the late 1970s.

Stasi files opened up after the *Wende* showed that Mielke's men had noticed East German punks and skinheads in 1982. The blinkered bureaucrats had trouble sorting out the far-left punks from the far-right skinheads. Jailing the rowdies brought some of them into contact with real Nazis, former SS and Gestapo men who were now political prisoners and marked Hitler's birthday in jail by sporting toilet paper armbands with swastikas marked on them.[4] The Stasi did not start taking right-wing radicalism seriously until 1987, but it was interpreted as the result of ideological diversion from the West.[5] Officials insisted there were neither the ideological nor the socio-economic bases for an extreme right in East Germany.

THE ASYLUM DEBATE AND NEO-NAZI VIOLENCE

With borders opening across Europe, reunited Germany attracted ever more immigrants from eastern Europe, Africa and Asia. Since Bonn had no immigration law, there were only two legal ways to settle in this Eldorado. East Germans and German minorities from eastern Europe had open access, thanks to Bonn's ethnically based citizenship laws. All others had to enter as real or supposed political refugees and hope the bureaucracy would recognise them as oppressed people deserving shelter. Bonn's 1949 constitution, drafted in conscious rejection of the Nazi period, had one of the broadest – and easiest to misuse – guarantees of political asylum that could be found in the West.

And so the great migration began. The total of arriving asylum-seekers soared from 57,379 in 1987 to a peak of 438,191 in 1992. And this was only part of the problem. In 1989, West Germany received a total of 842,227 East Germans and ethnic Germans from further east. This was more than the population of Frankfurt. There was also illegal immigration, a problem that by definition could not be neatly measured. From 1992, Germany also temporarily took in over 300,000 refugees from the war in former Yugoslavia. Cities and towns had to use sports halls, hostels and trailers to house them all. According to government figures, Germany's percentage of the EC's overall intake of asylum-seekers rose from 52.6 per cent in 1989 to a peak of 78.8 per cent in 1992.[6]

Anti-foreigner violence, an occasional scourge in divided Germany, soared to unimagined levels following reunification. After a total of 308 incidents in 1990, the number of violent attacks by right-wing extremists leaped to 1,489 in 1991. The trend peaked the following year at 2,640.[7] Marauding youths, often on weekend drinking binges, grew increasingly brazen as they saw how little resistance they met. A Mozambican died in Dresden in April 1991 after being shoved out of a moving tram by right-wing radicals. When visa-free travel for Poles began in April, neo-Nazis blocked traffic at two border crossing points and pelted Polish buses and cars with rocks. The police stood by without intervening.

The radical right seized its chance to sow chaos. Some of the best-known neo-Nazi leaders from western Germany and Austria converged on eastern Germany looking to stir up trouble. In June 1991, over 2,000 neo-Nazis paraded through Dresden, openly breaking the law by shouting "*Heil Hitler!*" and giving the straight-arm salute right in front of the passive police. "What a victory," crowed one of the organisers, Heinz Reisz. "We've learned how to make this state look ridiculous."

Copycat attacks multiplied. In September, skinheads in Hoyerswerda, between Cottbus and Dresden, found that townspeople cheered them on when they pelted an asylum-seekers' hostel with stones. They came back the next day with Molotov cocktails and fought a pitched battle with the Mozambicans living there. After six days of intermittent rioting, the town sent four buses to the hostel and shipped the foreigners out. Violence had paid and even won public approval.

The dozens of smaller attacks that followed across eastern Germany confirmed the state could not stand up to the skinheads. Discredited because of their role under the communists, the police were unsure how to react and vastly underequipped. The region was effectively lawless, a "Wild East". Skinheads roamed the streets "slapping up Fijis" (beating up Vietnamese) and bullying "briquettes" (blacks). A neo-Nazi youth culture spread across the region to the beat of "Oi" music, a hard-driving punk style that glorified Germany and urged Germans to take out their frustration on foreigners.

> Violence had paid, and even won public approval

Bonn was at a loss to say what was going on or even where to look for explanations. The domestic security agency, the Office for the Protection of the Constitution (BfV), was still fixed on fighting the dwindling threat of left-wing violence. Primed by the fight against the Red Army Faction (RAF) that terrorized West Germany in the 1970s and 1980s, politicians and police reacted by looking for an organised conspiracy behind the violence. When none was found, they breathed a premature sigh of relief.

Germany clearly had to get these two unsettling trends – uncontrolled immigration and spreading anti-foreigner violence – under control. Prompt and firm action could have at least helped to fight the trend. But local authorities were overwhelmed by the twin challenges. In Bonn, the parties got entangled in sterile political struggles that only heightened the sense that the state was powerless. The CDU insisted the liberal asylum law enshrined in Article 16 of the constitution had to be amended. The SPD, which saw this article as Bonn's response to the way the Nazis drove their critics into exile, refused to consider any change. The dispute degenerated into a polarised fight, with the CDU accusing the SPD of blocking a solution. Wolfgang Schäuble, who had become the CDU parliamentary leader in November 1991, bitterly attacked the opposition after every wave of firebombings, arguing that only an amendment could solve the problem.

The fruitless wrangling in Bonn sent an explosive message to extremists across the country. The CDU and CSU had simplified the issue to a single premise: foreigners were the problem and radical measures to keep them out were the solution. With so much public frustration over the issue, bomb-throwers felt they were in the vanguard. They were ready to act where the politicians would not.

The politicians didn't seem to be getting much else right at the time. Inflation was rising and interest rates were at record levels. Official unemployment levels almost doubled in the east during 1991, spreading concern about job losses among western workers. Two state elections in April 1992 gave voters a chance to send a message to Bonn. In Baden-Württemberg, Germany's richest state, the Republicans bounced back from the 1990 setbacks to win 10.9 per cent in the state assembly. They were suddenly the third-largest party there, ahead of the Greens or the FDP. Up north in Schleswig-Holstein, the German People's Union (DVU) came in third in the state poll with 6.3 per cent of the vote.

CONFUSION AS VIOLENCE SPREADS

The year 1992 turned out to be Germany's *annus horribilis.* On warm summer weekends, so many violent attacks occurred that news broadcasts sometimes only added up the total and mentioned one or two of the worst incidents. The overall picture was frightening. The total of 2,640 attacks worked out to a daily average of more than seven a day for the whole year. Official statistics counted 17 people killed in extreme right-wing violence. "Anti-fascist" groups, which kept close tabs on the far right, claimed that as many as 34 victims died that year.

The opinion-making elites – politicians, academics, the media – worked overtime trying to explain behaviour they thought Germans would never engage in again. The facts seemed to butt in to contradict the latest explanation. The high level of violence in the east at first made it look like a regional problem, but it soon spread to the west. Another view saw unemployment as the main culprit and massive job programmes as the solution. This looked shaky when it turned out that quite a few of the extremists had apprenticeships or normal jobs. Not all victims were foreigners, either.

> 66 The opinion-making elites worked overtime trying to explain behaviour they thought Germans would never engage in again 99

In fact, 10 of the 17 people officially reported as being killed by far-right violence in 1992 were Germans. A strikingly high number were simply homeless men who had been murdered, as one skinhead killer explained at his trial, "out of general feelings of hate".[8] The firebombers often used Nazi symbols or slogans, but they did not seem to be organised. In fact, most were drunken teenagers.

The full extent of official impotence went on alarming display in late August in Rostock, where there were three days of rioting against an asylum hostel. A crowd about 2000 strong cheered as hundreds of teenage rowdies hurled stones and Molotov cocktails at the building. Carloads of neo-Nazis from Berlin and Hamburg arrived to join in the action. The thin line of police trying to defend the hostel was helpless. Riot-hardened reinforcements from Hamburg finally roared into town to break it all up. Once they were gone, though, the rowdies set the building ablaze and then lit the next building. Vietnamese workers living there had to scramble on to the roof to escape.

With tension rising, the SPD announced in late August that it was giving in on the asylum issue. It agreed with the CDU to deny asylum to people from countries Bonn considered free of political persecution. This applied to transit countries as well, so anyone arriving from France or Poland would also be turned back. Anyone refusing to cooperate with inquiries about an asylum request would be deported.

Rostock was a shot in the arm for the mob. In the two months that followed, police recorded an astonishing total of 1,000 acts of far-right violence. Neo-Nazis burned down the so-called Jewish barracks at the former Sachsenhausen concentration camp in September, only two weeks after Israeli Prime Minister Yitzhak Rabin had visited an exhibition there on anti-Semitism in the Third Reich. With the situation crying out for moral leadership, the main parties planned a "march for human dignity" in Berlin on 8 November. President Richard von Weizsäcker promptly signed up for it; Kohl went along reluctantly. About 350,000 people – several times more than the number expected – emerged from the ranks of the silent majority to protest against the violence. At the final rally, however, about 400 anarchists interrupted the speeches by bellowing "Hypocrites! hypocrites!" and hurling paint bombs and stones. Weizsäcker stopped speaking when he was hit by an egg. He resumed only after a phalanx of riot police had taken up position and an aide held up an umbrella against further eggs. Instead of projecting a new confidence, Germany looked more than ever like a helpless giant.

Then came Mölln. On 23 November, two neo-Nazis firebombed a Turkish family's house in this small town near Lübeck, killing a woman and two girls. Violence was now turning towards Germany's biggest minority. The 1.8 million-strong Turkish community had roots in Germany going back three decades. Once limited to doing the dirty work Germans would not touch, many in the second and third generations had started businesses, bought houses and traded Islam and tradition for modern European city life.

Mölln called the bluff of anyone who blamed the unrest simply on the asylum crisis. Racist violence was now aimed at integrated foreigners, a step up on the scale of Nazi-style targets. Pent-up public anger at official inertia exploded. Frightened by their country's sinking image, 22 German tourist firms and airlines took out a full-page advertisement in Turkey's mass circulation daily *Hürriyet* to condemn the killings and proclaim their solidarity with foreigners. But the main responsibility for countering this violence lay with the institution that had the legal power to do so, i.e. the state. "Do something!" pleaded Pro-Asyl, a refugee lobby group. "For God's sake, do something out of patriotism, or for our export chances or just for humanity. Motives are unimportant now."

> 66 How many times had skinheads murdered foreigners, burned asylum hostels or growled illegal Nazi slogans without provoking a response? 99

Federal Prosecutor General Alexander von Stahl took over the case the same day, a sign that far-right violence was finally a high-priority issue. Within eight days, federal authorities had arrested two suspects who confessed to the crime. Instead of the usual mild charges such as disturbing the peace, they pressed for triple murder charges along with attempted murder and arson. At the same time, Interior Minister Rudolf Seiters declared war on neo-Nazi groups. It took only four days for him to ban the Nationalist Front, a small pro-Hitler party, and have police search its premises in 40 cities around the country.[9] By Christmas, the authorities had banned four far-right organisations and confiscated large stocks of neo-Nazi propaganda, weapons and home-made bombs.

Welcome though the belated decisiveness was, several disturbing questions remained. Stahl had long refused to investigate attacks on foreigners because he saw no political motivation or organisation behind the violence. But Mölln promptly became a federal case, ostensibly because an unknown person who had telephoned police to report the fire had ended the call with the cry *"Heil Hitler"*. "This indicates that the unknown attackers want to re-establish a National Socialist dictatorship in Germany," Stahl claimed. How many times before had skinheads murdered foreigners, burned asylum hostels or growled illegal Nazi slogans without provoking a strong response? If the crackdown on the far right was now sending a clear warning signal to neo-Nazis, what message did the previous response send?

Kohl rejected calls to attend a funeral service for the Mölln victims in Hamburg. Television pictures of the chancellor grieving under the half-crescent flag would have sent a powerful message. Kohl was no racist and he publicly condemned far-right attacks. But he always made sure he avoided political risks while doing it. Even in such clear cases, he would never denounce far-right violence without mentioning left-wing terror in the next breath. Attending a service for the Turks would amount to admitting Germany was an immigration country after all – a red rag to the right wing, where the CDU and CSU were nervous about losing votes to the Republicans. So he opted to sit it out.

Nothing illustrated the gulf between the people and the politicians as well as the *Lichterketten* ("chains of light") that followed Mölln. Disgusted with all the violence, the silent majority – led by local churches, artists and entrepreneurs – organised candlelight processions of protest. They shut out politicians to avoid being hijacked by narrow party interests. The first and most impressive of the *Lichterketten*, held in Munich on 6 December, drew more than 300,000 people. The demonstrators stood shoulder to shoulder, sometimes seven deep, along 40 km (25 miles) in the historic city centre and along major arteries leading out of town. They formed a shimmering star of light that passing aircraft could spot from miles away. "We have to show that we are the majority. Germany is not a radical right-wing country," said demonstrator Gabrielle Schmidthammer. It sounded like "We are the people," transplanted to the west. The civil society, a term more commonly applied to the East European states, was talking back to its leaders.

This was the starting signal for dozens of other such demonstrations all across Germany. By the end of January, an estimated 2.9 million people had protested against the violence. The marches filled an important gap. They said that society wanted to defend its moral values even if its leaders could not find the right way to do so. These were the kind of political symbols needed in those confused times. If some neo-Nazis still thought they were in the avant garde of the silent and frightened majority, the *Lichterketten* told them clearly they were not.

The shift in public mood stuck out like an earthquake on a seismograph printout. Polls showed the total number of Germans rejecting the call "Foreigners out!" soared from 43 to 69 per cent. The number of those expressing understanding for neo-Nazi violence fell from 33 to 12 per cent. Most importantly, the wave of attacks ebbed and stayed considerably below the all-time peak of 561 assaults in September 1992.[10]

The danger did not completely disappear. On 29 May 1993, another firebomb killed five Turks in Solingen. A feeling of helplessness and dismay set in. Had all the *Lichterketten* been for nothing? Weren't the bans on neo-Nazi parties and the crackdown on immigration enough? Kohl's spokesman Dieter Vogel expressed the helplessness felt by the government about the arsonists. "They do not belong to any political parties, some are drunk, they act spontaneously, they make use of far-right symbols – probably without knowing what they mean – because these provoke general revulsion. It seems this violence is the behaviour of a few apparently feeble-minded people who are venting their frustration rather than expressing political thoughts."

The federal prosecutor's office promptly took over the Solingen investigation. Police arrested four suspects on charges of murder on five counts, attempted murder and arson. These suspects told police they had set the house on fire in revenge when three of them were thrown out of a bar following a fight with two foreigners. Unlike those in Mölln, Solingen's Turks fought back. Youths rampaged through the city smashing store windows and skirmishing with police. The backlash pointed to a deeper problem caused by Germany's refusal to solve its "foreigner problem". Stubbornly denying that Germany had become an immigration country was creating a minority that could turn away from the state that refused to integrate them.

Once again, the question arose as to whether Kohl would attend the funeral. Weizsäcker promptly announced he would go, as did Kohl's foreign, interior and labour ministers. Pressure mounted even within his own party for him to visit the Cologne mosque for the service. Again, he refused.

REBELS WITHOUT A CAUSE

The crackdown after Mölln showed what the justice system could do when it was determined to act. The main suspect was sentenced to life imprisonment on three counts of murder, 39 counts of attempted murder and an additional charge of aggravated arson. The Solingen arsonists met with similar firmness, with the only adult defendant getting 15 years on five charges of murder, 14 attempted murders and aggravated arson. The other three were tried as juveniles and sent to prison for ten years.[11] The crackdowns could not stamp out racist views or violent tendencies; that was a longer-term educational project challenging other European countries as well. But it could draw a line in the sand and treat crime as crime. There were copycat attacks after Solingen, too, but the number then fell back and continued to decline through the following year. The total of right-wing extremist attacks dropped from the 1992 total of 2,640 to 2,332 the following year, and 1,309 in 1994.[12]

Apart from the hard-core neo-Nazis, most of the racist rowdies of the early 1990s could be called "rebels without a cause". Sociologists saw their behaviour as essentially juvenile delinquent in nature, with a violence which deserved a firm police response from the beginning. Their political views were racist, but without any structured ideology or strategy. "Whoever wonders what goes on in the minds of violent right-wingers comes to the conclusion that nothing much is happening there. They are breathtakingly unreflective and apathetic. Some maintain quite credibly that they acted out of pure boredom," sociologist Claus Leggewie wrote. "The young right wing is less extremist than 'extremely normal', despite its martial get-up."

> 66 The post-war methods of teaching children about the evils of Nazism were starting to lose their sting 99

The Nazi symbols these youths used were as much a provocation as a political statement. Most of them did not know much about the Third Reich. But they knew the taboos of present-day Germany quite well. "Right-wing slogans have a strong provocative effect on people who share the fundamental political and moral values of this society," Leggewie wrote. "Repeating them coolly leads to a reaction one can otherwise rarely get in a climate of general apathy."[13]

Ironically, the young rowdies were rebelling against the society that the student protest generation had created. The "1968-ers" introduced a dose of moralism into the political culture as a reaction to the way their parents tried to hush up or forget the Nazi years. Now in their 40s, the opinion elites of that generation – the politicians, teachers and journalists – openly admitted Germany's guilt, rejected nationalism and stressed their country's duty to foster peace and human rights. It presented an ideal taboo for rebellious youths to break.

The post-war methods of teaching children about the evils of Nazism were starting to lose their sting. Educators had to find new ways of getting the message across, an effort that would take years and might never fully succeed. In the meantime, though, the government had to take determined steps to promote integration. The first would be to stop repeating that Germany was not an immigration country. The country needed a modern democratic immigration law to handle the population movements that would only increase in the future. Even more importantly, Germany had to change its blood-based nationality law to allow the growing community of German-born "foreigners" to be fully integrated. This would be the strongest sign to the racists that Bonn actively rejected them and their views. There actually was a majority for citizenship reform in the Bundestag during the 1990s, but it cut party lines, from the left across the FPD and into the ranks of the CDU. Right-wing Christian Democrats and the CSU opposed the idea and no progress could be made.

NOTES

1   US Secretary of State George Schultz was devastating about Kohl's thick-skinned determination to stage a gesture of reconciliation at any cost. "Kohl's unbending iron will did seem to demonstrate a massive insensitivity, on the one hand, to the troubles he was causing Ronald Reagan and, on the other, to the trauma this episode caused in the Jewish community around the world and, beyond the Jewish community, to all who remembered the Holocaust and its horrors." See Schultz, George (1993) *Turmoil and Triumph*. New York: Charles Scribner's Sons, page 560.

2   The US post-war re-education programme is a favourite target of the far right, which sees in it a humiliation of Germany's national pride and the start of a liberal political correctness about the Third Reich. See Assheuer, Thomas and Sarkowicz, Hans (1992) *Rechtsradikale in Deutschland:* Die alte und die neue Rechte. Munich: Verlag C.H. Beck, pages 45–6.

3   For more on East German dissent in the early 1980s, see Wolle, Stefan (1999) *Die heile Welt der Diktatur*. Bonn: Bundeszentrale für politische Bildung, pages 235–79. On the grass-roots group, see Eckert, Rainer "Die revolutionäre Krise am Ende der achtziger Jahre und die Formierung der Opposition" in *Enquete-Kommission*, Volume VII/1, pages 667–757.

4   Hasselbach, Ingo with Reiss, Tom (1996) *Führer-Ex*. New York: Random House, pages 60–3.

5   Geiger, Hansjörg "Rechtsradikalismus in der DDR", *Enquete-Kommission*, III/1, pages 178–86.

6   For intake figures, see "Zur Situation der Ausländer in Deutschland" (Bonn: Presse- und Informationsamt Bundesregierung, Auslandsabteilung, January 1995), page 36.

7   "Zur Situation der Ausländer in Deutschland" (Bonn: Federal Press Office, 1995), page 40.

8   For fuller details, see Borchers, Andreas et al. (1995), *Un-Heil über Deutschland*. Hamburg: Gruner and Jahr, pages 242–75.

9   Members didn't believe the state would crack down until police actually raided their offices. During a telephone interview with me on 27 November, an arrogant young man at the party's headquarters in Detmold was making fun of Seiter's threats when he suddenly panicked, yelled "The police are here!" and hung up.

10   There was a small increase in mid 1993, when the total rose to 242 in June following the Solingen murders, but the overall trend was down. Only 51 violent racist crimes were reported in June 1994. For the figures, see *Zur Situation der Ausländer in Deutschland*, page 38.

11 For more on the courts' response to right-wing violence, see *"Germany for Germans" – Xenophobia and Racist Violence in Germany*. New York: Human Rights Watch, April 1995, pages 41–8.

12 *Zur Situation der Ausländer in Deutschland*, page 40.

13 Leggewie, Claus (1993) *Druck von rechts*. Munich: Verlag C.H. Beck, pages 56–61.

9

ANOTHER PAST TO LIVE DOWN

WHO SHOULD PAY FOR 40 YEARS OF COMMUNISM? Which East German leaders were to blame and what should be done with them? The wartime allies had arrested the top surviving Nazis and tried them in Nuremberg; the Romanians had summarily executed Nicolae Ceauşescu.

> 66 We wanted justice and got legalism instead 99

After reunification, the communist hierarchy, its subordinates and almost all their secret files were under western-style jurisdiction. The single-party dictatorship, the injustice, the lack of fundamental freedoms, the harassment, discrimination, sometimes even torture and death – common sense said all this was wrong. But how many years should Erich Honecker get for moral responsibility? Political justice was not the task of the western courts.

Trials of the old elite and the border guards who had shot fleeing defectors ran throughout the united state's first decade. Instead of promoting the feeling that justice had been done, the main cases left an ambiguous impression. Politburo members were tried on charges that seemed secondary to their acts. Even the biggest case of all, the murder trial against Erich Honecker, ended not with a bang but a whimper. As a disillusioned Bärbel Bohley put it, "We wanted justice and got legalism instead."

Probably only a dramatic revolution with rolling heads would have provided a real catharsis. But the east Germans opted for a "peaceful revolution". The closest they got to rough and ready justice came with the "Stasi mania" as the agency's files gave up their secrets. Proof or even just rumours of collaboration with the hated Stasi sufficed to end political careers overnight. This method, however, decimated the front ranks of the new political generation in eastern Germany rather than punished the old one. For *Ossis* yearning for clarity, very little seemed clear.

DIFFICULT TARGETS

The problem was translating indignation into indictments. East Germans were outraged when, right after the Wall fell, the media revealed the quaint luxury in which their leaders had lived. Accusations of corruption and fraud flew when they saw that the Politburo compound at Wandlitz was well stocked with the western appliances and fresh fruits the average citizen never saw. East German prosecutors scrambling to adjust to a new culture of accountability brought vague indictments against Politburo members for "the anti-constitutional media policy" or "misuse of trust". The charges rarely stood up when examined by western jurists.

The Harry Tisch case was the first of many that started high and ended low. The former boss of the Free German Trade Union Federation (FDGB) was arrested in early December 1989 and accused of "seriously damaging public property and the people's economy through abuse of power". The charges focused on several cases of apparent embezzlement and fraud in relation to FDGB funds. By the time the trial opened in January 1991, the dossier had been passed to the western prosecutors who took over after reunification. Since the charges were basically economic, the first trial of a Politburo member was held in a west Berlin commercial court.

Only two weeks into the trial, the court's three judges dropped one charge of "breach of trust" over renovations to the official FDGB hunting lodge. There was no equivalent in the western penal code. The other two charges of "embezzlement of socialist property" led to long lectures from Tisch's eastern lawyers on how meaningless official budgets had been under communism, since everything was paid by the state anyway. The prosecution's case slowly melted down to the charge that Tisch had used union funds for his vacations. The total came to the princely sum of 77,468.85 *Ostmarks*. He was given an 18-month sentence that was waived because he had already spent almost a year in pre-trial custody. One of East Germany's leading politicians walked out of the court a convicted white-collar criminal – and quite a small-time one at that.

Erich Mielke, the "Master of Fear", was second to Honecker in terms of power in East Berlin. As minister for state security, Mielke commanded a vast network that spied on colleagues, friends and even spouses. Stasi agents tapped telephones, opened mail, rigged elections and manipulated groups that they infiltrated. The ministry sheltered terrorists on the run from West Germany. But Mielke was not brought to trial for the things that most East Germans hated him for. Instead, the prosecutors reached back to 1931, when Mielke was a communist street thug in Berlin suspected of killing two policemen. He fled to the Soviet Union and was convicted *in absentia* for murder. The Tisch trial and other smaller ones like it had shown it was difficult to nail a Politburo member for crimes as a leader in the communist regime. East Germans were growing impatient as they watched the old guard dodging justice. The murders offered the unique opportunity of trying Mielke on a concrete criminal case in which all available evidence pointed to him as the main suspect. It was a strange way to try the Stasi chief, but it promised a quick trial and certain conviction.

The trial heightened the feeling of unreality. By now 84, Mielke claimed on the first day not to remember his date of birth and refused to answer any other questions. He sat out the rest of the trial impassively, like an old crocodile in a terrarium. The verdict was finally read out in October 1993 – six years in prison on a murder conviction. The disappointment in the east was palpable. "It would have been better to hand Mielke over to the former East Germans," said Walter Janka, a dissident communist who was a victim of a 1950s show trial. "We would not have needed three years to give him the punishment he deserved."

Not all guilty verdicts were the same. Prosecutors won the most convictions in cases against the border guards known as the "Wall shooters". They were the ones who carried out the shoot-to-kill orders on East Germans trying to flee to the west. Often motivated by the extra pay, these volunteers were trained to "defend" the border against "illegal crossings". A clean hit or a killing was rewarded with a pay bonus, extra vacation and a medal. In all, the border guards killed 264 people trying to scale the Wall or cross the no-man's land between East and West Germany.[1] Despite all this, three-quarters of east Germans surveyed late in 1991 said the sentries should not be treated as criminals.

The trials often turned into wrenching sessions where families finally learned how brutally a son or brother had been killed. Some young guards sobbed as they told of their fear and remorse. Others coldly testified that they were just following orders. Although they had to use East German law in the trials, the western judges insisted that a higher moral code annulled the communist law meant to protect the border guards. Making direct parallels to the Nuremberg Trials, they argued that the shootings were like an execution and the laws authorising them did not merit obedience. One judge lectured guards that they should have applied a "pro-human rights interpretation" to the law. But every *Ossi* knew there had been no "pro-human rights interpretations" in East Germany. Easterners soon had the impression that the western judges were making the small fish fry while the big ones got away.

In the end, the courts found it hard to punish the guards harshly while the men who issued the orders they had followed were still free. Most ended up with convictions for manslaughter and were sentenced to two or three years in jail. But almost all sentences were suspended because the courts could not square the circle between the eastern and western systems. Tough sentencing was reserved for the most cold-blooded killings. One guard got six years for shooting dead a West Berliner whose motor boat had strayed across the unmarked demarcation line in a canal. Another was sentenced to ten years for mowing down a would-be defector who had already given himself up.

> 66 The trials often turned into wrenching sessions ... Some young guards sobbed as they told of their fear and remorse 99

THE MAN WITHOUT A FACE

Prosecutors went to remarkable lengths to convict the murkiest figure of them all. Markus Wolf, who headed the foreign espionage arm of the Stasi for 33 years, was a legendary figure whose spy network was among the best in the world. The man said to be the model for the cunning spy Karla in John le Carré's thrillers (he modestly denied this) had planted "moles" as high as the Bonn chancellery, NATO headquarters and West Germany's counter-espionage service. His agents had kidnapped, blackmailed and tortured people. "Romeo agents", a Wolf speciality, had seduced lonely secretaries in Bonn and Brussels to lure them into the espionage game. Being at the centre of this spider's web, it seemed, Wolf had to be implicated in any number of crimes.

Looking like an ageing Paul Newman, Wolf, 70, was as urbane as the other East German leaders were bland. Tall, trim and dapper, he was a frequent television chat show guest. When his trial for treason and bribery opened in Düsseldorf on 4 May 1993, Wolf challenged the court's right to try him. How could he be accused of treason against the Federal Republic when he had been a citizen of the German Democratic Republic? "Which country am I supposed to have betrayed?" he asked. Why did the west protect its own spies but treat East Berlin's as criminals? "A result of this inequality is that I, as former head of the intelligence agency of one German state, am in court while the former head of exactly the same agency in the other state is now foreign minister of united Germany," he said.

> 66 Being at the centre of this spider's web, it seemed, Wolf had to be implicated in any number of crimes 99

His reference to Klaus Kinkel, who as head of West Germany's Federal Intelligence Service (BND) in the early 1980s had been Wolf's direct counterpart, pointed to the Achilles heel of the western case. Every sovereign state had an espionage agency whose dirty tricks were protected from the law. Trying the easterners for this while ignoring western spies smacked of 'victor's justice' against the east. Bonn had considered absolving spies from both sides at reunification, but dropped the idea because of strong public opposition to a "Stasi amnesty".

"The court will find me guilty," Wolf said as the proceedings closed in November. "It would have been more honest to say openly, in the name of the victors of German reunification: Now we've got you, now you're getting what's coming to you and you have to pay." The court sentenced Wolf to six years in prison on three counts of treason and seven of bribery. But he could not be jailed until the Federal Constitutional Court ruled on whether united Germany could convict East German spies at all. As expected, the supreme court decided in May 1995 that espionage was not a crime like any other. Wolf and his control officers who had operated from East Germany could not be prosecuted, it said. The suave spy supremo was no hero for most Germans in east or west, but many were pleased that "victor's justice" did not prevail.[2]

THE HONECKER TRIAL

On 12 November 1992, Erich Honecker was escorted into the court at Moabit Prison to face his trial. Although 80 years old and stricken with terminal liver cancer, he walked in holding his head high. Honecker, who oversaw the building of the Wall in 1961, embodied more than anyone else the state behind the barbed wire and concrete walls. The charges against him were 12 cases of manslaughter for deaths by shooting at the Berlin Wall, and by mines and automatic shooting devices along the border with West Germany. Apart from Honecker, the court also levelled the manslaughter charge against Mielke, former Prime Minister Willi Stoph, former Defence Minister Heinz Kessler, his deputy Fritz Streletz and Hans Albrecht, former SED boss in Suhl district. All belonged to the National Defence Council, the highest body of party and defence officials, and the group responsible for enforcing the shoot-to-kill orders.

Honecker had fled to Moscow in 1991 to escape the trial, but the 1991 coup against his host, President Mikhail Gorbachev, sounded the death knell for his refuge. When Russian President Boris Yeltsin ordered him to leave in December, he took shelter in the Chilean embassy and held out there until July. After he was denied asylum in Chile, where his daughter lived, he gave himself up in July 1992 and returned for trial in Berlin.

Speaking in his own defence on 3 December, Honecker denounced the proceedings as "a Nuremberg Trial against communists." The western authorities wanted to come to grips with the communist past in a way they never did with the Nazi era, he said. Honecker recalled that West Germans had courted him only a few years earlier. "Today they call criminals the same people that yesterday they welcomed with honours, as state guests and partners in a common effort to prevent war from ever starting again on German soil," he said. In an ironic twist, he then went on to deny what he had spent decades trying to make the West believe – that East Germany was a sovereign state. He rejected the charge that he or anyone else in East Berlin bore responsibility for building the Wall in 1961. "The truth is that the construction of the Wall was decided at a meeting of the Warsaw Pact member states on 5 August 1961 in Moscow.

66 Honecker denounced the proceedings as 'a Nuremberg Trial against communists' 99

The GDR was an important link in this alliance of socialist states, but not the leading power." His statement finished, Honecker sat down and kept his silence for the rest of the trial.[3]

He didn't have to say anything else. The trial soon fell apart of its own accord. Honecker's lawyers repeatedly focused the discussion on his growing cancer tumour and then, outside the courtroom, bemoaned the depressing effect that talk about his failing health had on Honecker himself. In early January, the presiding judge had to step down after asking Honecker's lawyers to have the communist autograph a map of Berlin for him. A week later, Berlin's Constitutional Court ruled that Honecker was too ill to stand trial further and should be released. The city sent

Honecker off to the airport in a dark Mercedes limousine with a police motorcade. He was reunited with his family in Santiago and died there on 29 May 1994.

PRISONERS OF GERMAN HISTORY

With the collapse of the Honecker trial, the Germans lost the hope of seeing the law make amends for the crimes of their leaders for the second time this century. The experience of two authoritarian regimes over the past 60 years had left Germans looking for a catharsis to sweep away all the complicated and embarrassing baggage of their past. But once again, the main symbols of those regimes just slipped out of their grasp. There were few people in Germany who believed the communists as guilty as the Nazis, or wanted harsh punishment or death for Honecker and his friends. But the fact they got off legally was a bitter lesson for eastern Germans about the limits of the law in dealing with politics and morality.

One of the most scornful reactions came from Kohl's eastern protégée Angela Merkel. The federal minister for youth and women, a CDU politician with no nostalgia about the "good old days" under commun-ism, she suddenly found a gut preference for the East German way of doing things. "This is not an example of how to convince people that the injustice of a dictatorship can be dealt with by the law," she complained. Her western colleagues differed. Kinkel, who was justice minister before taking over the foreign ministry in 1992, said, "I consider this trial against Mr Honecker a good example of the legal system we can be proud of." In fact, many *Ossis* had more sympathy for Honecker than *Wessis* did. Protestant pastors showed the same independence of thought that made them moral authorities in the confused days of the *Wende*. Asked how he felt, the prominent eastern churchman Friedrich Schorlemmer replied, "I feel a certain relief that this court focused on the dignity of a dying man. I think this shows the generosity of the (western) legal system. It does not act as Honecker and his state behaved towards other people."

The "Honecker trial" continued without Honecker until September 1993. In the end, the remaining defendants – Kessler, Streletz and Albrecht – were given jail sentences of between four and a half and seven and a half years. The second judge in the trial concluded that men in charge of East Germany's borders were ideologues rather than killers. They accepted the killings as part of a strategy to defend the communist state. "The court was always conscious of its historical bias," judge Hans Boss reflected when he handed down the sentences. "In the defendants' favour, we had to consider that they were prisoners of German history – as are we all."

HISTORY AND HYSTERIA

There was another way to deal with the past and it could be swift and sharp. No legalisms were needed, few explanations were heard. All one had to do was fling the charge "Stasi contacts" and an east German could be irrevocably tainted. Rumours and innuendo were often enough to ruin reputations or end careers. From the time the Wall fell, journalists competed avidly to uncover ever bigger and more staggering scandals. Politicians gladly turned the spotlight on to any dark corners of a rival's past. The mind-boggling extent of Stasi snooping made all kinds of charges seem possible.

This "Stasi mania" rarely exposed the full truth. Life under the century's second German dictatorship was full of grey areas that eluded easy moral judgements. Some people had reasons to talk to the Stasi, some were pure opportunists and some just went along. Besides, who could cast the first stone? Too many *Ossis* had gone along with the system. Too many *Wessis* knew they could have done the same.

The first wave of Stasi accusations cut down two promising new eastern politicians just as they reached national prominence. Wolfgang Schnur was a former human rights lawyer in East Germany who headed the Democratic Awakening party just before the March 1990 Volkskammer election. Helmut Kohl often seemed more comfortable campaigning with him in the east than with apparently more compromised eastern CDU veterans like Lothar de Maizière. A week before the vote, Stasi files showed he had informed on his dissident clients for 16 years. Schnur quit in disgrace. Over at the SPD, front-runner Ibrahim Böhme basked in the attention he got from Willy Brandt and other western Social Democrats during the campaign. A week after the vote, however, *Der Spiegel* reported he had been working for the Stasi since the mid-1960s. He denied the charges but had to step down because of the scandal. The full extent of his spying on the dissident scene became known when the Stasi files were opened to the public in 1992.

> 66 Rumours and innuendo were often enough to ruin reputations or end careers 99

No *Ossi* rose as high and crashed as badly as de Maizière. Painfully shy by nature, he steered East Germany to reunification and was made Kohl's deputy chairman in the united CDU. After the 1990 election, he had a good chance of being elected speaker in the all-German parliament as well. But in early December 1990, both *Der Spiegel* and *Stern* named de Maizière as an informer who had reported to the Stasi almost monthly since 1982, on the Protestant church and dissidents close to it. Suddenly, none of his former allies wanted to know de Maizière. Kohl said nothing in his defence and Schäuble damned him with faint praise. Unable to disprove charges flung at him almost daily, de Maizière finally gave up on 17 December and quit his cabinet and party posts.

De Maizière's case was more complex than the others. As one of only a few dozen independent lawyers in East Germany, he insisted, he had to have contact with the Stasi because of his legal work. The Stasi controlled the legal system, running investigations in dissident cases and telling prosecutors and judges which way the trial should go. The only way to help a defendant was to try to influence the procedure from the start. It was a question of how long a spoon was needed to sup with the devil. "At no point did I sign a declaration obliging me to work for the Stasi, deliver reports, or receive money or any other privileges," he repeated wearily, but to no avail. De Maizière was not the only easterner who suspected the Stasi scare was being used to keep *Ossis* at arm's length in Bonn.

INSIDE THE BEAST

Each scandal revealed more about the Stasi and hinted at how much more remained to be unveiled. The Ministry for State Security (MfS) was a swamp of conspiracy and betrayal. The sheer size of the MfS and the extent of its paranoia was the first surprise. It had dossiers on about six million people – four million East Germans (i.e. a quarter of the country's total population) and two million West Germans. That added up to 100 km of files in the central archives in East Berlin. Another 80 km of files   gathered dust in the 15 capitals of East Germany's districts. One room at the headquarters had jars containing samples of some dissidents' clothing, so that search dogs could recognise them by their smell.[4]

Reasons to work for the Stasi were many and varied. Full-timers had probably shared the same mix of conviction and careerism as did members of the SED, which they all had to join. The MfS paid higher salaries and gave employees priority for scarce items such as apartments,

East German leader Erich Honecker greets Soviet President Mikhail Gorbachev in East Berlin for the 40th anniversary of the German Democratic Republic, only a month before the Wall fell. Honecker wanted to show he could resist the changes sweeping the communist world, but the Cold War-style event turned out to be his last hurrah. Photograph by Gaby Sommer, 6 October 1989.

A West German border guard welcomes East Germans with flowers as they stream across the open border to the West in their Trabis the day after the Berlin Wall opened. The sputtering Trabi, mocked in the west as a power lawnmower with headlights and seats, came to symbolise the East Germans' new freedom to travel. Photograph by Sven Creutzmann, 10 November 1989.

East Berliners cross the old no man's land into West Berlin after a section of the Wall was torn down to create a new border crossing at Potsdamer Platz, which before World War Two was the busiest intersection in Europe. Hitler's chancellery, with the underground bunker where he committed suicide, stood on the open ground visible to the left of the street on the eastern side. Photograph by Wolfgang Rattay, 12 November 1989.

Showing the strain of the initial post-reunification period, Chancellor Helmut Kohl loses control and lunges at demonstrators after they pelted him with eggs and tomatoes during a visit to the eastern city of Halle. The crowd was protesting against the wide-scale layoffs that scarred the east after the communist system was scrapped. Photograph by Reuters, 10 May 1991.

Erich Honecker gives the traditional communist clenched-fist salute in a Berlin court at his trial for manslaughter, the most spectacular of the post-unity court dramas in which western authorities attempted to make East German officials pay for 40 years of communism. Although Ossis were often disappointed with the verdicts, the exercise highlighted the primacy of the law in Germany's post-war democracy. Photograph by Lutz Schmidt, 26 November 1992.

Several hundred Turkish residents mourn the victims of a neo-Nazi arson attack on a house in Solingen, near the western city of Düsseldorf, in which five Turks died and three were injured. Many Germans were shocked by the attacks on the Turkish minority but Chancellor Helmut Kohl failed to show moral leadership and join other prominent politicians – including President Richard von Weizsäcker – in attending their funeral. Photograph by Reuters, 30 May 1993.

Chancellor Helmut Kohl and French President François Mitterrand listen to their national anthems during farewell ceremonies for Allied forces leaving western Berlin. The two men worked closely to place reunited Germany within a new Europe that would be further integrated by forming a common currency. Kohl never found the same harmony with Mitterrand's successor, Jacques Chirac, and the traditional "French–German motor" driving EU integration stalled. Photograph by Lutz Schmidt, 8 September 1994.

The Wrapped Reichstag, a modern-day take on history that symbolised the Germans' new self-assurance, draws tens of thousands of curious and cheerful visitors to Berlin 50 years after the city was the last battlefield of the collapsing Third Reich. The two-week wrapping by the Bulgarian-American artist Christo marked the end of the post-unity confusion and the real start of the transition towards the "Berlin Republic." Photograph by Reinhard Krause, 25 June 1995.

After the government tried to squeeze its budget to qualify for Europe's monetary union, coalminers protesting against cuts in state subsidies for their uncompetitive industry block a main intersection outside Helmut Kohl's chancellery in Bonn, brandishing banners reading "Kohl must go!" Kohl's government hesitated to make the unpopular cuts at home that were needed to meet the single currency goal he championed so single-mindedly abroad. Photograph by Michael Urban, 11 March 1997.

One of the models for Berlin's Holocaust memorial, a vast symbolic graveyard due to be built in the former no man's land near the Brandenburg Gate. Plans for the controversial project changed over the years as younger generations of Germans sought new ways to understand the Nazi slaughter of the Jews and keep its memory alive. Photograph by Fabrizio Bensch, 25 August 1998.

Gerhard Schröder celebrates his victory as Germany's new chancellor with his partner and rival Oskar Lafontaine. The almost seamless cooperation that produced the SPD victory over Helmut Kohl lasted little more than five months before the ambitious Lafontaine quit in frustration over his role as second fiddle to the more popular Schröder. Photograph by Michael Dalder, 27 September 1998.

The changing face of the Christian Democratic Union – former party chairman Helmut Kohl, newly-elected head Wolfgang Schäuble and the soon-to-be leader, easterner Angela Merkel, sit together at a special CDU party congress in Bonn after Kohl's defeat. Photograph by Michael Urban, 7 November 1998.

Right-wing extremists demonstrate in the northern city of Kiel against a controversial exhibition documenting the crimes of the Wehrmacht, the German army during World War Two. The exhibition provoked protests wherever it was shown in Germany because it highlighted the role the Wehrmacht played in atrocities against Jews, Communists and nationalists on the eastern front. Photograph by Christian Charisius, 30 January 1999.

Foreign Minister Joschka Fischer, who reconciled much of the German left with the idea of armed intervention in humanitarian missions, is hit by a paint bomb by protesters during a raucous Green Party congress in Bielefeld, where the traditionally pacifist party debated its stand on Kosovo. Photograph by Reuters, 13 May 1999.

Jubilant Kosovar Albanians greet German tanks and troop carriers arriving in Prizren, in western Kosovo, as part of the NATO-led KFOR peace-keeping force, after Serbia agreed to withdraw from the province. German soldiers, on their first combat mission since World War Two, were astonished to find they were hailed as liberators in a country the Nazis had once occupied. Photograph by Peter Müller, 14 June 1999.

The German parliament, now based in the renovated Reichstag building in Berlin, commemorates the 10th anniversary of the fall of the Wall with a solemn ceremony addressed by former presidents George Bush of the United States and Mikhail Gorbachev of the ex-Soviet Union. Former Chancellor Helmut Kohl stole the show so effectively that former aides wondered if he was planning a political comeback. Photograph by Michael Urban, 9 November 1999.

telephones and cars. Why "unofficial collaborators" (IMs) betrayed friends and colleagues was harder to say. A typical informer was recruited while still a student, lured by promises of a job in exchange for occasional reports on professors and fellow students. People caught trying to flee to West Germany might be offered short jail sentences if they later helped the MfS. Some sought the Stasi's help to change things, believing its agents would use their influence to right some wrong somewhere. Motives could be as individual as the informers themselves. Easterners were shocked in 1995 to learn that the region's most popular radio talk show host, Lutz Bertram, had been an IM. The uproar died down when he recounted how glaucoma had slowly made him blind as a teenager. He desperately hoped that helping the Stasi would earn him a visa, so that he could have an eye operation in West Berlin.

> **66** The Stasi files spilled out a revolting mixture of betrayal and banality **99**

One of the last decisions of the Volkskammer, before it disappeared, was to name Joachim Gauck as head of an agency to oversee the Stasi files. His office, soon known as the "Gauck agency", collected the archives and provided information from them for the government and judicial authorities. There were repeated leaks and the accused could not defend themselves. When the agency finally opened its files for the public on 2 January 1992, Gauck declared, "We are now moving from the hysterical to the historical phase of dealing with our past." He could not have been more wrong. The Stasi files, now available for those mentioned in them as well as researchers and journalists, spilled out a revolting mixture of betrayal and banality. The MfS had pursued its goals with a thoroughness worthy of the Nazis.

Some of East Germany's best-known dissidents turned up on the first day to read their files. Bärbel Bohley, Vera Wollenberger, Rainer Eppelmann, Gerd and Ulrike Poppe each got a pile of thick binders retelling the Stasi version of his or her past. The Poppes, among the most active of peace campaigners in East Berlin, found 40 binders of files, each stuffed with 300 pages apiece. Bärbel Bohley thought her 25 binders were boring. They were so detailed there was even a photograph of her taking out the rubbish. "If that was my life, what was it all about?" she asked in slight bewilderment.

Vera Wollenberger already knew the files' worst secret before she opened them. Just before Christmas, the press revealed that her husband Knud (alias "IM Donald") had for five years passed details of her role in the underground peace movement to the Stasi. Wollenberger looked shaken after reading her dossier. "These files are a quite dangerous mixture of fiction and truth," she commented. "Anybody who wants to look into the files must be aware that nasty surprises might be awaiting them."[5]

STOLPE SLOWS THE STEAMROLLER

The Stasi steamroller was rumbling along at full throttle when Manfred Stolpe, the popular premier of Brandenburg state, held up his hand and cried, "Stop!" His gesture looked suicidal. Unprompted, he revealed in *Der Spiegel* in January 1992 that he had had about 1,000 meetings with SED, state and Stasi officials in his 30 years as a lawyer for the Protestant church. Stolpe said he hoped his report from inside the lion's den would add depth to the superficial debate about East Germany's past. "Many people have never understood and cannot understand how a dictatorship works," he wrote. "Today, after the Soviet empire has fallen apart and East Germany has come home to a western Germany, history's winners seem to be those who were tough anti-communists or who waited things out and hibernated. Whoever tried to work for change inside East Germany, which nobody thought would disappear quickly, now look worn out, suspicious, maybe unfit for a future in a united Germany."[6]

Both the media and Stolpe's critics went into a feeding frenzy. For months afterwards, fresh charges and new details popped up almost daily. The Gauck agency, whose director had long been critical of Stolpe's high-level contacts, called him "a classic IM" but had no proof he had agreed to spy for the Stasi. Calls for his resignation piled in from left and right.

Stolpe had been one of the most influential men in the east. During the communist period, dissidents, conscientious objectors, critical clergymen, would-be emigrants – all came to him for a solution to their problems, and many found one. The Social Democrat's name came up regularly in speculation about who would succeed Richard von Weizsäcker as Germany's president in 1994.

He refused to buckle under the intense pressure, however, and insisted his actions could not be understood out of context. "The party depended on the third pillar of power, the ministry for state security, in its decision-making. That is where it got its information, its assessment of a situation and the basis for party guidelines meant to secure their power," he explained. "Anybody wanting to exert influence from outside had to take that into account."[7]

But even this consummate diplomat could not reconcile all the conflicting interests he dealt with. After the Wall fell, some dissidents accused him of helping East Berlin to expel them to the west. Many asked why he had not been as courageous as they were. Maybe reform could have come much earlier, they argued, if influential people such as Stolpe had not acted in a way that stabilised the communist system. But Stolpe never claimed to be a revolutionary. His goal was to maximise the church's freedoms.

Stolpe was from the "Class of '53", the generation of East Germans who remembered how Soviet tanks had crushed the workers' uprising of 17 June 1953. They saw the SED build the Wall in 1961. All-out opposition was futile, even dangerous, they believed. "I was no hero, I was no resistance fighter," Stolpe admitted. "I tried to use the chances I had to win more freedom at a time when I could not assume the Soviet empire would fall apart in the 1990s and set us free." Judging East German history from its origins rather than its end produced a different view.

> His case blurred the lines between East Germany's culprits and its victims

The serious debate Stolpe said he wanted never took place, partly through his own fault. After revealing his Stasi contacts, he fought on as the press uncovered ever more damaging details about how closely he had cooperated. His state government almost collapsed in dispute over his half-hearted confessions. Stolpe's national image was battered and his chances of becoming Germany's president were long gone, but he kept on fighting. Brandenburg's voters spoke the final word. In September 1994, he won re-election with a stunning 52.4 per cent – a 14-point leap over 1990. Stolpe explained this by saying he gave Brandenburgers self-confidence in difficult times. He also helped them gloss over the compromises they had made with the communists. His case blurred the lines between East Germany's culprits and its victims.

CRIMES AND CULPRITS

The Stasi files were hardly opened before the calls came to close them up again. The MfS seemed to be getting a hold on united Germany. The files were biased, poisonous documents that could not be taken at face value in court. The best thing to do, said respected dissident pastor Friedrich Schorlemmer, was to burn the files in a bonfire and get on with everyday life. "I don't want the Stasi to have power over us after the fact," he explained. Helmut Kohl joined the chorus of file-closers in November 1993. "The Stasi files are ... poisoning the whole atmosphere these days. Nobody knows exactly how much in a report is written to please some superior and how much is fact. They let off a very foul odour ... If I could decide completely freely, I'd know what to do with the files. We'll get no satisfaction from them and historians won't get any later either."[8]

But nations need to remember. The store of shared experience is one of the foundations of a society. With so many painful memories, the temptation in Germany to suppress failures and stress successes is understandably strong. But the negative lessons from the past also help shape the collective memory. The workings of Germany's two repressive systems had to be uncovered and understood. The Stasi files offered some keys to that understanding and Gauck won enough support to keep them open.

Imperfect though it was, the Germans' second attempt to clean up after a dictatorship has probably done better than the first. The Stasi hysteria and the seemingly inconclusive trials aroused cynical criticism about how reunited Germany was not doing any better than post-war West Germany. But, with some distance, it became clear the trials played an important part in reaffirming the rule of law. They chose neither to punish the culprits harshly nor to absolve them. In the end, they upheld the rule of law by clearly condemning crime. The short or suspended sentences they handed down reflected the unique situation the east Germans were in and the flexibility of the western system to integrate them. Developing a democratic legal system after the war was one of the most important steps the West Germans took to learn the lessons of the past. It struggled and sometimes slipped trying to square the circle in seeking justice for east Germany's past. In the end, it proved its worth by sensibly opting for reason rather than revenge.

NOTES

1   This is the offical figure Germany's state prosecutor's office use. The 13 August Working Group, which researches crimes along the border, said on 11 August 1998 that as many as 1,000 people may have died trying to flee East Germany since 1949.

2   Prosecutors put Wolf on trial again in 1997 for abduction, coercion and causing bodily harm in three HVA kidnapping cases dating back to the 1950s and 1960s. He was found guilty and given a two-year suspended sentence. "I suppose I can live with this," he remarked dryly.

3   For full text of Honecker's speech, see Wesel, Uwe (1994) *Ein Staat vor Gericht: Der Honecker-Prozess*. Frankfurt: Eichborn, pages 64–83.

4   The exact number of MfS employees is unclear because many files that might have provided the total were destroyed. The Modrow government told the Round Table there had been 85,000 full-time employees, but the Gauck agency later revised this to 97,000. Gauck himself normally spoke of "about 100,000". The last SED government also claimed there were only 109,000 informal collaborators, but former Stasi general Heinz Engelhardt put the figure around 180,000, while dissidents spoke of several hundred thousands. Historian Karl Wilhelm Fricke, a western specialist on the MfS, considers the dissidents' estimate closest to reality. See Fricke, "Das Ministerium für Staatssicherheit als Herrschaftsinstrument der SED – Kontinuität und Wandel" in *Enquete-Kommission*, VIII, page 15.

5   For her sad story, see Wollenberger, Vera (1992) *Virus der Heuchler*. Berlin: Elephanten Press.

6   *Der Spiegel*, 20 January 1992.

7   Stolpe, Manfred (1992) *Schwieriger Aufbruch*. Munich: Goldmann Verlag, pages 115–21.

8   *Enquete-Kommission*, V/1, page 928. Kohl's comments appeared in a different light years later, during the uproar over his illegal party financing schemes, when the ex-chancellor tried to stop the Gauck agency from releasing transcripts of telephone calls tapped by the Stasi in the 1980s that included references to his slush funds. Kohl's cabinet decided in 1990 to destroy unread several boxes of transcripts of tapped West German telephone conversations that East Berlin's CDU-led government handed over that spring.

10

THE BLOSSOMING LANDSCAPES

THE MOST CELEBRATED CAR OF 1989 WAS THE SPUTTERING LITTLE TRABANT. Hardly more than a power lawnmower with headlights and seats, the two-stroke "Trabi" transported tens of thousands of East Germans to the west before and during the *Wende*. When the Wall fell, West Berliners showered flowers and sprayed Sekt on Trabis as they inched through the packed crossing points. The boxy plastic-bodied car became the symbol of the *Ossis'* freedom to travel wherever their hearts desired. It even became the leading "character" in a comedy film, *Go, Trabi, Go,* about a Leipzig family's first trip to the west – in their Trabi, of course.

Halfway through 1990, Trabis became as unsellable as last year's calendars. The introduction of the deutschemark in the east stood the communist economy on its head. The waiting times of up to 15 years for a Trabi vanished. Prices plummeted. With hard cash in their hands, east Germans went for western cars that left Trabis in the dust on the bumpy eastern autobahns. The outdated Trabi factory in Zwickau closed down to make way for a new Volkswagen plant.

Most of the east German economy suffered the same fate as the Trabi, going into an uncontrolled skid after the full force of capitalism hit. Output plummeted, factories closed and jobs considered secure for life disappeared. Western consumer goods filled department stores and grocery shops. Abroad, the east European markets that once soaked up East Germany's exports also collapsed. The shock of the overnight economic merger helped maintain Germany's east–west split even while the two states were coming together. It created start-up conditions that ensured the two regions would remain different for decades.

MAKING AQUARIUMS OUT OF FISH SOUP

There have been so many debates about the myriad mistakes made in uniting the two economies that some basic facts have to be recalled. In the early months of 1990, the exodus of East Germans to the West threatened to destabilise both German states. Bonn had to take dramatic decisions very quickly to stem the flow and give the East Germans some hope for the future. There were only two options. Bundesbank President Karl Otto Pöhl wanted the two economies to adjust to each other over several years before sharing a single currency. This could be economically sound but politically unpredictable. Helmut Kohl's path to quick unity would deal with the exodus and East Germany's stability, at an unknown cost. Kohl's approach prevailed and the merger went ahead at breakneck speed. The August 1991 coup against Mikhail Gorbachev delivered chilling proof that he was right about the politics, diplomacy and timing. If Bonn had taken the slower path, the two Germanys might not have reunited and the result could have been more instability in the heart of Europe.

> 66 There was probably more worst-case planning in 1989 for earthquakes than for reunification 99

There was probably more worst-case planning in 1989 for earthquakes than for the event enshrined as a national goal in the western constitution. Bonn's Ministry for Inner-German Affairs had no contingency plans for reunification. Marxist academics had written for decades about "the transition to socialism" but no thought had been given to "the return to capitalism". As Poland's first non-Marxist finance minister, Leszek Balcerowicz, liked to describe the problem, "We all know how to make fish soup out of an aquarium – you just put the fish through a blender. But could somebody please tell me how to make an aquarium out of fish soup?"

There was one study, though, that read like a blueprint for Kohl's approach. In September 1953, Bonn's Economics Minister Ludwig Erhard published a short article about the complexity of reintegrating the communist zone one day. When the time came, he said, Bonn would have to introduce the deutschemark there quickly and force the East to conform to western ways. Men and markets would take care of the rest, he predicted. "The misery of those people still living under tyranny, their hunger and lack of all the things that make life worth living will prove to be a powerful force propelling them forwards and providing almost unimagined possibilities for human labour," he wrote.[1] Helmut Schmidt, who like Erhard also went on to become chancellor, drew up an SPD plan for economic reunification in 1959 that advised a gradual transition spread out over five years. Although Schmidt was by no means a model for Lafontaine, the SPD candidate in 1990 advocated a unity plan that echoed this long-forgotten study.[2]

Kohl was gripped by Erhard's optimism as he watched East German communism collapse. He campaigned vigorously for the eastern CDU in the Volkskammer election with the old Erhard slogan "Prosperity for All". Since 1990 was a double election year, one important part of the master's message was played down. Erhard's essay included a dire prediction about the effects of the rapid monetary union he advocated. "The economic situation of the Soviet zone will be ruthlessly exposed and there can be no doubt that the result will be depressing, yes often even shocking," he wrote.

Erhard's optimism was a powerful vision, but it belonged to another era. The western economy in 1948 had to recover from the war, but so did competitors in other countries. Four decades later, East Germany joined a capitalist world economy with well-established markets and suppliers. Industrial production jumped by 50 per cent in the west within a year of Erhard's 1948 currency reform. In eastern Germany, factory output dropped by one-third once the deutschemark was introduced there. Bonn waited nine years before making its deutschemark convertible. In 1990, by contrast, the East German economy lost overnight the exchange rate tool that struggling economies use to make themselves more competitive in the world economy. By taking the deutschemark, the region's currency was effectively revalued by 450 per cent without any comparable jump in productivity to justify it. "The result, as you know, was a disaster," Pöhl told the economics and finance committee of the European Parliament in March 1991.[3]

ERHARD'S WORST FEARS COME TRUE

East Germany's last communist government was confident it had an impressive dowry for the marriage with West Germany. It boasted it was the world's tenth industrial power, although it was not clear where this ranking came from. East Germany estimated its total national income in 1990 to be between 1,000 billion and 1,600 billion marks. In October, Treuhand President Detlev Rohwedder gave the first rough western estimate: "The whole mess is worth about 600 billion marks." When western-style balance sheets for east German firms were finally published in 1992, the estimate of the region's overall value plummeted to 260 billion marks. Against this stood liabilities of 520 billion marks.[1] It turned out that east Berlin had far overestimated the value of fixed assets that would have been written off decades before in the west. Some equipment was so old that western firms actually bought up machines they had manufactured before the war to display in their company museums.

> 66 City and local governments were caught in an unimaginable cash squeeze 99

The switchover had dramatic effects for eastern companies whose debts were suddenly denominated in deutschemarks. Under the communists, debt was little more than an entry in a ledger signifying funds an enterprise had received from East Berlin. Capitalist-style levers such as interest rates meant little. These debts, exchanged at the rate of two-to-one, were transformed overnight from sleeping dogs to growling lions. Up and down East Germany, firms were strapped with debts before they even had a chance to operate. Many faced the stark choice of shutting down immediately or plunging deeper into debt to stay alive.

City and local governments were caught in an unimaginable cash squeeze. Heinrich Lehmann-Grube, who had an investment budget of 400 million to 500 million marks a year when he was chief administrator of Hanover in the west, got a start-up budget of 50 million marks when he was elected Lord Mayor of Leipzig in May 1990. The two cities were equal in size with a population of about 500,000 each. But Leipzig's funds were barely enough to continue the apartment building already under way and do the absolute minimum work needed for schools, hospitals and municipal construction. Although it needed to desperately, Leipzig could not launch federally funded job-creation schemes because it had no money to hire the bureaucrats needed to set them up.

Another familiar neighbourhood fixture, the local grocery store, changed beyond recognition. Shopping became a trip to a local wonderland. Soon after the Wall fell, western products began brightening up drab East German store shelves. By the spring, hundreds of thousands of East German pigs, about 30 million eggs and tons of vegetables could not be sold because western goods had taken their place. Just before monetary union came, shelves emptied as shopkeepers held back western goods until they could be paid for in deutschemarks. Then, after 1 July, western products drove most of the old brands of meat, yoghurt, beer and other goods out of the shops. Other stores cleared their shelves to make way for Japanese radios, Italian shoes and western clothes.

The sudden success of western goods was not driven only by new consumer preferences. The big western supermarket chains that bought up eastern grocery stores filled them mostly with goods from their own suppliers in the west. Once the new delivery patterns were set, there was little space left for eastern suppliers who came around months later with new products or better packaging. It would take two to three years before eastern products made any headway in their own markets.

The switchover also killed off what was meant to be the region's lifeline for the initial transition to a market economy. In many industrial sectors, about half of all output "made in GDR" had been exported to the other members of the Comecon trading bloc. This seemed to ensure a dumping ground for at least some of the goods that could not be sold in the west. But these former communist trading partners would have to pay for east German goods in hard currency from the beginning of 1991. Why should a Czech factory buy east German machinery if South Korea offered better quality at lower prices? How could any East Bloc camera maker compete with photo equipment from Asia? In the second half of 1990, exports from eastern Germany to eastern Europe and the Soviet Union plunged by more than 50 per cent. By the end of 1992, they had fallen by more than 75 per cent from their 1989 levels – while west German sales to the east rose by 23 per cent.

THE TREUHAND

None of the exciting new ideas of early 1990 turned out to be so off the mark as the Treuhand agency. It takes a special effort now to remember that this jobkiller incarnate, second only to the Stasi in terms of the public contempt it provoked, was the brainchild of the opposition parties around East Berlin's Round Table. The Treuhand (the word means "trustee") was proposed by theologian Wolfgang Ullmann as a way to save state industry from the clutches of West German capitalists. Since state-owned companies were known in communist jargon as *volkseigene Betriebe* (literally "companies owned by the people"), Ullmann reasoned that the people should share the profits when they were sold off. He proposed a new government agency to privatise state companies and either issue shares for all employees or set up some kind of public mutual funds to spread the wealth around. Estimates of these shares' value for each citizen ranged up to 40,000 marks – a nice nest egg for starting a new life under capitalism.

The Treuhand, whose directors were appointed by the government, was also supposed to prop up shaky companies with funds from dividends from healthy firms. Within months, however, it was laying off workers en masse and selling factories for only one mark to whichever *Wessi* carpetbagger would take them. Its transformation was so fast and complete that there was hardly time for it to masquerade as a wolf in sheep's clothing. East Germans quickly saw the Treuhand as a vicious wolf that was tearing apart their economy.

It is also hard to imagine the sheer size of the Treuhand agency. Since its writ extended over almost all state-owned businesses in a communist economy, it was the largest holding company in the world. As its start, the Treuhand controlled about one-third of all property in Eastern Germany. Almost 3.6 million people, about two-thirds of the East German workforce, worked in Treuhand companies. From industrial conglomerates with 60,000 workers to corner grocery shops with two employees, nothing was too big or too small to escape its grasp. It started off owning 8,000 different companies. This total swelled to about 14,000 as East Germany's many conglomerates were broken down into their component parts.

Detlef Karsten Rohwedder, who took over the Treuhand in August 1990, was one of the few West German managers with experience in both business and politics. Rohwedder rose to become a state secretary in Bonn's economics ministry before leaving for a top post at the ailing Dortmund steelmaker Hoesch. Over the next decade, he slashed the staff by 50 per cent, reduced Hoesch's reliance on the struggling steel sector and expanded into new high technology branches. When he went to the Treuhand, Rohwedder was confident he could finish the job by the year's end and return to Hoesch.

For the uncertain east Germans, Rohwedder's pin-striped suits and ironic smile came to personify the west German takeover of their country. As layoffs multiplied in early 1991, he and Kohl were vilified as heartless jobkillers in protests around the east. After a few months on the job, though, his views began to change. Reconstructing the eastern economy, he began to say to colleagues, was "a task of awesome dimensions" that might need 40 years to finish. He saw a growing need to restructure companies rather than just sell them off or shut them down. But his time at the Treuhand was too short to translate this insight into a new policy. On 1 April, a gunman fired three bullets through a window into his Düsseldorf home and killed him on the spot.

The first major victim of the new order was the Dresden camera maker Pentacon, one of East Germany's most prestigious exporters with 10 per cent of the world market. The announcement came on 3 October, Unity Day itself. Pentacon was a textbook example of communist inefficiency. It spent about DM 1,000 to produce a camera that sold abroad for only DM 200. Production facilities were spread out over 17 different factories and 41 more warehouses and office buildings. Of the 5,456 staff in mid-1990, only 232 were left a year later.

The state airline Interflug was the next big name to go down in a tailspin. Up to 20 western investors showed an interest in its fleet of 22 Soviet-built planes and three Airbuses. The main contenders were Germany's Lufthansa and British Airways, which was eager to build Berlin into a continental hub. As the negotiations were going on, the looming Gulf War and the spectre of terrorism cut deeply into world air traffic. When BA pulled out in January and Lufthansa dropped its bid in early February, the Treuhand announced it would liquidate the airline because no buyer could be found. A month after Interflug was shut down, Lufthansa moved into its offices and took over its operations. The Western airline, 52 per cent of which was owned by the German government, ended up taking Interflug's place without taking over its debts.

Within a year of the German–German monetary union, overall unemployment in the east hovered above 30 per cent. Officially, it only measured about seven per cent. But the legions of workers shunted off into state-funded retraining schemes or short-time work were really not fully employed. There was a wave of new jobs, but they were mostly in video shops or ice cream parlours. East Germany's infrastructure was crumbling but about 200,000 workers in construction, the classic sector to kick-start a recovery, were out of work for lack of public contracts.

While the *Ossis* watched their jobs disappear, the western economy was booming. Western producers had a windfall new market of 17 million people eager to buy their cars, washing machines, video recorders and other consumer goods. Thanks to this unleashed demand, employment in the west rose by nearly a million jobs in the first year after the German–German monetary union. The economy in the west grew by 4.5 per cent in 1990 and through the first half of 1991.

One deceptive ray of hope for *Ossis* was the trade union drive to boost their wages to western levels. At reunification, eastern workers earned only about 60 per cent of western wages. So in 1991, powerful western-based unions pushed for wage deals guaranteeing full parity by 1994. This was divorced from all economic reality. Productivity was far lower in the east and would not rise to western levels that quickly. But the western-based unions had no interest in a cheap labour pool next door that could compete with their rank-and-file. Like the Bonn government, they wanted to dissuade eastern workers from moving west. After the whopping pay hikes were agreed, western companies began exporting jobs to Poland or Czechoslovakia where hourly wages were as low as one-tenth of German pay levels. In the end, these dramatic pay hikes killed off almost any hope of keeping most factories competitive.

At the same time as introducing its "solidarity tax" in 1991, Bonn created the *Aufschwung Ost* (Upswing East) programme. This was to pump 24 billion marks of state funds over two years into roadbuilding, municipal construction, housing, business subsidies, worker retraining schemes and other government-funded pump-priming projects previously out of official fashion. It also gave local governments another 5 billion marks to repair hospitals, schools and old age homes – a quick way to get struggling carpenters, electricians, painters and plumbers back to work. Combined with overall west-to-east transfer payments of about 150 billion marks that year, this meant every east German got an average of 9,600 marks in subsidies from the west in 1991.

After Rohwedder's assassination, his successor Birgit Beuel became the *Wessi* the *Ossis* loved to hate. This convinced free-marketeer quickly moved into place and started forcing the pace of selling. There was such pressure to sell off companies quickly that Treuhand managers dreamed up eye-popping incentives to get staff to shed their share on time. The Halle regional office, for example, set a bonus of 88,000 marks for directors and 44,000 marks for department heads if the branch sold everything by October 1992. The agency soon reached a pace of over a hundred sales a week. Its workaholic salesmen had a favourite joke: "Question: Do you have to ask an investor his name before you sign a contract with him? Answer: You can if you like, but it slows down business a lot."

Putting so many companies on the block created a huge buyers' market. Several companies went for the symbolic price of one mark, which the eastern staff often took as an insulting statement of how little western investors valued their work. It did not take long for scandals to harden popular resentment against the slick western "yuppie" managers who made quick life-or-death decisions about their jobs. "Skinheads in pinstripes" was one of the more polite epithets hurled at them from protest marches outside Treuhand offices around the country.

Kohl normally kept his distance from these deals, but made one large exception. In May 1991, the chancellor heard desperate appeals for help when he visited chemical plants around Bitterfeld. None of the four outdated plants in the area, one of the cradles of the German chemical industry, could survive capitalist competition. At a gloomy meeting with 500 workers, the chancellor announced, "I will do everything to ensure that this chemical industry is preserved and developed further." But west Germany's chemical giants all declined his invitation to invest there.

> 'Skinheads in pin-strips' was one of the more polite epithets hurled at slick western 'yuppie' managers

Kohl and François Mitterrand then agreed to make this a flagship project to demonstrate Franco-German friendship. The French state-run oil company Elf Aquitaine started negotiating with the Treuhand. Germany's Thyssen and Russia's Rosnaft were brought in as partners and the deal to build a new 4.3 billion mark refinery on the Leuna site was announced in 1992.

The forced march into the free market attracted carpetbaggers of all sorts and plunged the Treuhand into repeated scandals. Because the agency operated in relative secrecy, accountable only to the finance ministry in Bonn, it was often hard to say whether corruption or sloppy management was more to blame for the mess.

The Treuhand office in Halle achieved notoriety by selling 21 companies to a single western fraudster who juggled funds from one firm to another. Within three months of buying one company, he had plundered more than half of its 35 million mark reserves to prop up his other companies.

Some east German money flowed halfway around the world. Two Indian businessmen bought two textile factories from the Treuhand in 1991. Nine million marks of their 40 million mark Treuhand start-up credit ended up in their company in Kuala Lumpur. Wary about real estate sharks buying companies for their property, the Treuhand tried to sell off east Germany's leading publisher, Aufbau, while keeping possession of its headquarters in the heart of east Berlin. But the contract, signed with a Frankfurt property tycoon, failed to specify this. When he spotted this error, the new owner sold the building to one of his subsidiaries to ensure the Treuhand could not claim it back from him. The Treuhand did get it back, but only after paying the tycoon 9 million marks.[5]

These cases paled when the story of the Baltic coast shipyards' privatisation came to light. The shipyards, once a major producer for the Soviet fleet, had 1950s technology and costs that were about 20 per cent higher than those of the main competition in South Korea. They looked doomed to sink, but the Treuhand worked out a deal in 1992 to sell three yards to Bremer Vulkan, western Germany's largest shipbuilder. Bremer Vulkan paid 1.25 million marks for its shipyards, but got 1.2 *billion* marks in subsidies in the bargain. When Bremer Vulkan went bankrupt four years later, it emerged that its chairman had syphoned off 854 million marks of Treuhand funds to prop up his shaky business in the west.

THE TURNAROUND

The true weakness of the eastern economy was as ruthlessly exposed as Erhard had predicted. The result was "depressing, yes often even shocking" in more ways than Mr Prosperity had imagined. People who had thought unity would help them step up to the western way of life felt trampled by change. Money, fraud, competition and status symbols, all things that played a minor role under the communists, overwhelmed them. The secretive ways of the Treuhand also frustrated them. Bonn had originally considered creating a reconstruction ministry, with Günther Krause at its head. But that would have landed the responsibility for a very unpredictable project squarely on Bonn's shoulders. From the government's point of view, the Treuhand was a conveniently distant lightning rod. It made the tough decisions and acted as a fire wall for the political heat that arose as a result.

By mid-1992, the "blossoming landscapes" that Kohl had promised were sprouting only in scattered patches. A construction boom was starting and the puny service sector was rapidly expanding, helping the eastern economy to grow by an impressive 7.8 per cent. But that had to be set against the 30 per cent drop the previous year. Figured separately, the region's "gross national product" amounted to only seven per cent of that of united Germany. The wells meant to irrigate those "blossoming landscapes" also began to run low. In 1992, the west German economy slowed down dramatically. The next year, the worst of the recession, it contracted by 1.9 per cent. Bonn was running out of tax revenues in the west, just as its need for them to give the east another kick-start rose.

Saxony's premier Kurt Biedenkopf, an old Kohl rival, finally cried "Stop!" when the Treuhand tried, in late 1992, to close down a steelworks in Freital. Closing the plant would throw 2,200 people out of work, while financing a restructuring for a few more years could save the factory. Biedenkopf accused the Treuhand of taking a blinkered view of the east. A shutdown might be cheaper for the agency, but not for the state government which would have to pay out jobless benefits. After a few days of discussion, Bonn gave in and the Treuhand agreed to keep the steelworks afloat. The days of fast-forward privatisation were ending.

During a visit to Schwerin in November, Kohl announced that "core industries" in eastern Germany had to be saved. This was the final admission from Bonn that the Treuhand's policies were pushing the region towards deindustrialisation. The business weekly *Wirtschaftswoche* saw Kohl the campaigner lurking behind the conversion: "It seems the push for the new states is timed to arrive right in time for the general election in 1994."[6]

The trade unions' dream of bringing eastern wages up to western levels by 1994 faded. Early in 1993, engineering sector employers threw out a benchmark agreement that aimed for wage parity the following year. Unit labour costs were sometimes 70 per cent higher than in west Germany, they complained. In some eastern factories, wages were as high as those in the United States but productivity as low as in Mexico. In response, workers walked out in the region's first official strikes, following 60 years of Nazi and communist rule. Well choreographed by the western-based IG Metall, the protests spread across the whole region. After three weeks, the two sides finally agreed to delay full parity until 1996. This helped the employers, but still left eastern wage levels too high to attract many investors there.

When Breuel dismantled the Treuhand's nameplate from the entrance to its Berlin headquarters on 30 December 1994, the agency had only 65 companies still on its books. "We have laid the groundwork," Breuel said in self-defence in her farewell address. "It was the only conceivable way to give these companies a chance for the future." But what kind of future? The region emerged seriously deindustrialised. Roughly three-quarters of all east German industry was shut down. Only about one-third of the three million jobs in manufacturing survived the transition. Exports, including to former West Germany, shrank dramatically. In all but six per cent of the Treuhand companies, ownership went over into western hands. What was left was a region at a long-term structural disadvantage vis-à-vis western Germany.

Jobs weren't the only baby that went out with the industrial bath water. Research and development (R&D) departments were often the first to be cut when a western firm bought out an eastern one. Of the 75,000 jobs in East German R&D in 1989, two-thirds had disappeared by 1991. Industry accounted for only 9,000 of them. Eastern factories were often reduced to the role of "extended workbenches", production units dependent on the western headquarters.

Eastern Germany also became a market economy with few markets for its products. The old Comecon markets and the few western outlets East Germany had before 1989 disappeared. The cost advantages East German products used to enjoy were wiped out. Marketing, an art practically unknown in the old communist economies, developed slowly in the east.

The West German "economic miracle" of the 1950s turned out to be the wrong prism through which to see the region's future. Within a year of monetary union, the most frequent comparison heard was to the *Mezzogiorno*. Eastern Germany, it was said, would turn out to be like Italy's poor south – backward, with little industry, an area that bought its goods from the prosperous north and sent its youth there to find work. Noting the structural imbalance emerging in Germany, some economists went even further and saw parallels between the east and the Third World. *Ossis* were understandably upset when they heard western academics comparing their region to Sri Lanka, Honduras or Tunisia.

> **66** What was left was a region at a long-term structural disadvantage vis-à-vis western Germany **99**

The real parallel was much closer to home. The region risked becoming hooked on a long-term flow of west-to-east subsidies without fully reaching the "take-off" stage that all development strategies aim for. West Germany lived for 40 years with this dilemma in West Berlin, where the local economy could not have survived the Cold War without the subsidies that Bonn provided. Unification seemed to put an end to this kind of massive support, but it appeared to be coming back on a far larger scale.

NOTES

1   Erhard, Leudwig (1953) "Wirtschaftliche Probleme der Wiedervereinigung," in *Bulletin des Presse- und Informationsamtes der Bundesregierung*, Number 174 (12 September), pages 1453–4.

2   See Schmidt, Helmut (1993) *Handeln für Deutschland*. Berlin: Rowohlt, pages 27–8.

3   That unguarded remark outraged Kohl and was one of the reasons for Pöhl's resignation a few months later. Pöhl later told the parliamentary committee investigating the Treuhand that he thought no journalists were present until he saw a Reuters correspondent rush out of the room to report his frank comments. See *Beweisprotokoll zur 11. Sitzung des 2. Untersuchungsausschusses "Treuhandanstalt"*. Bonn, Deutscher Bundestag, 9 December 1993, page 23.

4   Breuel, Birgit (ed.) (1993), *Treuhand intern*. Frankfurt: Ullstein, pages 102–4.

5   Details of several fraud cases can be found in *Treuhandanstalt: Bericht des 2. Untersuchungsausschusses des 12. Deutschen Bundestages*. Bonn: Deutscher Bundestag, 1994, pages 299–330.

6   See *Wirtschaftswoche*, 27 November 1992.

11

TOWARDS A GERMAN EUROPE?

THOMAS MANN WAS THE GERMAN SPEECHWRITERS' favourite author in 1990. Nobody needed a good reassuring quote more than German politicians. Suspicion and doubts about reunification were rife abroad and at home. What would happen when Germany reunited? Would it dream of dominating the rest of Europe again? With questions like this in the air, Bonn's wordsmiths unearthed just the quote they needed. "We do not want a German Europe," Mann said in 1945, "but rather a European Germany." "*Wir wollen kein deutsches Europa, sondern ein europäisches Deutschland,*" became the official mantra of German foreign policy. Mann's quote seemed to say it all. No, it told the doubters, there would be no repetition of history. Yes, it said, Germany would cooperate with its neighbours in Europe. Germany would change, too, to become even more open and pro-European than ever before.

> 66 The choice was not between a European Germany or a German Europe. Reality would be somewhere in between 99

In fact, the reuniting Germans no longer had the either/or choice that Mann's reassuring words portrayed. Western Germany was Europeanised to a far greater extent than the author could have imagined. Domestic and European factors were so intertwined in many policies that Germans spoke of "*europäische Innenpolitik*" ("internal European politics"), a phrase that made deal-making among leaders of EU member countries sound much like politicking among senators from American states. Bonn was not so pro-European that it forgot to defend German interests; but it now did so in a multilateral context, where compromise was the rule.

The question in the 1990s was how German the new Europe would become. Now the largest member by a clear margin, Germany was bound to exert influence. It had to do this, however, in a multilateral web of partnerships and compromises that the last united German state had never known. It could win almost across the board on one point, for example on Europe's monetary union, but fail to achieve the political union it considered its necessary balance. The choice was not between a European Germany or a German Europe. Reality would be somewhere in between.

TWO SIDES OF THE SAME COIN

No other policy issue brings the Germans' hopes, fears, dreams and schemes together in a more complex mix than Europe. After the war, the Germans had to find a way to resume normal relations with countries they had only recently overrun. As Konrad Adenauer saw it, they had to be bound up with the fate of their neighbours so much that they would never "go it alone" again. European integration offered the decisive helping hand. Over the decades, a pro-European "post-national" outlook became a firm part of West German politics and culture. It didn't replace the Germans' national identity, but added a comforting level of identity over their weak national feelings. It convinced them the old-fashioned nation-state was dying out. This attachment remained strong among west Germans even when certain policies, such as the EU's currency union that would abolish the deutschemark, were unpopular.

As is often the case with high-minded policies, there were solid national interests behind the German position. Germany does half of its trade with other members of the EU. By 1989, neighbouring France, the Benelux and Austria were already part of a "D-mark bloc" with the Bundesbank at its core. This gave business an important advantage, but it could not last for long without the neighbours chafing under Germany's new economic domination. Much as Bonn's diplomatic and military power had to be channelled through the EU and NATO, its economic influence would have to be integrated into a wider European context.

"If Europe does not create a common currency, the mark will fairly certainly dominate Europe in 10 or 15 years thanks to the size and strength of the German economy – just as the US dollar dominated the whole world in the first few decades after the last world war," Helmut Schmidt argued. "Germany's private financial institutes, its banks, insurance companies and the Bundesbank would thus win a dominant position in markets far from Germany's borders, causing discomfort, annoyance and envy in other countries. Why should we burden ourselves with such an annoyance?"[1]

Kohl always said (in another well-worn phrase, borrowed this time from Konrad Adenauer) that "German unity and European unity are two sides of the same coin." When he surprised his allies with the Ten Point Programme, however, doubts arose in European capitals. A reunited Germany, with 80 million people, would throw out of kilter the old balance in the EC, where the "big four" – Britain, France, Italy and West Germany – all had between 50 and 60 million citizens each. It could slow preparations for the Single Market due to be launched in 1992, especially if Bonn became increasingly interested in trade with eastern European countries that were toppling communist rule.

François Mitterrand was deeply convinced that Germany was a country "hesitant between its callings, either as a nation firmly fixed in the European union or the unspoken heir to the imperial ambitions of the Hohenzollerns and the Habsburgs".[2] He did not oppose reunification as such, but was alarmed at the possibility that it could lead Bonn to drift away from Brussels. Mitterrand first hoped to slow the merger down. At the same time, he stepped up the pressure on Kohl to agree to speed up the so-called "deepening" of the European Community. France had long seen further European integration as the best way to balance off west Germany's strength. The best way would be to absorb the deutschemark, the most powerful expression of Germany's influence, into a wider European currency. Standing above this would be a European Central Bank, where France would have a voice rather than be excluded when the Bundesbank made decisions that effected the rest of Europe.

> 66 Thatcher wrongly assumed that Bush, Gorbachev or Mitterrand would line up with her to slow down the merger 99

Mitterrand held out for a deal that would be crucial for both Germany and Europe. Although Kohl was initially reluctant, the president insisted he agree to start a conference in December 1991 to prepare for a monetary union. His aide, Jacques Attali, noted with bemusement in early December 1989 that "It's grotesque – German reunification is happening before our very eyes and François Mitterrand and Helmut Kohl confine themselves to talking about a date for a European monetary conference that won't take place for another 18 months!"[3] In return, Bonn won clear EC support for its long-stated goal that "the German people regain their unity through free self-determination".

In contrast to Mitterrand, Thatcher took a narrow view of how to react and came out with nothing to show for her efforts. She wrongly assumed that Bush, Gorbachev or Mitterrand would line up with her to slow down the merger rather than try to use the inevitable for their own purposes. This policy lost its basis when the others concluded that rapid reunification was the best guarantor of stability. Each of the others found a way to use the trend – Mitterrand to push for a European currency, Gorbachev to get more German aid and Bush to reinforce US ties with the country he saw as Washington's most important ally in Europe. "If there is one instance in which a foreign policy I pursued met with unambiguous failure, it was my policy on German reunification," Thatcher later wrote, in a rare admission of defeat.[4] Kohl could not understand her approach. "In her place, I would have done everything to make sure reunited Germany was tightly integrated into the European Community. But this was a strange idea to her ... I had the impression that Margaret Thatcher lived in the pre-Churchillian era, in the balance of power mind-set of the nineteenth century."[5]

THE ROAD TO MAASTRICHT

Once Bonn had made it clear it would respect the Oder–Neisse line as Poland's western border, France and Britain lost the last major hurdle they could put in the way of reunification. Kohl had won over his partners' minds, even if not their hearts. A special summit in Dublin on 28 April announced that the EC "warmly welcomes German unification ... We are confident that German unification, the result of a freely expressed wish on the part of the German people, will be a positive factor in the development of Europe as a whole and the Community in particular."

The reason for the change in tone was a deal cut by Kohl and Mitterrand only days before the summit opened. The two agreed to push the EC ahead towards another new goal, a "political union" parallel to the monetary union already on the agenda. Back in step again, they suggested that preparations for both projects should start in late 1990. The treaty, which came to be known as the Maastricht Treaty, would be signed and ratified by member states by the end of 1992. The unspoken assumption was that German reunification was still a while off and would also take place at that time.

France and Germany fleshed out their plan in December, just before the two intergovernmental conferences were to open. "The political union should include a genuine common security policy which should ultimately lead to a common defence," it said. The conference should review how the Western European Union could eventually become the military arm of the political union. Foreign policy should also become a Community affair, with the European Council – the six-monthly EC summits – setting the main lines. The EC should also take on more responsibility for policies on immigration, visa policies, the right of asylum and the fight against drug smuggling and organised crime. The European Parliament, which had little say over Brussels, should exercise "co-decision-making" for legislation and confirm the appointment of the commission president and his commissioners.

> 66 Kohl became increasingly enthusiastic about Europe's prospects ... barriers would fall more easily than people thought 99

The vision of this new Europe, presented by Kohl in his opening speech to the new Bundestag, was the most ambitious yet. "We cannot in any way be satisfied with what we have reached," he said on 30 January 1991. The Chancellor stated that Bonn's main goal was the political unification of Europe. "No matter how important the realisation of the economic and monetary union may be, it will only be patchwork if we do not achieve a political union at the same time. In my view, Germany can only agree if both are realised at the same time. Both projects are inseparably linked to each other."

A few months later, when the new British Prime Minister John Major had shown he did not share Thatcher's visceral distrust of Germany, Kohl was even more enthusiastic about Europe's prospects. The EC would expand to take in other western European states such as Austria, Switzerland, Sweden, Norway and Finland. Further down the road, it would offer the option of membership to the ex-communist countries of Eastern Europe. "The building of the United States of Europe will be the world success story of the 1990s, not the Japanese," he declared in May. Apparent barriers to Europe's integration – Britain's reluctance, for example – would fall more easily than people thought. "I believe the dynamics of developments will simply sweep many obstacles out of the way."

Kohl's main partners meant different things by the same word, "Europe". Britain preferred a minimalist vision, a free trade zone with little more integration of policies among its members. London recognised that many rules governing trade had to be harmonised to ensure the efficiency of this Common Market. But the integration of areas such as monetary affairs, social policies and immigration, or giving up powers to a multinational body, were unacceptable. No matter what new "security structures" were created in Europe, Britain felt, real security only rested in NATO and in a firm partnership with the United States. Since the sights for this Europe were set low, bringing in new members – "widening" the community – was no problem. A loose Europe of 16 or 25 members was the best guarantee against the Brussels centralism Thatcher and Major wanted most to avoid.

France saw Europe as a tighter community of nation-states. Each member should remain proudly sovereign but all should work more in unison to build up Europe as a force in the world. This harmonising of national policies could "deepen" into core areas of the state such as monetary policy; France hardly had much remaining leeway anyway, because its *franc fort* policy linked the franc tightly to the deutschemark. This suited longer-term French goals such as gaining a say in European monetary decisions or loosening Europe from American military predominance. Much of the structure and operation of the EC already had a French style to it. France was at the centre of that old EC, with the other members mostly positioned around it, and deepening this constellation was in its best interests.

As often happened, Germany straddled these positions. The transfer of sovereignty that "deepening" involved posed few of the problems that Britain had with the idea. As a divided and defeated nation, West Germany had already broken with many of its national traditions, whereas its partners still jealously guarded theirs. Given its success under limited sovereignty, giving up more to a "deeper" community could be the logical next step. "Widening" also fitted in with a high German priority, the integration of Eastern Europe into the democratic mainstream. With communism dead and Russia in retreat, one of Bonn's most urgent tasks was to ensure the gradual progress of the reborn eastern states into democracy. But Germany was neither able nor willing to undertake such a massive task alone. The most effective way to aid their economies and stabilise their democracies would be to take them under Western Europe's wing.

In one point, though, Germany was distinctly different from its two main partners. It was a genuine federal state, with power divided between the national and state governments. With its strong upper house of parliament for the states and the Federal Constitutional Court for the judiciary, it had a system of checks and balances it believed was the guarantee of a modern democracy. This served as the basis for its view of how a political union should look. A powerful Commission would need an ever stronger watchdog that was elected and had teeth. The European Parliament met the first condition and Bonn wanted to give it more power to meet the second. Even the (federally structured) Bundesbank agreed a political union was the best way to ensure the single currency succeeded. As its president Helmut Schlesinger said in late 1991, "A monetary union will prove permanent only if there is a dominant political will to take social measures to deal with the serious economic effects ... In the last resort, this calls for a political union too."[6]

Kohl and Mitterrand took another step forward in October when they unveiled an outline for a European army. The plan was to upgrade the Western European Union (WEU) from a defence discussion forum into the military arm of the EC's political union. A common defence was still seen as far off, but Kohl and Mitterrand pointed out the route to take. The existing Franco-German brigade of about 5,000 men could be the nucleus of a European corps – up to 100,000 troops – including forces from other member countries, they said.

Kohl admitted to the Bundestag in late November 1991 that he could not convince his partners to increase the powers of the European Parliament at the Maastricht summit. Preparations for monetary union would go ahead but another summit later in the decade – it turned out to be the Amsterdam summit in June 1997 – would then assess progress and propose further steps. It was a gamble with his dream but it was the best he could get. Germany was ready to be flexible, "on the condition that these compromises do not put into question the basic tendency of the treaty, namely that the unification process is irreversible," he explained. "We want a treaty that makes it very clear that the Economic and Monetary Union and the Political Union are irreversible – underline this word again, it is very important."

> 66 A powerful Commission would need an ever stronger watchdog that was elected and had teeth 99

When the wheeling and dealing was finished in Maastricht, united Germany no longer looked as all-powerful as its critics feared. Kohl failed to win the decisive step forward towards a political union that a real strengthening of the European Parliament would have meant. There was little progress on formulating joint policies in foreign affairs, defence, immigration or legal issues. Bonn did not even get the 18 extra seats it sought to reflect Germany's larger population since reunification. The German vision of an ever closer European union went too far beyond what its main partners wanted.

Germany still won in the area that mattered most, however. The new European central bank would be independent of national governments and dedicated to strict anti-inflation policies just like the Bundesbank. Would-be members of the single currency club could have annual budget deficits of no more than 3 per cent of their gross domestic product (GDP). Their overall debts could be no more than 60 per cent of their GDP. Inflation and interest rates had to be close to the lowest rates prevailing in the community. This was an economic fitness test set up to meet German standards of budgetary discipline.

THE MONETARY MESS

While politicians worked on ever more elaborate models of Europe, an economic time bomb was ticking away at its core. The Exchange Rate Mechanism (ERM), the currency grid launched in 1979 to keep Europe's money closely linked, was the foundation for the planned Economic and Monetary Union (EMU). In the ERM, most currencies could fluctuate within a band of 2.25 per cent above or below their central rates. Britain, Spain and Portugal had a wider margin of six per cent. Once those limits were reached, central banks had to intervene to buy or sell the currency back into line. The benchmark for the system was the deutschemark. Pegging other currencies to its exacting standards was meant to bring those economies into line with Bonn's.

> 66 After reunification Bonn went on the kind of spending spree it warned its neighbours against 99

The assumption was that Germany, as anchor of the system, would be more stable than other countries. It played that role well during the 1980s. After reunification, though, Bonn went on the kind of spending spree it warned its neighbours against. The government plunged into debts that soared to 6 per cent of its gross national product. Inflation, at historic lows before the Berlin Wall fell, crept up relentlessly. The Bundesbank saw no alternative but to jack up interest rates in response. The discount rate rose from six per cent in 1989 to eight per cent just a week after the Maastricht Treaty was signed. The Bundesbank had long been wary of Kohl's dream of a single currency. It thought even less of his decision to finance reunification by borrowing rather than raising taxes or cutting spending in his budget. A showdown over how to run the economy was looming.

The ERM made the battle spill out over Germany's borders. Not wanting to devalue against the deutschemark, other ERM countries (i.e. all EC states except Greece) had to boost their interest rates every time the Germans hiked up theirs. But seven of the ten other members had inflation rates lower than Germany's. They were in recession, with unemployment rising dramatically, and needed lower rates to help their economies spring back to life. The logical option would have been to realign parities within the ERM, but this had not happened since 1987. Opting to do so now, the politicians thought, would be an embarrassing admission that their economies could not keep up with the Germans.

By mid-1992, the whole system was teetering on the edge. Then, on 2 June, a referendum in Denmark unexpectedly rejected the Maastricht Treaty. The "no" camp won by only 50.7 per cent and sent a shock wave throughout Europe. The next day, Mitterrand frayed nerves even further by calling a referendum in France for 20 September. A undercurrent of anti-treaty sentiment swelled to challenge him. In this charged atmosphere, the Bundesbank once again disregarded calls for moderation and on 16 July hiked its discount rate to a post-war record of 8.75 per cent. Speculators knew it was only a matter of time before some kind of revaluation came. The run on the pound, lira and peseta became a stampede.

On 13 September, EC finance ministers agreed the lira had to be de valued by seven per cent. When the Bundesbank disappointed the markets with a half-point rate cut the next day, Schlesinger let his central banker's discretion slip by suggesting to the business daily *Handelsblatt* that the ERM realignment should have been broader. That was the signal that sterling was doomed. The following day, 16 September, was "Black Wednesday" in London. The Bank of England spent about £16 billion in a frantic attempt to save sterling from devaluation. It failed and had to bail out of the ERM in humiliation. The lira dropped out, too, and the Spanish peseta and Portuguese escudo were devalued by six per cent.

Europe's *erster Geldkrieg* (First Money War), as German commentator Josef Joffe called it, brought another sobering insight. Reunited Germany was powerful enough to destabilise the rest of Europe economically, just as it could militarily during the *erster Weltkrieg* (First World War). But in this as well, Germany was not big enough to win the struggle in the end. A total collapse of currency coordination in Europe would have set off a stampede on the mark. The currency would have soared, pricing Germany's exports even out of markets just across its borders. So the ERM crisis ended up stiffening Bonn's resolve to push ahead with a true European monetary system to replace the ERM cocktail of currencies.

    ❝ The Maastricht project, as headline writers gleefully wrote, 'ended in tiers' ❞

The French referendum that followed four days after the ERM rout was a near-death experience for Maastricht. The anti-treaty forces tapped an undercurrent of defensive national pride, not least with an emotive and outdated warning against domination by an aggressive Germany. The "yes" camp won, but with only 51.05 per cent backing the treaty.[7] The Maastricht project, as headline writers gleefully wrote, "ended in tiers". European integration, other wags said, was at "half-Maastricht". No sooner was the result known than talk of a "two-speed Europe" or "multi-tiered integration" began racing around EU capitals again. Countries willing to move forward to higher stages of unity, for example a common currency, should proceed in a smaller group. Any country opposed to any specific plan could simply opt out of it.

WIDENING, DEEPENING, NARROWING, EXCLUDING

After the razor-thin French majority, the pro-Europeans lost patience with the Eurosceptics. In the months and years that followed, Bonn turned to an approach of "as much Europe as possible". For Kohl, it was essential that French–German cooperation was at the core. A common currency was a must and the community had to expand to the east. All else was basically negotiable, as long as there was momentum.

This less ambitious approach also reflected the growing anti-Brussels feeling welling up even in pro-European Germany. Extreme-right parties such as the Republicans and the German People's Union surged in state elections in 1992 on platforms that included emotional attacks on European unity. Edmund Stoiber, the new CSU premier in Bavaria, railed against a Brussels juggernaut threatening his proud state. "We Bavarians have struggled against all attempts at centralisation in Germany and we are not ready to sacrifice our Bavarian statehood now on the European altar," he argued.[8] Germans generally still saw Europe as a good thing, but felt increasingly left behind in its leaders' rush to move towards a closer union.

While deepening took on a different character, widening proceeded apace. With the Cold War over, rich neutral states like Austria, Finland and Sweden suddenly had nothing to stand apart from any more. In Bonn's eyes, they were ideal candidates for the EU – potential net contributors to the budget, natural allies within the community – and the Germans championed their cause.

With criticism of Europe mounting, Kohl sought to reassure German voters that they could learn to love the inevitable. Germany's resolve to have the European central bank located in Frankfurt stiffened into a dogma. Amsterdam, London, Barcelona, Lille, Lyon and Strasbourg all announced their interest, but Bonn was adamant. Only a "Eurofed" in Frankfurt, the home of the Bundesbank, could convince Germans that the new single currency was as strong and stable as their beloved deutschemark. "The boss was on the phone with other European leaders, twisting arms constantly," one Kohl aide later said. "If you want to talk about Germany throwing its weight around after reunification, this was one of the most important occasions. It was done behind the scenes and little of it leaked out. But it was brutal."

Wolfgang Schäuble and Karl Lamers, the CDU parliamentary leader and foreign policy spokesman, mapped out the new German approach in their proposals for a "hard-core Europe" in September 1994. They argued that the 12-member European Union could not survive expansion to 20 states if it maintained rules made for a club of six. It needed more flexibility so that a "hard core" could integrate further without being held up by other states. The Commission in Brussels should develop into a kind of government and the European Parliament be turned into a real legislature. The European Council, the six-monthly leaders' summit that sets out the main lines of Union policy, should become a kind of upper house of the European Parliament representing member states' interests. The EU should also turn the WEU into its military arm.

> 66 If you want to talk about Germany throwing its weight aroung after reunification, this was brutal 99

Schäuble and Lamers broke diplomatic taboos by naming names. Germany and France would form the "core of the hard core" and Belgium, Luxembourg and the Netherlands would coordinate policies more closely with them. Denmark and Ireland might also qualify for the monetary union, which the authors described as "the hard core of the Political Union". The other Europeans would not be in the hard core, but Italy, Spain and Britain would be welcome "as soon as they have solved certain current problems and shown themselves ready to commit themselves."[9]

Italy, the only founding member not included in the hard core, protested loudly at being left out. Critics in several countries suspected it was a German ploy to dominate Europe. Even though Britain did not want to be in the hard core, John Major was uneasy about seeing one actually emerge. "I see a real danger in talk of a 'hard core', inner and outer circles, a two-tier Europe," he said.

By laying their cards on the table, the two Christian Democrats got Europe to focus on several pressing issues. The setbacks of 1992 had made European leaders wary about daring any further leaps ahead just yet. They needed to square this circle and the CDU paper offered a blueprint for consideration. For those who listened, the paper was also an offer to continue seeking ways to fit the larger Germany into a constructive European context. This was "a German message Europe must heed," wrote the former Dutch ambassador to Germany, Jan van der Tas. "The rest of the continent needs to respond positively to Germany's request to be bound irreversibly to a politically and economically integrated continent ... even if we are confident that the Federal Republic will never again follow a 'special path' outside the European mainstream, we would ignore at our peril Germany's call for European solidarity and integration."[10]

NOTES

1   Schmidt, Helmut (1993) *Handeln für Deutschland*. Berlin: Rowohlt, pages 228–9.

2   Mitterrand, François (1996) *De l'Allemagne, de la France*. Paris: Editions Odile Jacob, pages 129–30.

3   See *Verbatim III, 1988–1991*, page 355.

4   *The Downing Street Years*, page 813.

5   *Ich wollte Deutschlands Einheit*, page 196.

6   Speech in Rotterdam on 8 November 1991, cited in Marsh, David (1993) *The Bundesbank*, London: Mandarin, page 244.

7   Interestingly, the French regions Alsace and Lorraine along the German border, Rhone–Alpes near Switzerland and Pyrenees–Atlantiques on the Spanish border all turned in strong pro-Maastricht majorities. The part of Denmark bordering on germany also supported the treaty more than other regions in the Danish referendum.

8   Conversation with the author in Munich, 7 October 1993.

9   For the text and reactions to it, see "Das Schäuble–Lamers Papier – Nationale und internationale Reaktionen." Konrad-Adenauer-Stiftung: Sankt Augustin, October 1994.

10   *Financial Times*, 16 September 1994.

12

OSSIS AND WESSIS

Even the dial tone on the telephone is different now. – Bärbel Bohley, *Ossi*

In this new system, we are what I call secondary illiterates. I'm as naive as a 20-year-old, but I'm no longer 20 years old. The experience we have accumulated during our lives is now more or less worthless. – Jens Reich, *Ossi*

I do not want to be reunited. – Erich Böhme, *Wessi*

Our mid-life crisis has broken out in the form of German unification. We would have been ready for impotence, prostate problems, false teeth or menopause, for a second Chernobyl, cancer, death and the devil. But not for Germany, united fatherland! – Patrick Süskind, *Wessi*

GREAT CHANGES SPAWN THEIR OWN VOCABULARY. Jacobins, Bolsheviks, Cold Warriors, Thatcherites – history is full of terms coined to label groups, movements and ideas. Probably because much of it took place among the wise-cracking Berliners, the *Wende* produced a host of its own neologisms. Some were linguistic shooting stars, but two words quickly found their way into everyday German around the country – *Ossis* and *Wessis*. This linguistic dividing line cropped up in late 1989 and survived for years.

Ossi and *Wessi* could have the force of a curse or be spoken with affection. They described differences so well that they spawned more new constructs, including *Besserwessi* (a cross between *Wessi* and *Besserwisser*, or "know-it-all") and *Jammerossi* (complaining easterner). Rough-and-ready hybrid forms such as *Wossi* (a westerner living in the east) also emerged. The two words became the most durable neologisms of the unity period because they expressed differences that lingered after the border disappeared.

Not long after the Cold War barrier collapsed, Germans began talking about a "wall in the head" that lived on in their minds. In many ways, the mental wall seemed to grow with the years. Berlin's newspaper market, for example, remained deeply divided no matter how hard the *Berliner Zeitung* tried to sell in the west or the *Tagesspiegel* strained to win over eastern readers. Advertising was different, too. The west preferred abstract "lifestyle" ads and sly jokes, while the east wanted fact-filled publicity to tell them what they were buying. "We've created something new with this united Germany," Kohl reflected in August 1993. "If we're honest with each other, we have to admit that these 40 years of division have left a deep impression on the way we deal with each other. I didn't think it would be like this and I see now that I made a big mistake. We have to get over this."

WE ARE THE PEOPLE! WHO ARE WE?

The Germans had a feeling of togetherness long before the nation-state brought them together. Even before their first unification in 1871, they saw themselves as a *Kulturnation* ("cultural nation") that transcended the shifting political frontiers. A common language, culture and traditions stretched from Cologne, Strasbourg and Basel in the west out to Königsberg, the Volga region and Transylvania in the east. Germany's post-war division put this *Kulturnation* theory to a severe test. The two political systems were bitter rivals and made the Germans look in opposite directions.

When East Germans began quitting their state in droves in the summer of 1989, West Germans spontaneously opened their arms and hearts to them. It was a show of national solidarity without overt nationalism, a happy reunion of the *Kulturnation* to which they all belonged. When the Wall fell in November, even *Wessis* who had totally ignored the east also felt freed of a terrible burden. The threat of an East–West clash over Germany and all the *Angst* it produced dissolved overnight. The ugliest symbol of the Cold War was suddenly nothing more than a traffic bottleneck. The people penned in behind it were free.

Once *Ossis* and *Wessis* got a closer look at each other, the stereotypes blossomed. The mental antennas that pick up accents and gestures were suddenly overloaded with confusing signals, even though they were coming from fellow Germans. Both sides fell victim to what Freud called "narcissism of small differences", the tendency of similar communities to find fault with each other the most. To the westerners, *Ossis* all wore stone-washed jeans (long out of fashion in the west) and spoke with nasal Saxon or working-class Berlin accents. They were wide-eyed hicks in the big city – *Zonenzombies* (zombies from the Soviet zone) in West Berlin slang. All they wanted was bananas, an exclusive luxury in East Germany that became a symbol with which to ridicule *Ossi* materialism. Seen through eastern eyes, the *Wessis* were spoiled and arrogant. Easterners saw west German society as cold and selfish, with little sense of the solidarity they knew at home. The typical westerner was jealous of his prosperity, more attached to his money than his country. Many *Wessis* faced west emotionally as well, identifying more with France, Italy, Britain or the US than they did with their cousins east of the Elbe.

Even after stereotypes were swept away, something separating them persisted. "People point to differences in dialect, in everyday behaviour, in body language," the New Forum co-founder Jens Reich said. "Of course, we are Germans and to the foreigner we look very much alike. The language is the same. You must be very subtle to hear the differences. It's not as though we're different nations or a different continent. But there are subtle differences and it's the subtlety of the difference that makes it so perceptible and so stable. In 1989, nearly everybody was clear that we belonged together and the division of Germany was something very irrational and couldn't last for centuries. But now after marriage, as it were, you see the more subtle differences."[1]

> 66 To the westerners, *Ossis* were wide-eyed hicks ... through eastern eyes, *Wessis* were spoiled and arrogant 99

OSSIS

Who were these other Germans who had lived behind the Wall? One of the first things western visitors observed was that the *Ossis* were "more German" than the *Wessis*. The *Ossis* seemed more obedient, shy, less self-assured and individualistic than westerners. As a group, they were more authoritarian in their views than west Germans. Easterners valued the relative equality they enjoyed more highly than the liberty that had seemed beyond their reach. After so many decades of censorship, the rush of free speech after 1989 brought them as much confusion as relief. "There were a lot of things you could not say in East Germany, but everybody immediately noticed what was not said," observed Daniela Dahn, a best-selling eastern author almost unknown in the west. "In west Germany, you can say anything, but nobody notices what you say."[2]

One of the mistaken assumptions of reunification, especially in the west, was that these differences would quickly fade away. Many eastern regions had strong traditions and roots that westerners hardly knew about. "The mental differences between eastern and western Germany are centuries old," said Reich just before the fifth anniversary of unification.[3] "There is the notion of *Ostelbien*, a country and culture east of the Elbe River which had for centuries quite a different culture and way of life ... There is some sort of mental cleft between both parts ... which is quite similar, incidentally, to the north-south rift in Germany, between Bavaria and the northerners ... I think east and west will continue for some time, maybe for generations, to be very different in general outlook and culture ..."

> 66 Career skills such as taking initiative or thinking critically did not 'come back' to people taught to avoid them 99

One of the most common complaints *Ossis* had was that their lives and skills counted for little in the new Germany. For most people over 40, the switch to an open society was a wrenching experience. Career skills that westerners pick up in their youth, such as taking initiative or thinking critically, did not "come back" to people taught to avoid them. The heavy doses of ideology permeating most official disciplines were a serious disadvantage for anyone working in the liberal arts or social sciences. Prominent communists were weeded out of school and university staffs. East Germany's diplomatic corps was put out to pasture en masse.

The gap between what east and west had experienced was often so great that easterners spoke defensively about having their "own biography". It was hard to argue it had been better. Their lives seemed duller, slower and sadder than what they saw in the west. Their offices, hospitals and factories were decades behind the times. The usual tools of the information age – computers, fax machines and portable telephones – were complete novelties at first. The western-based media repeatedly reinforced the feeling by highlighting each case of backwardness.

Reunification's biggest losers, without any doubt, were east German women. About 90 per cent of East German women had jobs (compared to 50 per cent in West Germany) and the state did what it could to make life easier for them. Up to three years' maternity leave, free kinder-gartens, cheap baby clothes and access to scarce apartments were among the means used to encourage childbearing. Women's wages were usually about one-third below those of men, but family benefits more than made up for that. Parents paid little or nothing for the crèches, school trips, sports clubs or music lessons that can weigh on a family budget. All this was subsidised by the state and just about all of it disappeared when East Germany gave up the ghost.

In its place came a West German system that not only lagged behind East Germany, but was also behind other west European countries. The west-ern system, with far fewer kindergartens and shorter school days, was based on the premise that mothers stayed at home to raise children. Many working mothers in the east found they could not afford the baby-sitters they needed to allow them to go out to work. Since day-care centres were no longer linked to the workplace, mothers had to worry about the unfamiliar problem of transporting their children to the few nursery schools and kindergartens that survived the switch.

Women were among the first and the worst hit when the waves of lay-offs broke over the East German economy, even before Unity Day in 1990. Roughly two-thirds of the unemployed in eastern Germany after unification were women. When recession hit eastern Germany in the early 1990s, about half the women who had taken maternity leave found their jobs were gone when they tried to return to work. Many thought having no children would improve their chances of getting or keeping a job in such a tight market. The number of women who had themselves sterilised in Brandenburg state, for example, rose by over seven times – from 820 to 6,000 – in the years 1991 to 1993.

Few statistics illustrated the shock of unification better than the alarm-ing slide in eastern Germany's birth rate. Nine months after the Wall fell, births dropped off in a slump that became the most severe in the 200 years since records were kept. It was even worse than the decline that the bombed and then conquered city of Berlin experienced during and right after World War II. From the 1989 level of 198,900, births fell continu-ally to 174,700 in 1990, 107,800 in 1991, 88,300 in 1992, 80,500 in 1993 and 78,700 in 1994. During the same period, western Germany's famously low birth rate stayed steady and was at least twice as high as that in the east.

"Eastern Germany's adults appear to have come as close to a temporary suspension of child-bearing as any large population in the human experience," the Washington-based demographer Nicholas Eberstadt wrote in 1994. "Eastern Germany's marriage rate is today lower than that of any other society in which such formalised adult unions prevail."[4] Early marriages, once the rule, suddenly became the exception and slumped by 62 per cent. Curiously, divorce also dropped by 80 per cent, a phenom enon sociologists explained as a refusal to give up the known at a time when so many other factors were unknown. The brightening outlook for the economy seen by mid-1994 finally turned the tide and births slowly rose to 82,000 the following year.[5]

OSTALGIE

The fall of the Wall created within weeks what the SED couldn't manage through decades of effort – a feeling of a separate eastern identity. At best, the great East German sports machine created a kind of national pride for the *Ossis*. If there was anything that united them, it was their inability to visit West Germany. "Somewhere over the rainbow was a country that GDR people could only dream of. It was the end station of their yearnings and desires. This illusion was a unique luxury reserved for East Germans – a surplus of hope that helped them put up with reality," east Berlin journalist Jutta Voigt recalled nostalgically in 1991.[6]

The confrontation with those dreams changed all that. The first visit to a western department store showed wide-eyed East Germans how far behind the West their country had slipped. They felt looked down upon by arrogant *Wessis* and wanted to catch up as quickly as possible. In the first year or so after the Wall fell, one of the strongest feelings in the east was the need to make up for lost time. *Ossis* bought shiny western cars, took vacations to Spain and redecorated their flats and houses – just as the westerners did. The shopping areas in the main cities began looking like western pedestrian zones. There were even enunciation classes so that *Ossis* could learn to suppress nasal Saxon or working-class Berlin accents in favour of more western-sounding High German.

By 1993, the mood was visibly changing. East German pop music came back into fashion. Eastern products such as Spreewald pickles and local beers were again in demand. The most bizarre fad was the tongue-in-cheek "*Ossi* party", a disco night with a distinctive retro touch. The entry fee was called the *Zwangsumtausch* (the "mandatory money exchange" West Germans had to make when they visited East Germany). Old GDR aluminium coins were used as drinks tokens. Anyone turning up in the deep blue shirt of the *Freie Deutsche Jugend*, the once-omnipresent communist youth organisation, got in for free. Bartenders and waitresses wore SED lapel pins or old National People's Army uniforms. For the climax of the evening, an Erich Honecker look-alike delivered a speech in appalling communist jargon or partygoers hurled eggs at someone wearing a Helmut Kohl mask.

Far from being just an escape into the past, this wave of *Ostalgie* actually marked a new phase in the easterners' adaptation to their new life. "They're adapting and getting down to work," east Berlin sociologist Rolf Reissig explained. "If you ask the people if they want to go back to the GDR, 80 per cent say 'For God's sake, no!' This east German identity is now a symbolic construction, a reaction to the way that everything became different at once. People need an anchor to hold them steady during this radical upheaval. It's actually a positive reaction. You get to know the rules and then say, but wait a minute, my whole previous life – I can't throw that away. I may have thought so in 1990, but not any more."[7]

66 We gave away ... the right to influence our own destiny 99

Reich, who kept his job as a microbiologist at an east Berlin research institute when a western scientist took over its management, also saw this as a natural defence mechanism. "Without this self-esteem and self-assurance, the easterners wouldn't tolerate the problems they have with unification and its relative drawbacks for their personal position. But what we gave away is something like the right to influence our own destiny. That is something that cannot be compensated by simply having a better pension or salary. There is an everyday feeling that you are what I call a secondary illiterate. I'm unable to really influence decision-making at the institute. I don't know how these things are done in Bonn and how to apply and whom to call. When money is needed or a decision is needed, I don't know anybody in the Berlin government, which is a west Berlin one, so I have no influence at all. Normally you would have a lot of exper ience in the network where you have lived for 20 or 30 years. But I'm helpless compared to the director here, who comes from Heidelberg and knows whom to ask."

What that meant in political terms became clear in December 1993, when the PDS, the successor party to East Germany's old communists, scored strong advances in Brandenburg state's local polls. As the only completely eastern party in the race, the PDS skilfully struck a chord with a clever mix of *Ostalgie* and pocket-book issues. The party that westerners thought would wither away came in second with 21.2 per cent of the vote, behind the SPD's 34.5 per cent. The biggest surprise came in the state capital Potsdam, where a 46-year-old former Stasi informer fell just short of winning election as mayor. Rolf Kutzmutz never tried to hide the fact he had once written a few short reports for the security police. In fact, he proudly campaigned with a slogan that echoed what many *Ossis* felt – "My biography didn't start in 1989."

WESSIS

There was no better symbol of the satiated 1980s in West Germany than the zebra stripes at the street crossings in Sindelfingen. Flush with money, this town with a population of 60,000 west of Stuttgart imported slabs of gleaming Carrara marble from Italy to pave the town's intersections. White paint just wasn't good enough any more for a town that could afford five public swimming pools, four libraries, two art galleries, two exhibition halls, free parking garages, a high-tech hospital, a museum, a soccer stadium and an indoor sports centre of nearly Olympic proportions. Over at the huge Mercedes plant, whose taxes were the source of much of Sindelfingen's wealth, the well-paid workers had six weeks' vacation and a wide array of other paid privileges.[8]

> " All this seemed so secure that public *Angst* turned to such 'post-modern' topics as dying forests and recycling "

The white-collar workers weren't doing too badly either. The West German middle class enjoyed a prosperity that anyone old enough to remember 1945 would never have thought possible. Although a Christian Democrat sat in the Bonn chancellery, West Germany in the 1980s was closer to the Social Democratic ideal of a flourishing welfare state. Summer vacations abroad were the rule, not the exception, and a winter getaway to the ski slopes or a sunny beach was no longer reserved for the rich. All this seemed so secure that public *Angst* turned to such "post-modern" topics as dying forests and recycling.

Despite all his clumsy comments and little scandals, Helmut Kohl helped West Germany feel more comfortable with itself. "Kohl, the canny power politician … showed West Germans that politics was a pragmatic business," social critic Cora Stephan explained. "It could get by without flag-waving and lofty speeches and didn't need a *Führer*, statesmen and heroes … After the tensions of the 1970s and early 1980s, West Germany experienced a wave of modernisation under conservative auspices. The old German authoritarian state had disappeared."[9]

Seen from inside this cocoon of stability and prosperity, the sudden rush to reunification was hardly a cause for joy. The shock seemed worst for the forty-something West Germans who had grown up with the Federal Republic. The novelist Patrick Süskind, author of the world-wide best-seller *Perfume*, called it a mid-life crisis. "After 40 years of ... a solid and apparently immutable European post-war order, our feet are slipping out from under us. We grew up in this order. We didn't know any other."[10] Sociologist Wolf Wagner saw this post-war identity as a kind of security blanket. "For me and other members of my generation, it was comfortable not to have this greater Germany anymore. So I could say I had nothing to do with the Germany of the concentration camps and the Holocaust. The Federal Republic I grew up in was not Germany, only West Germany ... Over all these years, I had built up an anti-heroic and, as I understood it, an anti-German identity. And then these refugees arrived calling out *"Deutschland!"* from the train windows."[11]

With so many psychological factors linked to the nation's division, East Germany was a kind of never-never land of the West German mind. Many West Germans simply ignored it. Only people with close family ties travelled there regularly enough to get some idea of the place. If Saul Steinberg had sketched a poster of the *Wessis'* mental world as he did for New Yorkers, West Germany and its favourite tourist destinations France, Italy and Spain would have dominated the picture. Soviet nuclear missiles would have loomed large on the eastern edge, the bright lights of Broadway and Hollywood on the western. Bangkok's brothels and Bali's beaches would shimmer off to the southeast. At best, the other German state next door would have intruded with a small sketch of the Wall or the Brandenburg Gate. Behind it would have been little more than a shadow.

LIFE IN A REDIVIDED LAND

Few social trends merit their own prime-time television series. Even fewer deserve two. The post-unity mistrust and misunderstanding between *Ossis* and *Wessis*, though, got double exposure on ARD television in 1992 – once from each side. First came *Motzki* – the name derivesfrom the verb "to complain" – about a bigoted west Berliner who wanted the Wall rebuilt immediately. "I thought, uh oh, this riff-raff will go straight for your wallet!" moans Friedhelm Motzki. When his *Ossi* sister-in-law Edith looks baffled by life in the west, he fires back in a blast at all easterners: "You've been Germans for three years now – how long will it take before you catch on?" Later on that year, it was the easterners' turn with *Trotzki*, the saga of a Leipzig taxi driver's family struggling with their new lives. Their name stemmed from the verb "to defy". In one scene, Herbert Trotzki mumbles, 'If only I'd thought of buying a Kalashnikov from those Russian soldiers,' when another slick *Wessi* salesman tries to swindle him.

Pollsters had a field day measuring the gap. The Allensbach Institute, Germany's oldest polling group, kept a special eye on the pulse of the nation. When asked in November 1990 whether they agreed with the slogan "We are one people," 54 per cent of the *Wessis* and 45 per cent of the *Ossis* agreed. By July 1994, the "one people" quotient had dropped to 47 per cent in the west and only 28 per cent in the east. Asked whether democracy was the best possible form of government, 75 per cent of those surveyed in the west said yes; in the east, only 32 per cent agreed.

> **❝Anyone who has to pay the same prices for fewer services or poorer goods realizes where he comes from❞**

The western pollsters were alarmed at the growing eastern scepticism towards the western system. "Democracy is not taking root in eastern Germany," Noelle-Neumann warned in early 1994. Easterners seemed less worried about the split. "The majority who were lost in daydreams in 1990 have woken up," Jens Reich wrote in mid-1992.[12] "They feel like *Ossis* because they are *Ossis*. Anyone who earns 60 per cent of the salary of his western counterpart feels like a former East German now, while in 1990, he may have had the illusion that this would all pass away quickly. Anyone who has to pay the same prices for fewer services or poorer goods realises where he comes from ... I realise it when I compare the co-op apartment prices in the *Berliner Morgenpost* with my own bank statements ..."

NOTES

1   Conversation with the author, 20 September 1995.

2   Dahn, Daniela (1996) *Westwärts und nicht vergessen: Vom Unbehagen in der Einheit*. Berlin: Rowohlt Berlin Verlag, page 162.

3   Conversation with the author, 20 September 1995.

4   Eberstadt in *Europe–Asia Studies*, May 1994, quoted in *The Economist*, 23 April 1994.

5   For a critical east German view of the post-unity situation for women, see Niederstadt, Jenny "Vereinigung zu Lasten der ostdeuschen Frauen' in Dümcke, Wolfgang and Vilmar, Fritz (eds.) (1995), *Kolonialisierung der DDR*. Münster: Agenda Verlag, pages 255–75.

6   *Die Zeit*, 2 February 1991.

7   Conversation with the author in Berlin, 24 June 1996.

8   As long as business was good, of course. In the depths of the recession in 1993, the town's tax revenues fell to about 50 million marks from their peak of 267 million marks in 1986. Mercedes' sales had dropped dramatically. Long rows of unsold luxury cars stood in the vast parking lots behind the factory. Thousands of workers were laid off and the factory occasionally stopped working for a few days to hold back production. For more, see *Stern*, 11 February 1993.

9   Stephan, Cora. (1993) *Der Betroffenheitskult*. Berlin: Rowohlt, pages 25–6.

10 "Deutschland, eine Midlife-crisis", *Angst vor Deutschland*. Hamburg: Hoffmann und Campe, 1990 pages 111–22.

11 Wolf Wagner (1996) *Kulturschock Deutschland*. Hamburg: Rotbuch Verlag, pages 79–80.

12 *Wochenpost*, 20 August 1992.

13

ELECTING A LAME DUCK

THE CANDIDATE COCKED HIS HEAD BACK A BIT, surveyed the vast convention hall and chuckled at the thought that any of the delegates out there might ever doubt him. "People look at me like some kind of strange bird and ask how I can talk about winning this election," Helmut Kohl confided in mock amazement to his fellow Christian Democrats. "But I'm going on my own experience." Just forget all the bad opinion polls, he urged them, don't think about all the complaining going on out there. "We want to win these elections – our goal is victory, not second place!" he boomed out to the applauding audience.

It was in late February 1994, the dead of winter in snow-covered Hamburg, that the old war-horse limbered up for his fourth re-election bid. The CDU's prospects had never been worse. The post-unity years had been an ordeal for the country and the public mood was bitter. The Social Democrats had a strong head start in their campaign. In the midst of this gloom, a huge soft-focus photo of a relaxed Kohl dominated the entrance to the party's annual congress. Kohl spent three days spreading optimism among the 1,000 delegates. Eight months later, he was re-elected.

The 1994 general election displayed once again the crucial role of Kohl's legendary power machine. It was a rule of thumb in the old West German *Parteienstaat* (party state) that the candidate who mobilised his own voters best had a better chance of winning. Full support from the

CDU rank-and-file could balance out bad opinion polls. Kohl pulled out all the stops and finally prevailed over his challenger Rudolf Scharping.

The "super election year" – with 19 local, state, federal, presidential and European Parliament elections – would be the last time the old West German system would run so reliably. The party system was unravelling at the edges, with new parties such as the PDS upsetting the old balance of power. Never as monolithically structured as the CDU, the SPD was experimenting with new methods such as a primary vote to let its members choose their own candidate. The Greens were on the rise as the new kingmaker in the Bundestag, while the FDP, Kohl's only possible coalition partner, went into a possibly terminal tailspin. In the end, Kohl carried the day by a narrow margin, but he quickly became a lame duck.

SPD UP, KOHL DOWN

The SPD experimented with a primary election more by accident than design. Björn Engholm, the Schleswig-Holstein state premier who was elected party chairman after the 1990 election, unexpectedly resigned in May 1993 over a scandal in his home state. His weak leadership had left the party torn between its competing barons in the states. With no clear favourite to replace him, the party ducked a bruising power fight by opting for a primary, something unheard of in German politics. Rudolf Scharping, premier of Rhineland-Palatinate state, won 40.3 per cent of the vote to take the crown. Lower Saxony premier Gerhard Schröder, who campaigned for a "Red–Green" coalition with the environmentalists, scored 33.2 per cent and Heidemarie Wieczorek-Zeul, the favourite of women and leftists in the party, came third with 26.5 per cent.

At 45, Scharping was the youngest of the party's new generation. Neither as flexible as Schröder nor as flashy as Lafontaine, his main achievement to date had been to win Rhineland-Palatinate for the SPD in 1991 after decades of CDU control. The conservative western state was Kohl country; the chancellor had been premier in its capital Mainz before leaving in 1976 to become opposition leader in Bonn. Scharping rose from the grass roots with the same determination as Kohl, so much so that he was nicknamed *Rotkohl* ("red cabbage"). His quiet personal style reflected his political caution. Tall and trim with a neatly clipped beard, he seemed constantly on guard to control his every move. His hobby, cycling, fitted his image as a hard worker ready for the long run. In short, he was someone voters yearning for change could trust.[1]

As Scharping rose in the opinion polls, Kohl's luck went from bad to worse. His famous skills seemed to abandon him in the autumn of 1993 when he tried to find a candidate for president. Kohl had long said he wanted an eastern candidate, but there was nobody suitable in the eastern CDU. The party even considered the Leipzig conductor Kurt Masur, but he had no political ambitions and soon left to direct the New York Philharmonic Orchestra.

The chancellor finally settled on Steffen Heitmann, a slight and shy man almost unknown in Bonn even though he was justice minister in Saxony. Heitmann turned out to be too eastern for his own good. Naively unfamiliar with western Germany, he stumbled around breaking one *Wessi* taboo after another. Feminists howled when he said women should spend more time at home with their children. Liberals cringed when he complained about Germany being "swamped by foreigners". Heitmann's sceptical comments about European integration came close to an attack on Kohl's dream. The candidate also outraged Jewish groups by saying of the Holocaust, "The post-war period has finally come to an end with German unity and it is now time to put this event behind us." The World Jewish Congress in New York urged its members in 80 countries to protest to Bonn about him.

> 66 Heitmann stumbled around breaking one *Wessi* taboo after another 99

Kohl hunkered down for a bruising fight, determined to ignore what the others said, but found that Heitmann did not even have full support in the CDU ranks. The FDP named its own candidate, Hildegard Hamm-Brücher, to show its annoyance at Kohl for not picking someone it could support. Suddenly, Kohl was faced with the prospect of losing the presidential election if the FDP teamed up with the SPD. Heitmann took Kohl off the hook by withdrawing from the race in late November before any more damage was done. A few months later, the CDU nominated a safe candidate for the race, supreme court justice Roman Herzog.

THE SUPER ELECTION YEAR

The super election year dawned in what Fritz Stern, one of the leading US historians of Germany, described as "exuberant pessimism". With unemployment at 3.7 million and rising, the press was drawing exaggerated parallels to the last days of the Weimar Republic – even though the figures were nowhere near the Depression levels that helped the Nazis rise to power. The Labour Ministry was so concerned about the "highest unemployment since Hitler" lines in the press that it took the unusual step of issuing a statement rebutting the Weimar comparison.[2] In late 1993, protest voters had made deep inroads in Hamburg's election and in local polls in Brandenburg. Stern saw the mood as a reflection of the deep uncertainty the Germans still felt about their history, their nation and the role it should play. Neither Kohl nor other leaders had done much to help them find their way. "There is a lack of political leadership that helps to explicate deep issues like that," he argued. "There is not enough moral authority in this country."[3]

Kohl had a few aces up his sleeve when he started his campaign at the Hamburg CDU congress. No post-war election had ever voted a sitting chancellor out of office. While low in the popularity polls, the legendary "Kohl system" ensured he was unparalleled when it came to support within his own ranks. The "blossoming landscapes" might not be evident everywhere, but construction was booming in the east. Optimism was on the rise there too, in contrast to the morose mood in the west. With a little luck in the coming months, the first signs of a recovery would be visible and a mood of confidence would come back.

Schröder got the SPD off to a good start by winning an absolute majority in the Lower Saxony election on 13 March, allowing him to drop his Greens coalition partners and govern alone. But Scharping's carefully laid plans went astray later that month when he bungled the introduction of a major tax reform proposal. It was supposed to look like a "soak-the-rich" plan with a tax hike for the top 15 per cent of taxpayers, and cuts for everybody else. But the starting point for the "rich" was a DM 50,000 annual income for single people and DM 100,000 for married couples – so low that skilled industrial workers reached it easily. The reaction was sharp and swift. *Bild* printed pictures of a dozen workers who would be hit by the surcharge and asked in a bold headline: "Are we rich, Herr Scharping?" After a few days of this, Scharping revised the plan and stumbled again when he tried to present it.

This broke his stride and Scharping started tripping up on other issues as well. Encouraged by the FDP's rebellion against Heitmann, he made the unlikely bet that the liberals would abandon the CDU to vote for the SPD's presidential candidate Johannes Rau in May. When the Federal Assembly – a joint session of the Bundestag and Bundesrat – voted as expected for Herzog, Scharping's patience snapped. His hopes for a national coalition with the FDP were gone.

The European Parliament election on 12 June was another setback for the Social Democrats, who slumped by five points to 32.2 per cent, their worst result in any national poll since 1957. The CDU/CSU rose 1.5 points to win 38.8 per cent, while the FDP crashed out. The Republicans, whose 7.1 per cent result was the headline news of the 1989 poll, limped in with only 3.9 per cent this time.

Once again, the SPD missed the public mood. Its campaign had focused on fighting unemployment and rising crime, the gloomy issues of the previous winter. Kohl showed much better timing with his bet on rising optimism. Although unemployment was stuck at around 3.8 million, Germany's longest post-war recession was ending. The outlook was for one per cent growth that year in the west and a booming 7.5 per cent in the east.

The SPD got caught embarrassingly short on foreign policy as well. The supreme court put an end to years of fruitless debate when it ruled on 12 July that the constitution did not bar German troops from military missions outside NATO. The ruling put into sharp relief the narrow corner into which the Social Democrats had placed themselves on this issue. With the Bosnian tragedy dragging on, even moderate Greens such as Joschka Fischer and Daniel Cohn-Bendit were saying that Germany would have to play a bigger part in ensuring security for all of Europe. The SPD position had also isolated it from Germany's two main allies. President Bill Clinton was visiting Berlin when the supreme court decision was announced. Asked what he thought of Germans taking up arms again, he said, "I am completely comfortable with that." Two days later, German troops marched down the Champs Elysees in Paris for the first time since the 1940–44 Nazi occupation. The Bundeswehr unit was part of the new Eurocorps and were welcomed as warmly as the French, Belgian and Spanish soldiers they marched with.

> 66 Once again, the SPD missed the public mood ... Kohl showed much better timing 99

THE RED SOCKS

The growing drift between east and west set a novel trap for Scharping's campaign and he had little choice but to drive straight into it. As the east regained some self-confidence after the upheaval of reunification, state politicians began to chafe under the guidelines they were getting from Bonn. The biggest bone of contention was how to treat the PDS, the reform communists. While *Wessis* saw them as Stalinists to be shunned,

Ossis appreciated all the grass roots work the ex-communists did to defend eastern interests. Two-thirds of eastern voters felt the PDS was a democratic party, a view shared by less than a quarter of the electorate in the west. Outside of Brandenburg, the only hope the eastern SPD had of forming a state government was to cooperate with the party the western SPD abhorred.

The dilemma arose in late June when the vote in Saxony-Anhalt produced a result unimaginable in any western state. Both the governing CDU and the opposition SPD ended up with 34 per cent, with Kohl's party ahead by a fraction. The PDS came in third with 20 per cent. Since both opposition parties had gained votes and the CDU had lost, state SPD leader Reinhard Höppner insisted on trying some kind of left-wing government rather than the CDU–SPD grand coalition that Bonn thought was the only alternative. Easterners would accept it, but what would the reaction be in the west? In the end, Höppner formed a minority government with the Greens. The PDS would not join the cabinet but would cooperate in the state assembly as long as it was consulted. Keen to show it was serious about change, the SPD headquarters in Bonn gave its blessing to Höppner's plan. At the same time, it nervously swore to western voters it would never do such a deal in the Bundestag.

> 66 The CDU couldn't believe its luck ... Scharping had handed it a classic polarising issue – communism 99

The CDU couldn't believe its luck. After avoiding contentious positions for months, Scharping had handed it a classic polarising issue – communism. The party quickly whipped up some breezy commie-bashing ads. The best one was a poster showing a clothesline with two red socks – symbol of communists who still held positions of influence after 1989 – and the slogan, "Off into the future, but not with red socks!" Imagine their surprise, then, when even loyal eastern CDU leaders such as Angela Merkel, the shy women's affairs minister Kohl affectionately called *das Mädchen* ("the little girl"), promptly banned the poster in their states. What the CDU *Wessis* didn't understand was that a massive attack by a western party risked boosting the sympathy vote for the PDS in the east. CDU westerners knew it would go down well in the dominant part of the country.

The CDU overtook the SPD in opinion polls in June after trailing it since mid-1991. Kohl also surpassed Scharping as the favoured candidate that month for the first time. Saxony-Anhalt weakened Scharping within the SPD, where critics began asking whether he was the best candidate they could have chosen. If the SPD was now aiming for a red–green coalition, wouldn't Schröder have been a better choice?[4] The ambitious Gerhard

Schröder stepped up his sniping from the sidelines. The SPD had turned cold on its last two candidates halfway through their campaigns. Would Scharping be the third in a row?

The SPD stopped its free fall in late August by relaunching the faltering Scharping as the head of a leadership "troika" with Schröder and Oscar Lafontaine. Schröder, who had spent his time since his primary defeat building up his media image as a pragmatic manager, was earmarked to be a "super minister" for economics, transportation and energy. Although weakened by scandals back in Saarland, Lafontaine was still popular in the party and keen to try his luck as shadow finance minister. Kohl's response cut straight to the point. "Is that a troika?" he laughed. "As far as I can see, those are three people who all want the same job. All three want to become chancellor – one wants to do it earlier, the other later and the third has already tried."

THE SECOND ALL-GERMAN ELECTION

In the last two weeks before the 16 October election, Kohl seemed to run out of steam. Scharping, helped by the troika, fought his way back. Polls showed the coalition at or slightly below the absolute majority, but it was too close to call. For lack of any better issues, Bonn journalists speculated as to whether the chancellor would run again in 1998. In an unguarded moment, Kohl remarked that this campaign would be his last, a remark he quickly corrected.

Kohl's coalition ended up just a nose ahead with 48.4 per cent, as opposed to the combined opposition total of to 48.1 per cent. The CDU/CSU slipped two points to 41.5 while the FDP lost almost half its deputies and limped in at 6.9 per cent. Although the coalition lost 124 seats in the Bundestag, it still had a ten-seat edge over the opposition. The SPD advanced by three points to 36.4 per cent, a respectable showing for Scharping, while the Greens were up two points at 7.1 per cent and could bring their western deputies back into the parliament. Stumping western sceptics, the PDS almost doubled its parliamentary group to 30 seats. Its nation-wide result was still short of the 5 per cent cut-off point, but it returned to the Bundestag by winning four direct mandates in east Berlin constituencies.

Scharping seemed so relieved that he could have been mistaken for the winner. Beating Lafontaine's 1990 result put him in a good position in the SPD. He could now move to Bonn as opposition leader and focus on building up support, while the CDU faced an uncertain transition to the post-Kohl era. "We will certainly be governing in 1998, or earlier," he announced with confidence.

Just how thin Kohl's majority was became clear on 16 November when the Bundestag met to formally re-elect him as chancellor. Kohl needed an absolute majority of all seats (i.e. 337 out of 672) for this election. After an early-morning roll call and a last-minute rush to haul one late-sleeping deputy out of his hotel bed, he won re-election with only one vote to spare. There were dissenters in the ranks, probably among the FDP. Governing was going to be harder than ever.

> 66 The chancellor won re-election with only one vote to spare. There were dissenters in the ranks 99

SINGLE COUNTRY, SPLIT ELECTORATE

The PDS daily *Neues Deutschland*, once the *Pravda* of East Germany, coined the phrase that characterised the 1994 results – the "Berlin Wall at the ballot box". The best place to see this was in the capital. The reform communists dominated the east, the Christian Democrats led in the west and neither made headway in the other's backyard. The PDS won 34.7 per cent in old East Berlin and only 2.6 per cent in what used to be West Berlin. The CDU result was more balanced, with 38.7 per cent in the west and 19.5 per cent in the east. The Greens had almost twice as many votes in the west as in the east, the FDP almost four times as many. The most balanced result was for the SPD, which scored 33.1 per cent in the east and 34.6 per cent in the west. But it lost three of its direct Bundestag mandates in east Berlin to the PDS.

The split showed up in the national vote as well. Kohl won in the west, lost in the east and just barely carried the country overall. The government's share of the vote plunged by 11.5 per cent in the east (9.4 per cent of which was the FDP's fault) and five per cent in the west. "Red–Green" advanced at almost the same rate in both regions: 5.1 per cent in the east and 4.9 per cent in the west. As expected, the PDS had a totally lopsided result – 19.2 per cent in the east versus 0.9 per cent in the west.

The western states continued along the path of the four-party system – CDU/CSU, SPD, FDP and Greens – that had prevailed since the early 1980s. Beyond the Elbe, things moved in a different direction. After copying western voting patterns in the 1990 elections, the *Ossis* deserted the FDP and

Greens and voted in three-party state parliaments made up of the CDU, SPD and PDS. With the exception of the Greens in Saxony-Anhalt, the two west-ern-led "milieu parties" crashed out of all the east German state assemblies that year. The east still did not have the same class of well-off businessmen or "post-modern" ecologists who voted for these parties in the west.

The political fault lines also took different paths in the east. In many areas, the contest was between Christian Democrats and the PDS rather than between the CDU and SPD. In a reversal of western patterns, work-ing class *Ossis* tended to support the CDU (because of its role in reunification) while the middle class leaned towards the PDS or SPD.

CHANGE IN CONTINUITY

When the new Bundestag holds its first session after an election, its oldest member is asked to deliver the opening speech. This is usually a sign of continuity amid change. This time around, the opening speech in the Reichstag highlighted the change amid the continuity. Kohl and his cabinet were back. Speaker Rita Süssmuth presided as usual over the ses-sion. The first speaker, though, was Stefan Heym, a Jewish refugee from Nazism who returned in 1945 in a US Army uniform and later became one of East Germany's best-known writers. This lifelong dissenter, now 81, had been elected as an independent on the PDS ticket.

For once, the mischievous author was not his provocative self. His speech was measured, even conciliatory, and sprinkled with quotes from Abraham Lincoln and an aside on how he watched the Reichstag burn in 1933. Heym criticised what had been bad in East Germany but urged westerners not to overlook the good. "Money was not crucial, jobs were a right for men and women and housing was affordable," he recalled. While the other parties applauded politely, the CDU/CSU deputies sat in stony silence or demonstrably read their newspapers. Kohl had ordered a silent protest against the PDS and sat in the front row without once looking at Heym during the 25-minute speech. The whole scene looked oddly totalitarian, as if the Christian Democrats and not the PDS were the former communists.

66 Would the driving force behind Europe's unity get sand in its gears? 99

Change was looming on the foreign policy front as well. A long period of close Franco-German cooperation on Europe was coming to a close as François Mitterrand neared the end of his second seven-year term. The French were growing increasingly wary of their bigger and more powerful neighbour. The main Gaullist candidates for the presidential race in 1995, Prime Minister Edouard Balladur and Paris Mayor Jacques Chirac, were more reserved about Europe than Mitterrand. Would the "Franco-German axis", the driving force behind Europe's unity, get sand in its gears?

Just before Christmas, the long debate about Germany's new world role also neared a climax. Kohl announced he would send German fighter jets to Bosnia if NATO asked for help to defend UN peacekeepers during their planned pullout in 1995. The SPD agreed, if that was the only way to ensure that humanitarian aid flights to Sarajevo continued. Polls showed two-thirds of voters still opposed any military role for German forces, but the supreme court's decision had deprived Bonn of its last pre-text for standing aside. The growing threat from Serbian militia to NATO peacekeepers in Bosnia presented Bonn with a stark option – line up with your allies this time, or risk humiliation as an unreliable partner.

Slowly and unsurely, the new Germany was emerging. It was not the simple enlargement of the Bonn Republic, as many had imagined the reunited state back in 1990. Instead, it was a disunited Germany. The Berlin Republic would be western on all the big issues, but a mixture of east and west in the details. "Inner unity" was shaky, but it was starting to take hold. All Germany needed now was a symbol, a sign to everyone at home and abroad that a confident and reliable partner was emerging from the confusion. In the summer of 1995, that symbol emerged.

NOTES

1   For more on Scharping, see Rosenbaum, Ulrich (1993) *Rudolf Scharping*. Berlin: Verlag Ullstein; Leif, Thomas and Raschke, Joachim (1994) *Rudolf Scharping, die SPD und die Macht*. Reinbek bei Hamburg: Rowohlt Taschenbuch Verlag; and Bergs, Jürgen and Verheyen, Edgar (1994) *Scharping – Taktik, Strategie, Politik*. Munich. Publicom-Report.

2   The key number in the Weimar parallels was five million, the average figure for employment in 1933. The actual highpoint came in January 1933, the month Hitler became chancellor, when six million were out of work. That was 26.3 per cent of the workforce. Most received some meagre unemployment benefits but 23 per cent got nothing at all. The 1994 figures equalled 9.1 per cent of a much richer workforce and their benefits amounted to almost two-thirds of their last paycheque.

3   Interview with the author in Bonn, 12 January 1994.

4   A *Forschungsgruppe Wahlen* poll just before the October election showed many Germans thought the SPD would have done better with Schröder as its candidate. See Dalton, Russell J. (ed.) (1996) *Germans Divided: The 1994 Bundestag Election and the Evolution of the German Party System*. Oxford: Berg, page 219.

FOUNDING THE
BERLIN REPUBLIC

14

NORMAL AT LAST?

IN THE EARLY MORNING SUN, THE *WRAPPED REICHSTAG* shimmered like a frozen waterfall along Berlin's old dividing line. By midday, the fabric draping the once and future parliament shifted from silvery white to bluish grey. Nightfall saw the building bathed in a warm golden glow. The metallic fabric used by Bulgarian-American artist Christo had a magnetic effect, drawing ever more visitors in the summer of 1995 to gaze at the hidden monument. Around this symbol of Germany's brooding past, the atmosphere was light and laid-back. People picnicked, played music or enjoyed the jazz bands and fire-eaters. As in the dramatic days of the *Wende*, Berlin was again at the centre of the nation's attention. But there was neither drama nor euphoria this time. The centrepiece was not a moment of history, only a modern-day prank pulled on a symbol of history.

The two weeks when the Reichstag disappeared seemed to mark the end of the first post-unification phase. The highs of the *Wende* and lows of the recession were past. There was a new feeling in the air, one of finally being part of a success story. It started to feel "normal". The east no longer appeared as a depressed bloc, but a patchwork of prosperous and poor, dynamic and dozing. Germans also seemed more at ease with the new state that unity had created. In a small but symbolic step, the Post Office finally issued a stamp in April 1995 that

> 66 Berlin was again the centre of attention. But the centrepiece was not a moment of history, only a modern-day prank 99

identified the country of issue as *Deutschland*. No more beating around the bush with Federal Republic or Federal Post. Simply *Germany*.

The weight of the past also seemed to recede. The nation went through months of commemorations as the fiftieth anniversaries of the concentration camp liberations and finally the end of World War II came around. Then, in two major votes during the year, the Bundestag agreed to send German troops and fighter jets on the NATO peacekeeping mission in Bosnia. This would be the first deployment of German forces outside the alliance since the end of the war. The once-feared Iron Cross would reappear on planes and armour, but this time as an ally rather than a foe.

PAINFUL ANNIVERSARIES

At its start, 1995 promised anything but normal times. Five decades had passed since the end of World War II and it was time for a series of sensitive anniversary commemorations. For five months, from the liberation of Auschwitz anniversary in January to commemorations marking the fall of Berlin in May, world attention would recall the Nazis, the aggressors and the losers of the war. Kohl disliked events that underlined the difference between Germany and its post-war allies. In his striving for normality, he preferred to portray current-day Germany as a success and thus, in a way, a latter-day victor over Hitler. This could lead to some confusion among foreigners. In both 1984 and 1994, Kohl wanted to be invited to commemorate the D-Day landings in Normandy with his western allies, if they would see the event not as a purely military occasion but one that presaged their current alliance. Of course, the war's real victors – especially the tens of thousands of veterans planning to attend – wanted to commemorate that memorable battle. The chancellor was not invited.[1]

The year's first hurdle was the hardest. Auschwitz, which was liberated by advancing Soviet troops on 27 January 1945, was the Nazis' largest death factory. More a small city than a camp, it was the most powerful symbol of the industrial-style genocide Germany unleashed during the war. The Holocaust's six million victims, about 1.5 million of whom died in Auschwitz and its extermination centre in Birkenau alone, weighed heavily on the nation's conscience. Herzog, representing Germany at the commemoration in southern Poland, expressed his nation's complex feelings in the most eloquent way possible. He stood tall and solemn next to German Jewish leader Ignatz Bubis during the memorial service and said nothing.

As the months wore on, the anniversaries multiplied. April saw so many ceremonies marking the liberation of large and small concentration camps that it was hard to keep track of them all. Thousands of survivors returned to Germany from across Europe, Israel and the United States to pay homage to the fellow inmates they left behind. Survivors visited schools to share their experiences with young Germans. American and British veterans made the journey to tell of their shock when they opened camp gates and saw the walking corpses inside.

At the Bergen–Belsen commemoration, Herzog summed up the 50th anniversaries and the need to remember their message. "The generation of eyewitnesses is ending and another generation is emerging which faces the danger of regarding the experiences of Bergen–Belsen merely as history ... Now we must do our utmost to speak of the past, convey it and remember it in such a way that young people feel it is their own responsibility to make sure it can never be repeated. This is a decisive duty of our generation ... I am not sure we have found the correct forms for preserving this memory in the future."

> 66 Germans now saw 8 May 1945 not as a day of defeat but as the date of their liberation from Nazism 99

An abstruse debate just before the anniversary of the war's end shed light on how far German views of the past had shifted over the years. Opinion polls showed 80 per cent of Germans saw 8 May 1945 not as the day their country lost World War II but as the date of their liberation from Nazism.[2] President Richard von Weizsäcker set the tone for this in 1985 when, on the 40th anniversary of the war's end, he said the defeat was the founding act of West Germany's democracy. "From day to day it has become clearer that we have to say today: 8 May was a day of liberation," he said. "It freed us all from the inhuman system of National Socialist dictatorship." This cannot have been the feeling in 1945 and was not a widespread view for quite a while after the war. A group of about 280 conservative politicians and writers challenged this view with a manifesto saying the day also marked the start of the brutal expulsion of ethnic Germans from eastern Europe, oppression in eastern Germany and Germany's division. But the public reaction to their call was mostly negative.

This was a victory of positive psychology over painful memories. If successive generations saw 1945 only as a defeat, Germany might have fertile ground for nationalist resentment. The reinterpretation created a break between post-war Germans and pre-war generations they eventually could no longer understand. Younger Germans would identify increasingly with other Europeans of their age than with their own grandparents. The new view had some logical flaws; the term "liberation" normally describes the freeing of victims from slavery or foreign occupation, hardly the case of the Third Reich. But it was a constructive reading of the defeat, the opposite of Germany's resentment after 1918, and it helped build a positive post-war collective memory.

8 MAY

Bonn originally planned to mark the fiftieth anniversary of the war's end as a "family affair" – Germans only, please. Then François Mitterrand, bowing out of politics and stricken with prostate cancer, asked if he could join the gathering in Berlin to bid his official farewell to Europe. Kohl could hardly turn him down and, for protocol reasons, he invited the leaders of the other wartime allies to attend as well.

The commemorations turned into a four-day summit package tour right across Europe. London marked the start of the festivities on 6 May with a banquet for about 50 heads of state and government in the Guildhall. While other countries had only one dignitary present, Germany sent three – Kohl, Herzog and Kinkel – to dine in the medieval hall that had been so badly damaged during the Blitz. The dignitaries took the Eurostar train under the Channel for the tour's stop in Paris on Monday, 8 May. The French capital had seen victory parties all night, but they were celebrating Jacques Chirac's win in the presidential election the previous day rather than Germany's defeat 50 years earlier. When the ceremonies moved to Berlin that afternoon, the plan was for a few speeches and solemn music. Herzog and three foreign guests – Russian Prime Minister Viktor Chernomyrdin, US Vice President Al Gore and British Prime Minister John Major – delivered short speeches.

The hall fell silent when Mitterrand, 78 and visibly marked by his cancer, walked stiffly to the podium. He was one of the few present who had fought in the war, the president reminded his audience, and he was now taking his leave from the European scene. "Yesterday's enemy is today's friend," he observed. "Is it a defeat we are celebrating? Is it a victory, and which victory? It is the victory of freedom over oppression and above all, in my eyes, a victory of Europe over itself."

Pushing aside his text, Mitterrand leaned on the lectern and mused about his experiences as a prisoner of war in Germany. He had met many decent people during that time, he said, who helped him hope for a better future. His frail health seemed forgotten as he noted that the supposed hereditary enemies Germany and France were now allies. "The hereditary enemies are here; heredity did not prevail," he remarked, peeking up with an impish smile.

Mitterrand's speech reached a dramatic climax as he praised the bravery of the average German soldiers during the war. "It is not their uniform that is important for me, or even the idea that inspired their soldiers who were going to die in such great numbers. They were brave, they accepted the loss of their lives for a bad cause, but their gesture had nothing to do with that. They loved their country. One must realise that. We are building Europe, we love our countries. Let us stay loyal to ourselves. Let us join the past and the future and we can pass on the spirit of peace to those who will follow us."

> 66 This was an absolution from past sins, with Mitterrand playing the father confessor 99

Sitting in the front row, Kohl glowed with satisfaction. This was proof that Germany was accepted as a normal country. The months of commemoration, when Germany was symbolically in the dock, had culminated in the catharsis he had always wanted. Mitterrand had pronounced the average German blameless and his patriotism a virtue. This went beyond the formal reconciliation of former enemies. It was an absolution from past sins, with Mitterrand playing the father confessor. Ten years after one of Kohl's worst failures, Mitterrand delivered the message of Bitburg. "*It is not their uniform that was important ...*" German commentators were either so moved by Mitterrand's oratory or so tactful to the retiring statesman that few actually described his absolution of German guilt as such. In France, though, historians and war veterans accused Mitterrand of going too far in blurring the lines. The Paris daily *Libération* called Mitterrand's speech "The Great Absolution" and argued in an editorial, "Forgive, yes. Forget or misrepresent history, no."[3]

THE EUROPEAN NEIGHBOUR

After the summit tour finished in Moscow, Kohl turned his attention to some of the absentees. The Netherlands, Israel and Poland were three countries with traumatic memories of the war and traditional anti-German feelings. Dutch Prime Minister Wim Kok considered inviting Germans to his country's fiftieth anniversary ceremonies, but protests from veterans' groups forced him to back down. Kohl tried to persuade Israel's President Ezer Weizman to visit Germany on or right after 8 May, but he declined. Warsaw was upset at being left out of the Berlin ceremony so a Kohl visit was arranged to smooth ruffled feathers.

Kohl's visit to the Netherlands, where a much-publicised survey in 1993 had shown Dutch youths were as anti-German as earlier post-war generations, went off without a hitch. In Rotterdam, he gave an unqualified apology for the Nazi destruction of the city in the 1940 *Blitzkrieg* and for the murder of Dutch Jews. Addressing students, he said he understood how painful the memory of the war was for the Dutch and how wary they were of Germany. "But we cannot remain prisoners of the past, otherwise the past will have won in the end," the chancellor told them. The students gave him a standing ovation.

The chancellor got an even friendlier reception the next month in the country with most reason to be standoffish – Israel. Kohl was "Mr Europe" by now and Israel was interested in good relations with the increasingly important EU. The chancellor mastered the hardest parts, such as the visit to the Yad Vashem Holocaust memorial, with a dignity he failed to muster in his clumsy visit in 1984. For their part, the Israelis showed a warmth and goodwill no German until then could have expected to find. Ben Gurion University awarded him an honorary doctorate. Jerusalem's Hebrew University renamed its Institute for European Studies as the "Helmut Kohl Institute".

The Israel visit was part of a tour that started in Egypt, where Kohl discussed the Middle East peace process with President Hosni Mubarak. In Jericho, he gave PLO chairman Yasser Arafat 10 million marks to help build up the fledgling administration in Palestinian-controlled areas. Kohl then attended a short summit with Israeli Prime Minister Yitzhak Rabin and Jordan's King Hussain in Baqoura, just south of the Sea of Galilee. The EU was considering giving 700 million marks in aid to build two dams along the rivers here to provide water for both countries. The monarch praised the German effusively as "one of the greatest men of our times". Rabin told the chancellor, "Your involvement, your decision to come to visit here, gives us great hope."

Poland, the last stop on Kohl's diplomatic rounds, also looked to Germany as the door to Europe. Wary of the Russians, the post-communist government was determined to cement its turn towards the west by joining the EU and NATO. Even old communists who had stoked anti-German prejudices for decades converted to the new view. "The truth is that we will not catch up with the civilisational progress that characterises the west without direct help from Germany," wrote

Ryszard Wojna, a leading communist-era propagandist. "This is a new factor in Polish history. The road west leads through Germany and with Germany. We cannot circumvent it."

Addressing a joint session of parliament in Warsaw, the chancellor declared to loud applause, "Poland needs Europe, but Europe also needs Poland. Without it, it is just a torso." He later gave the timetable for joining the two western clubs as well, telling journalists, "I believe the major progress Poland has made allows us to assume that Polish accession will take place by the end of this decade of the 1990s." Touring Krakow after a visit to nearby Auschwitz, Kohl was greeted on the market square by hundreds of applauding on-lookers.

THE BOSNIA TORNADO VOTE

When Bonn wondered how to fulfil its new military role abroad, it dreamed of an ideal mission. During Kohl's Middle East visit, officials hinted that Bonn could send peacekeeping troops to patrol the Golan Heights after an Israeli withdrawal. The symbolism of defending peace between Jews and Arabs would be eloquent. Instead, Bonn had to march into a nightmare. After four years of war in former Yugoslavia, the policies that seemed so promising in the first flush of the post-Cold War period – economic sanctions, UN blue helmets, multilateral negotiations – had all proven ineffective. With the UN peacekeeping mission in Bosnia failing, Britain, France and the Netherlands decided in mid-1995 that a rapid reaction force was needed for a "more robust" response to the Bosnian Serbs. It also wanted up to 1,700 German troops – far more than the 500 or so logistics forces already helping behind the scenes there. With the deployment of actual combat troops and war planes meant to attack ground positions, post-war Germany would break a taboo and send fighting men outside the NATO area for the first time. And their first mission would be in former Yugoslavia, where Serbs vividly remembered Nazi atrocities against the mostly Serbian partisans and support for the fascist Croatian state during the last world war.

There was a sober mood of inevitability as the Bundestag met on 30 June 1995. PDS deputies arrived wearing T-shirts showing a blue helmet on a tombstone and proclaiming "We say No!" In the debate, the Social Democrats argued that the Tornado jets would only intensify the conflict rather than end it. "War in the air doesn't lead to peace on the ground," SPD chairman Rudolf Scharping argued. The SPD backed sending more medical and transport units and even Tornado jets designed simply for reconnaissance work. But it drew a fine line around the eight ECR Tornados because they were meant to shoot. The Greens went further, warning against a "remilitarisation" of foreign policy. Joschka Fischer called the mission "a caesura that we fear" and insisted Germany did not need to change its post-war foreign policy. The government won the vote and the Bundeswehr mission was approved. The 50-year taboo was finally broken in September when several ECR Tornados took to the skies to ride shotgun for the Rapid Reaction Force in Bosnia. NATO was bombing Bosnian Serb positions and Germans were on the team.

While most of Germany was focused on these flights, one politician took an overall look at Bosnia and got increasingly worried by what he saw. Fischer watched with horror as the UN "safe area" of Srebrenica fell to Bosnian Serb forces in mid-July. UN peacekeepers there were no match for "ethnic cleansing". It was a sobering moment when the Greens leader realised that the solutions he had proposed until then were not enough. Military force was needed. He put his thoughts down in a position paper that would mark a sea change in foreign policy thinking for the left. "The alternatives to a military guarantee for United Nations protected zones are only worse," he wrote. The next few weeks bore out Fischer's argument. The massive NATO bombing campaign stopped the Bosnian Serbs' advance and drove them back in some areas. The cruel shelling of Sarajevo finally ended.

THE SPD ON THE MOVE

The SPD was too wrapped up in its own problems during 1995 to look much further afield. Scharping stumbled from one setback to the next as the party's new leader in parliament. On 14 May, the SPD lost its absolute majority of North Rhine-Westphalia, forcing party elder statesman Johannes Rau into an unwanted coalition with the Greens. Voting the same day in Bremen, another "red" stronghold, brought more losses for the SPD and left it with only the CDU to take as a partner. Frankfurt's city hall switched from "red–green" to CDU in June. In October, Berlin handed the SPD its worst result there since 1945. Only 23.6 per cent of voters in Willy Brandt's city backed the SPD. In an unusual reversal of the normal trend, Kohl and the CDU were riding high in the opinion polls a year after the election.

In what seemed to be an SPD tradition, the party turned lukewarm on its own candidate. Gerhard Schröder let everyone know he thought he would have won the 1994 election if he'd been the candidate. Oscar Lafontaine backed Scharping on some points but made him look weak and dependent on others. Scharping hit back in August by dropping Schröder as the party's economics spokesman, but that did little to re-establish his authority.

The mood was glum and resigned when the SPD gathered for its annual congress in Mannheim that November. Grasping for straws, Scharping turned his opening speech into an all-out critique of the party's weaknesses, his own included. He had "done too much and achieved too little", he confessed, while others had undermined the party with their criticism. Disregarding Lafontaine and the anti-war left, Scharping endorsed German participation in the Bosnia mission, a policy the party leader's friends thought he supported but was too cautious to say. The congress clapped in polite disappointment.

The next day, Lafontaine stepped into the power void and whipped up the congress with a speech only he could give. The stocky Saarlander rolled out a litany of Social Democratic slogans that cheered the dispirited delegates. Jobs, shorter working hours, better welfare services, European integration, Germany as a "peaceful power" – they were all known positions, but his passionate oration made them seem like light in the darkness. A "draft Oskar" movement got started overnight. The next morning, the congress held a hasty leadership vote that ended with a shock – 321 for Lafontaine, 190 for Scharping. The defeated candidate sat numb on the podium as the delegates cheered their new leader. "Comrades, I thought we needed clarity. Now we have it," Scharping said bitterly.

> 66 He had 'done too much and achieved too little', Scharping confessed 99

The Greens conducted the debate the SPD should have held. Their annual congress in early December focused squarely on the military issue. Delegates had their choice among four different motions ranging from Fischer's call for military intervention to the quintessentially Greens proposal that Germany declare itself a conscientious objector ready to do alternative service around the globe. When Fischer stood up to speak, a dozen demonstrators in military uniforms and red berets rushed onto the platform for a short protest. Unfazed, he responded with the lesson of Srebrenica. "When a safe area became a place where thousands of unarmed people were handed over to their murderers and now lie cold in mass graves, then for me the line was crossed," he declared. In the end, the congress passed a resolution declaring economic sanctions the toughest weapon Germany should use against an aggressor, but leaving it up to the Bundestag deputies to decide how they should vote. More than a third of the delegates supported Fischer, a sign the party was moving in his direction.

ENTER THE NEW ERA

The post-war taboo against using the military abroad finally fell on 6 December when a wide majority in the Bundestag approved German participation in the NATO peacekeeping mission in Bosnia. The vote to send 4,000 armed troops was 543 for and only 107 against, a remarkable turnaround from the Tornado vote in June. Bonn's share of the 60,000-strong force was modest. Nearly all troops would be based in Croatia to avoid direct contact with Bosnian Serbs. Many would be logistics units assigned to rebuild damaged roads and transport supplies. Nevertheless, Germany's "vacation from history" was over.

It was Fischer's victory. Since returning to the Bundestag in 1994, the pudgy Greens leader had become the driving force in the opposition. His hard-hitting speeches and witty catcalls won him respect even from Kohl, who listened carefully whenever Fischer spoke and heckled him with gusto. With his background, the conversion to supporting NATO carried a convincing moral weight. It showed Germans the lesson to be drawn from their past was not "no more wars", but "no more aggression, no more genocide" – the lessons their allies had learned. In joining this consensus, Germany took another step towards being "normal". "Too bad he's in the wrong party," mumbled Fischer fans in the SPD.

A new mood was emerging in eastern Germany as well. As the fifth anniversary of unification came around, quiet optimism about the future was spreading. Bright shops and newly-painted houses were now the rule rather than the exception. Construction cranes dominated city skylines. Mere amateurs when they began in 1990, eastern politicians were getting better at their jobs. Economic growth of up to nine per cent and a continued flow of transfer payments from the west also helped. Unemployment was still high – 13.9 per cent at the underweighted official rate, compared to 8.2 per cent in the west – and the *Wessis* still had their say almost everywhere. But the good seemed to overshadow the bad.

The most telling shift came with the balanced view taken by the PDS on the eve of the fifth anniversary. The shrillest opponents of unification admitted for the first time that the overall balance was positive.

Unification "has brought noticeably more democracy, freedom and human rights for the large majority," the party said in a Unity Day statement. "The selection of material goods, services, art and literature has expanded at a rate that was inconceivable before 1989. Although equal standing with the western standard of living is still far off, there has been a rise in real wages and in most pensions." PDS leader Gregor Gysi admitted the party's arch-critical stand now only partially corresponded to what many *Ossis* felt and experienced in everyday life.

> 66 'The worst is over,'
> Jens Reich concluded 99

"The worst is over," Jens Reich concluded as he looked back over the initial post-unity period. "There are still a lot of conflicts, but now it's slowly calming down. It's settling in now. In a way, it's over."[4]

NOTES

1 Kohl denied ever asking for an invitation, which is strictly true since his aides stopped putting out feelers once they saw the ceremony would not paper over the past.

2 The Electoral Research Group (*Forschungsgruppe Wahlen*) survey noted about 87 per cent of Germans under 30 years old saw 8 May as a day of liberation compared to 67 per cent of those over 50. See the ZDF Politbarometer for April 1995 in *Süddeutsche Zeitung*, 29 April 1995.

3 See *Libération*, 10 May 1995.

4 Conversation with the author, 20 September 1995.

15

NO MONEY AT HOME, NEW MONEY FOR EUROPE

ONE OF THE HARDEST-FOUGHT POLITICAL BATTLES of the mid-1990s was also one of the most absurd. At a time when unemployment was on the rise and service sector jobs were booming in other countries, Germany clung to the most restrictive shopping hours in western Europe. Shoppers dreaded the last-minute rush to buy before the 6.30 pm closing time on weekdays or 2 pm on Saturdays. Department store turnover was stagnating. At the same time, petrol stations and train terminals, using a loophole allowing them to offer "travel provisions", expanded into little supermarkets selling everything from food and wine to toys and underwear on evenings or weekends. Bakers in Baden-Württemberg even installed electric golf cart rechargers so they could qualify as service stations and sell bread on Sunday.

Whenever a reform to the 1956 shop hours law was suggested, vested interests rose to strike it down. The department stores worried about hiring more staff. Employees complained they would not see their families anymore. Unions demanded higher pay. Change finally came in November 1996, when legislators desperate to do something about unemployment let shops open until 8 pm on weekdays and 4 pm on Saturdays. Bakeries were allowed to sell fresh bread on Sundays. It was a laughably modest reform, but at least one with a happy ending.

There was a long list of other reforms that Germany needed, but Bonn was too weak and deadlocked to achieve them. The federal budget had to be trimmed dramatically if Germany was to qualify for Europe's single currency. The tax regime needed an overhaul, as did the creaking pension system. Labour costs had to be brought down to keep jobs from being exported abroad. "Rhineland capitalism", the corporatist-style welfare state where capital, labour and government cooperated to produce prosperity, seemed to have run its course. Germany's successful drive to impose a strict "stability pact" for the euro currency gave the impression of a vigorous new leader in Europe. In fact, for many policies at home, the latest catchword, *Reformstau* ("reform backlog"), said it all.

CONSENSUS OR CONFRONTATION?

It was supposed to be a good year for Kohl. In October 1996, he would outlast his mentor Konrad Adenauer to become Bonn's longest-serving chancellor. His rule was undisputed in the CDU and he enjoyed a statesman's stature. But the pillars of his power looked shaky. The old West German model of high wages, high productivity and high job security was out of step with the competitive international markets of the 1990s. The great German gravy train had to be slowed down. But the chancellor had to hold off for months until a "Super Sunday" of elections in three western states had passed. His FDP coalition partners looked close to death after losing the last dozen elections. Three more defeats could effectively sink the party, leaving Kohl's CDU without its long-time coalition partner.

Looking further ahead, Germany seemed set to miss the targets for Europe's monetary union. The budget deficit had ballooned to 3.6 per cent of GDP in 1995 after only 2.5 per cent the previous year. Economic growth nearly ground to a halt late in the year while unemployment hit a record 4.2 million in January, or 10.8 per cent of the workforce. Economists expected the deficit to edge even higher in 1996 before dropping a bit in 1997, the year it would have to be at or below 3 per cent to make Germany eligible for the euro club.

66 **The great German gravy train had to be slowed down** 99

While the politicians hesitated, trade union leader Klaus Zwickel unveiled his "Alliance for Jobs" plan in late 1995. His giant IG Metall metalworkers' union offered to hold wage demands to zero in real terms for the next three years. In return, employers had to create 330,000 jobs and Bonn had to drop plans to cut benefits for the long-term unemployed. Zwickel wanted action. IG Metall had lost one-fifth of its membership since 1991, mostly because jobs were exported from high-wage Germany. Its members were now in direct competition with skilled Czechs, Hungarians and Poles who worked for one-tenth of their wages.

Zwickel's idea would not deal right away with non-wage costs such as welfare, social security and holidays, which could add up to 80 per cent to a factory worker's pay. Unless reforms tackled those issues, there seemed to be little hope of rolling back unemployment. But the Alliance for Jobs had the appealing pull of consensus about it, and most movers and shakers in the economy jumped on the bandwagon. A first "jobs summit" on 23 January pledged to halve unemployment to two million by the end of the century. Consensus carried the day on certain welfare cuts, tax reform and raising the minimum retirement age. The programme was vague on key points, but all sides wanted to believe it could work.

The long-awaited election day on 24 March turned out to be a Super Sunday for the government. The FDP came through more strongly than expected, the CDU gained ground and the SPD slumped everywhere. The best results for Bonn were in Baden-Württemberg, where the CDU was able to push the SPD out of the grand coalition there and take the FDP in as its partner. The SPD got mauled for campaigning against Europe's single currency and opposing further immigration of ethnic Germans from the former Soviet Union. The campaign seemed so right wing that several national party figures complained about it. On election day, the SPD vote plummeted by four points to its worst score ever in this state, 25.1 per cent.

Baden-Württemberg set the tone for the election strategies the parties would begin drawing up for 1998. The CDU saw the FDP's revival as the sign it was recovering from its slump. It also concluded that an anti-European campaign could not win, even if the majority did not like losing the deutschemark. The SPD would suffer "a terrible bellyflop" if it ever tried an anti-European campaign again, Kohl boasted. "The coalition will win the 1998 election, no ifs, ands or buts about it," he told journalists the day after the vote. "I'd get used to that idea if I were you."

His majority reassured, Kohl turned his back on the search for consensus. He had an "election-free zone" until early 1998, in which he could order the belt-tightening he would hardly dare to impose during a campaign. Two days after the state polls, the government announced it would stop negotiating reforms and ram its austerity programme through parliament. The SPD-controlled Bundesrat would be to blame if it did not become law. With consensus crumbling, the Alliance for Jobs talks stalled. Its last summit, in late April, ended in acrimony when the government sided with employers to demand cuts in the generous sick pay regime. Within days, Bonn announced plans to reduce pensions and unemployment benefits and impose a zero wage round for civil servants.

The main signal in all of this was that Kohl was determined to qualify for the single currency. The government had to slash 50 billion marks off its spending in 1997 to squeeze the budget into the Maastricht corset. "We have to try to reach consensus, but this striving for consensus cannot release political leaders, and especially the government and myself, from the task of taking necessary decisions when a consensus is not possible," he said.

There was a consensus, but not where Kohl wanted it. Polls showed over 70 per cent of voters opposed the austerity plan. No less than 90 per cent thought Bonn was favouring business and not doing enough to fight unemployment. Warning strikes broke out around the country, halting buses, stopping mail delivery and leaving rubbish uncollected. A shift in public opinion was taking place. Even CDU supporters began to fear the government was ready to get rough in a clumsy rush to downsize the welfare state. They understood Germany had to reform, but they wanted change to come gently.

REFORMING EUROPE THE GERMAN WAY

As Bonn surveyed the European scene in mid-1995, it did not like what it saw. The other European Union members did not seem to be preparing seriously enough for the looming economic and monetary union. Only Luxembourg already met the Maastricht criteria. France, Belgium, Italy and Spain seemed to be cruising along with high deficit or debt levels, confident that some last-minute Brussels deal would buy them entry into the new club. Potential members had to pass tight national budgets by late 1996 if they wanted to qualify.

The EMU clock was also ticking louder in Bonn's ears because of the fright it recieved from Jacques Chirac. After 14 years of close Franco-German co-operation, the new French President seemed ready to gamble away much of the progress Kohl and Mitterrand had made. His election campaign had focused on the fight against unemployment and social exclusion. The more he spent to create jobs, however, the less likely it became that France would qualify for EMU. A monetary union without France would be a hollow exercise, linking Germany in a deutschemark zone with the Benelux countries and Austria without really integrating Europe.

This was not the way to convince voters to love the loss of the deutschemark. A consistent majority of about 70 per cent rejected what populists called "Esperanto money". Decades of cheap vacations in Italy and Spain had created an ingrained contempt for "Club Med" currencies. Diluting the mark with them would produce inflation and force German taxpayers to transfer more to southern Europe, the argument went.

To convince the voters, Bonn first had to convince the Bundesbank. The Frankfurt "guardians of the currency" were the only authority the public would listen to on such an important matter. "Not all Germans believe in God, but all of them believe in the Bundesbank," European Commission President Jacques Delors liked to say. The bank had no formal veto over EMU, but its thumbs down could kill the project politically. Lukewarm at best about EMU, the bank felt there was too much leeway for countries to qualify through "creative accounting", and that it also lacked guarantees to ensure virtuous behaviour after the euro was launched.

Caught between their personal pro-European convictions and the bank's mission to ensure the stability of the German currency, Bundesbankers delivered lectures around the country giving a firm "yes, but ..." to EMU. If Germany would not lower its standards, their message went, the others would have to raise theirs. The franc, the lira and any other currency joining EMU had to be as strong as the deutschemark. EMU was a political project from the start and the Bundesbank was determined to ensure that the politicians made the figures add up.

> 66 Not all Germans believe in God, but all of them believe in the Bundesbank 99

Bonn responded with an arm-twisting campaign that showed the full force reunited Germany could muster when it was determined to win. Just how concerned it was about the lack of preparation for EMU came out in September when Theo Waigel told the Bundestag budget committee that Italy would fail to qualify in 1999. Belgium and the Netherlands would have difficulties, too. Foreign exchange dealers promptly dumped lire, francs and other EU currencies to snap up deutschemarks. The result was the worst turbulence on markets since the ERM crisis of 1993. The Italian government was up in arms. France said it saw no reason to tighten the rules on budget deficits. Amid all this, the market reflex to buy marks and drive up their value would bring the worst-case scenario that export-oriented Germany feared if EMU collapsed. There was no going back. Waigel had to convince his partners that they must qualify for the single currency on Germany's terms.

Waigel baptised his new plan the "Stability Pact", a name chosen with German voters' prejudices in mind. In it, he proposed that Maastricht's budget deficit target of three per cent of gross domestic product should be the absolute ceiling for state overspending, even at the worst of economic times. Any EMU member exceeding the three per cent limit would have to pay fines to the EU of up to 0.25 per cent of its GDP, a burden that would surely worsen its deficit. The money could only be reimbursed if the errant member returned to fiscal discipline within the following two years. Tightening the screw even further, he said the fines must kick in automatically. This mechanism would rule out the political horse-trading that reigned in Brussels. The Bundesbank applauded loudly.

The more Bonn spoke out for a single currency, the more its partners wondered whether Germany really wanted it. How could Bonn be 100 per cent behind a project that 75 per cent of the voters rejected? Working with Kremlinological fervour, economists, traders, journalists and diplomats weighed every nuance in Tietmeyer's talks and Waigel's wisecracks. Some analysts, especially in Britain and the US, were convinced the EMU was a pipe dream that was bound to end in a nightmare.

By insisting the euro would be as strong as the mark, Kohl and Waigel all but invited their critics to play the "more stable than thou" card and demand double and triple reassurances that it would be so. Gerhard Schröder, a pragmatic pro-European rather

66 Some analysts were convinced the EMU was a pipe dream that was bound to end in a nightmare 99

than a romantic one, deftly used the EMU debate to boost his popularity within the SPD. Keen to mark his differences with Scharping, in mid-1995 he began to pander to popular concerns about swapping the mark for a weak euro. Only a few states would qualify and the project would do little to create jobs, he argued, so why not put off the start for a year or so? Trying to raise the stakes, Scharping accused Waigel of not exerting enough pressure on EMU hopefuls to force them into line.

In the CSU, Bavarian state premier Edmund Stoiber pushed the party chairman Waigel into a corner. Eager to wrest control of the party from the finance minister, "Edmund Thatcher" – as the press dubbed him – demanded iron-clad terms for the euro. If Waigel failed to whip the other Europeans into line, his strategy went, his political career would be over. If the euro was a success, the self-appointed guardian of the Maastricht criteria would have been proven right. So Stoiber kept the heat on Waigel, scrutinising his EMU comments for any wavering from the strictest stand.

Waigel could not say only "three per cent"; he had to spell out "3.0 per cent" and remind his EU partners of this repeatedly to keep the Bavarians happy.

Bonn also faced several procedural obstacles. The Bundestag would have the final say on joining EMU. Any decision to join could also be challenged in the Federal Constitutional Court, where justices hinted they would reject it if the criteria were not respected fully by all future members. A last-minute Brussels fudge to admit unqualified members would not be strong enough to hold up to the withering scrutiny of a German judge.[1]

Kohl tried to tiptoe through this minefield, doing his best to avoid putting more emphasis on the criteria or the timetable. He could not allow the EMU decision to be pushed past its spring 1998 deadline. That would turn September's general election into a referendum on the euro, opening the door to anti-EMU campaigns that could whip up the vote for the extreme right. If it were decided on time, not the euro but his success in achieving it would be the campaign issue. Once again, Kohl conflated electoral strategy with international issues.

The chancellor had a trump card in his back pocket. No matter how much Germans seemed to wax lyrical about the deutschemark as their only national symbol, 60 per cent of voters did not really care about the issue. Stability of the currency was the crucial element. Surveys that simply asked "do you want to give up the deutschemark, yes or no?" were too superficial to catch this detail. They overlooked the fear of devalued money that had been fixed in Germany's collective memory since the great inflation of 1923. "They never want to have to experience again what they went through in the first half of this century," Renate Köcher of the Allensbach polling group explained. Even more reassuring for Kohl, most voters thought EMU was inevitable and trusted him far more than the SPD to make it work.[2]

"THE EURO SPEAKS GERMAN!"

After a brief period following Chirac's election when French support for the euro wobbled, Bonn ploughed ahead from one European meeting to the next getting a little bit more of its own way on EMU each time. The phrase "our voters would never accept anything less than this" soon grated in the ears of other Europeans. But each little step defused the euro issue that much more. Bonn fought off an Italian bid to postpone the 1999 launch. It made sure the statistics used to judge members' qualifications for EMU would be the final figures for 1997 instead of earlier estimates that could be manipulated.

Even the currency's name became an issue. France wanted to keep "ecu", which was both the acronym for the European Currency Unit and the name of an old French coin. The Bundesbank opposed this, so Waigel proposed adding the prefix "euro-" to national currency names to create "euro-mark" or "euro-lira". Somebody proposed "franc" but Spain torpedoed that because it sounded like the name of its former dictator Franco. Kohl insisted they agree on the safe name "euro". When Chirac tried to rescue "ecu" at the December 1995 Madrid summit by suggesting a referendum on the name, Kohl told him Germans would pick "deutschemark" if the issue were put to a vote. So "euro" it was.[3]

As the pressure mounted, Italy's new Prime Minister Romano Prodi suggested to his Spanish counterpart Jose Maria Aznar that they try to have the convergence criteria weakened. Rome's debts were 120 per cent of its gross domestic product (GDP), twice as high as the criteria allowed, and its budget deficit was 5.5 per cent rather than the three per cent Maastricht demanded. Aznar refused. He planned to slash spending in his 1997 budget to meet the EMU criteria. France swore it would clear the criteria hurdle as well. Prodi did an about-face. In late September, he unveiled deep cuts in Italy's budget and announced a one-off "Europe tax" to help reduce the deficit. Both Aznar and Prodi made pilgrimages to see Kohl in October and got warm encouragement to keep trimming their budgets.

This set off alarm bells in the Bundesbank. Concerned there was no political union to complement the monetary merger, Tietmeyer issued increasingly dire predictions about the need to respect the Maastricht criteria. "Fiscal discipline must be secured, or else the danger that the EMU could be torn apart is very high. Then we'd be worse off than we are today," Tietmeyer argued in November. But if Tietmeyer could raise the volume, so could Kohl. A few days later, the chancellor issued his most passionate defence yet of the single currency. "I will tie my own political fate to the founding of the European currency union," he announced to a banker's convention in Frankfurt. "The goal must be that many states meet the stability criteria and participate in the currency union from the start. But we take the criteria very seriously ... Anyone who thinks the Germans at the head of the federal government are so eurofanatic that they'll fudge the criteria in the end is wrong."

But not even reunited Germany could get its way across the board. With its tradition of political control over technocrats, France rejected the automatic fines for overspenders that Germany – which tends to think some issues are too technical to be left to politicians – insisted the stability pact must have. The fight went right down to the wire at the December 1996 EU summit in Dublin. When the unresolved issue came up on the agenda, Kohl and Chirac nearly came to blows in a corner of the conference room. "I have no room for manoeuvre," the chancellor bellowed straight into Chirac's face. "This is a matter of life and death for me. I cannot sell EMU in Germany without the Stability Pact. I absolutely cannot do without it. There is nobody in Germany who can champion the European idea as well as I can." Chirac roared back that arithmetic could not replace statesmen in making such important decisions.

Standing among the shocked onlookers, Dutch Prime Minister Wim Kok cheered Kohl on: "Helmut, be tough! Be tough!" Finally, one of Chirac's aides tapped him on the shoulder. "What do you want?" Chirac yelled. *"Monsieur le Président*, stop this discussion right now," the aide said. "It's useless. Let the ministers work it out." A truce was called. In the end, a narrow wiggle room for overspenders was defined. It was agreed that the EU's Council of Ministers, i.e. politicians, would have the final say in allowing a member country to exceed spending targets.[4]

> 66 'I have no room for manoeuvre,' the chancellor bellowed straight into Chirac's face 99

The compromise looked like a barometer of Germany's influence within the EU. Bonn had established an independent central bank, located it in Frankfurt, named the currency and imposed a Stability Pact to keep members in line. The "stability culture" the Bundesbank defended so ferociously would dominate the European Central Bank. The only chink in this heavy monetary armour was the decision to let politicians decide on exceptions to the rule, meaning a qualified majority could outvote Germany. Bonn could hardly complain. What had started out as a French project to rein in the Bundesbank had ended up as a German programme to spread its "stability culture" across the continent. As Waigel crowed when he returned to Bonn, "The euro speaks German!"

KING KOHL

Der Spiegel had written "Kohl kaputt" so often over the years that the chancellor refused to read it. When he wanted to refer to it, he spoke about "a Hamburg publication". The left-leaning news weekly lined up with the rest of the German media, though, to praise "the eternal chancellor" in autumn 1996. On 31 October, Kohl surpassed his mentor Konrad Adenauer's 14-year record in the chancellery. One could disagree with his policies, but there was no denying that Kohl had carved out his place in history. "Helmut Kohl is now – it's hard to use the superlative – the most respected statesman still in office in the world known to us," wrote *Der Spiegel* reluctantly. "Helmut Kohl is a man without scandals."[5]

To explain Kohl's political longevity, the media first of all commented on his plain ordinariness. Any man who had taken his summer vacation in the same resort in the Austrian Alps for 25 years exuded a solidity no PR manager could create. "Kohl is something like a mild sedative," the psychologist Horst-Eberhard Richter said. "He calms things down and puts conflicts to rest." Another of Kohl's strengths was his undisguised appreciation of power. He had no scruples about using it to cut down rivals or champion major issues such as reunification or EMU. "Power is important and necessary for me," he said in one television interview.

> 66 Helmut Kohl is a man without scandals 99

With hindsight, it is interesting to note that even Kohl's toughest critics apparently had no idea at this point that part of the chancellor's power was based on his slush funds.

Very little went well for Kohl after reaching this record. His coalition squabbled endlessly about tax and pension reform. Two of the austerity measures he had pushed through backfired. Companies could not impose the cut in sick pay benefits against union opposition. Daimler-Benz gave up trying when a single day of warning strikes cost about as much as it expected to save in a year from the reform. A cut in subsidies for "bad weather pay" for construction crews prompted builders to lay off workers in waves during the winter, more than doubling the sums the Federal Labour Office had to pay out in unemployment benefits.

Worried about their own careers, younger CDU leaders started to grumble about how Kohl blocked change at the top. Dubbed the "wild youngsters", these men – around 40 years old, mostly CDU leaders in SPD-run states – openly criticised the gridlock in Bonn. The CDU youth wing leader Klaus Escher won derisive laughs when he compared Kohl to a classic car: "Your collector's value rises steadily, but we can't get a new production line going with your model." The "youngsters" made no secret of their preference for Wolfgang Schäuble. But he was so closely linked to the chancellor that he could only wait until Kohl handed him the job. A palace revolt against Kohl would not be tolerated in the CDU. Schäuble's supporters got their hopes up after the March 1996 state elections and when Kohl reached his record in the October, thinking that this was the time for the chancellor to step aside and give Schäuble a chance to prove himself in the office before facing the 1998 election. Hanging on ran the risk of seeing everything slide downhill.

But what signal would Kohl send if he stepped down? That he didn't think he could win in 1998? Kohl had a mission to make European unification irreversible and was convinced that only he could do it. So the chancellor pulled the last rabbit out of his hat. On 3 April 1997, his 67th birthday, he announced in a television interview that he would run for chancellor again. The effect on the CDU (and on money markets) was reassuring. Helmut Kohl would not quit when he was needed most. He would ensure that Europe launched its single currency on time. His supporters were relieved to see Kohl run again, but couldn't say what he could do with another four years that he could not do at the time. The SPD majority in the Bundestag, which Lafontaine was skilfully using to block his tax reform plans, would probably continue for a few years. Kohl was not ready for other overdue reforms, such as modernising the citizenship law. He offered nothing but himself.

In mid-May, Waigel looked around frantically for a rabbit to pull out of his hat as well. Tax revenues were falling so far below target that the euro looked in doubt again. Grasping at straws, he dashed to Frankfurt for a crisis meeting with Tietmeyer. The Bundesbank had 95 million ounces of gold, very conservatively valued at $92 per ounce. Revaluing it closer to the market price of $340 per ounce would bring vast windfall profits for Bonn. Would the Bundesbank, the declared enemy of "creative accounting", consider helping out a bit this way?

The bank took two weeks to consider Waigel's request. Speculation about the euro's fate ran wild on the money markets. When it finally spoke, the bank's response thundered with indignation. Forcing it to revalue the gold "would go against the German tradition and the Maastricht Treaty's view on the independence of central banks." The government hit back minutes later with a declaration meant to cow the fabled bank into submission. Like lions baring their teeth, the entire coalition leadership signed the statement reminding the bank who made the law in Germany. "The coalition intends to revalue the currency reserves of the Bundesbank according to the principles developed by the European Monetary Institute," said the statement.

Germans were stunned to see the government so desperate that it would try to force the revered bank into the kind of sleight-of-hand they thought only the Italians capable of. Within days, several CDU and FDP backbenchers stood up to say they could not support the move. Stoiber warned Waigel to make peace with the Bundesbank or face defeat at the polls the next year. Waigel quickly worked out a truce with Tietmeyer. The Bundesbank agreed to revalue some assets, but the first payout of the new profits would not come until 1998. In the meantime, no gold would be sold and Bonn would have to look elsewhere to ease its deficit woes.

When EU leaders lined up in Amsterdam for the traditional "family photo" at their June 1997 summit, their Dutch hosts presented them with shiny new seven-speed bicycles. Tony Blair, Britain's boyish-looking new prime minister, leaped on his and sped off along the canal. His newly elected French counterpart, Lionel Jospin, and a pack of younger men such as Spain's Jose Maria Aznar and Viktor Klima of Austria promptly followed. Romano Prodi, a keen cyclist back home in Italy, eagerly joined the fun. Helmut Kohl and Jacques Chirac politely declined and stayed behind. Luckily nobody thought of giving them a tandem; they could not have agreed which way to go.

> **66 Germans were stunned to see their government so desperate 99**

The days when Kohl was larger than life were coming to an end. A new generation of leaders was sitting around the EU summit table. Chirac's gamble on a snap parliamentary election had just produced a left-wing coalition government with a quite different approach to EMU. The French socialists considered the Stability Pact a German obsession and insisted it should be linked to a job creation plan. They also demanded that Spain and Italy be in EMU from the start. All this smacked of the political tinkering Bonn had worked so hard to avoid.

Germany's federal states, led by a self-assertive Bavaria, were also chipping away at Kohl's clout in Brussels. The states scored a victory in 1992 when, in exchange for their support of the Maastricht Treaty, they won the right to be consulted on EU matters affecting their interests. They could shape Bonn's stand on issues such as culture, education or broadcasting that fell within their competence in Germany's federal system. The states lost no time in locking horns with Brussels. Mostly, they argued over subsidies, but Bavaria also thundered against majority voting on issues such as immigration and visa policy. All complained that Germany was paying far too much into the EU for what it got out.[6] "There are too many Thatchers in Germany," EU competition commissioner Karel Van Miert complained. "The possibilities for (Kohl) to play a pioneering role in Europe have been thwarted by Germany's state governments. Sometimes I ask myself whether some of these states are really part of the European Union."[7]

Hemmed in as never before, Kohl ended up blocking some of his own pet projects at Amsterdam. Germany had argued for years that the expansion to the east meant there would be so many members that they could not all have a veto, if the EU was to operate efficiently. The Amsterdam summit was due to approve this as part of a reform of the Maastricht Treaty. But the states opposed majority voting, fearing among other things that Brussels could then force them to take asylum-seekers who first arrived in other EU countries. So Kohl played the unusual part of blocking majority voting on legal affairs and immigration. The reversal of roles could not have been clearer. Even the churlish British were more willing to move forward on consensus voting. Kohl returned to Bonn saying he had defended German national interests well. It sounded like the statement a French or British leader might make after summit. It sounded normal.

NOTES

1   For more on the hurdles to EMU in Germany, see Pitchford, Ruth and Cox, Adam (eds) (1997) *EMU Explained: Markets and Monetary Union.* London: Kogan Page, pages 89–95 and 278–80.

2   *Frankfurter Allgemeine Zeitung,* 15 November 1995.

3   Milesi, Gabriel (1998) *Le Roman de l'Euro.* Paris: Hachette Littératures, pages 108–9.

4   Waigel described the scene in an interview for the last programme in the three-part BBC series "The Money Changers" shown in February 1998. For more on Chirac's side, see *Le Roman de l'Euro,* pages 142–7.

5   *Der Spiegel,* 30 September 1996.

6   The Finance Ministry said on 25 July 1997 that Germany paid about two-thirds of all net payments into the EU. Its net contribution of 22 billion marks amounted to about 65 per cent of all net payments, higher than the 50 to 60 per cent previously estimated. Neither Waigel nor his otherwise assertive Bavarian colleagues were keen to tackle the issue of farm subsidies that inflated the EU budget so much. A third of Germany's 530,000 farmers lived in Bavaria and were firmly opposed to the Commission's Agenda 2000 reform plan they said would cut their already low incomes by 20 per cent. For more, see *Neue Zürcher Zeitung,* 12 December 1997.

7   See *Die Welt,* 4 August 1997.

16

TIME FOR A CHANGE

WITH THE MUDDY WATERS OF THE ODER RIVER swirling below, Helmut Kohl surveyed the damage inflicted by the summer floods on Germany's far eastern frontier. The soggy dike beneath his rubber boots was holding against the tide. But the waters were still rising. Over on the Polish side of the river, the countryside was already under water. The tides could soon wash away this embankment and submerge dozens of villages north of Frankfurt on the Oder. Worried residents pressed forward to shake Kohl's hand and thank him for dispatching troops and relief workers to fight the floods. Germans east and west were united in their struggle to save the endangered region.

"This is where we have to prove that united Germany is one fatherland," Kohl boomed out to the crowd. As he spoke, his pep talk drifted to his dream of a united Europe. "A part of this river is Poland and a part of it is Europe, and that is why we have to do everything we can to ensure that this border loses its intensity, and that Poland is brought as quickly as possible into the European Union," he rambled on. German unity, European integration, two sides of the same coin – all the old clichés rolled off his tongue. The old war horse was gearing up for yet another election campaign.

The togetherness was impressive. For a few weeks in late July and early August 1997, the whole country watched anxiously as the Oder threatened villages whose names most Germans hardly knew. *Ossi* or *Wessi* made no difference when it came to pitching in to help. It was the kind of sponta-neous solidarity that seemed to have been missing in all those years since the autumn of 1989. Kohl's second big project of the decade was also hold-ing up, despite the hardships. The European economies were steadily converging. The euro looked likely to be launched. In a year's time, Kohl figured, Germans would look back at all he had achieved and thank him at the polls.

But while Kohl thought he was above the fray, his support was getting as waterlogged as the dike below him. The relentless currents of change were flowing past him, parting ways for the monument he stood on but then rushing on. A new generation was coming to power elsewhere in Europe and the Social Democrats were gearing up to follow suit. Globalisation was knocking ever louder on the door, demanding reforms that the exhausted coalition could not make. On the threshold of the Berlin Republic, Kohl had little more to offer than business as usual in Bonn. He had become, in Joschka Fischer's memorable words, "150 kilos of his-tory made flesh."

❝ On the threshold of the Berlin Republic, Kohl had become '150 kilos of history made flesh' ❞

"HELLO, CANDIDATE!"

Kohl lost one of his biggest advantages right at the start of the campaign. Since becoming chancellor, he had faced mostly weak opposition from the Social Democrats. The SPD lost its way in opposition and went through five chairmen and four candidates in 15 years. It had a tendency to sour on its candidates halfway through a campaign. But its new lead-ership was determined to win back the chancellery this time. Quite uncharacteristically, Oskar Lafontaine had devoted considerable time since becoming SPD chairman to preparing the party for 1998. The issue of who would challenge Kohl was not yet decided; Gerhard Schröder was keen to try his luck. But the two men made a crucial decision. They would not waste their energies tearing each other apart and handing Kohl the victory again.

Despite the uncertainty at the top, the Social Democrats had a tactical edge. They knew who their opponent was. A year before the vote, the SPD opened its campaign headquarters with a giant digital clock count-ing the days, hours, minutes and seconds left until Kohl would be gone. Clever campaign ads started to roll. One film clip showed Kohl in a Star

Trek sketch failing to muster up enough energy to get beamed up. The campaign had echoes of Clinton's Democrats and Blair's New Labour, whose campaigns the SPD studied carefully.

The chummy "Gerd & Oskar" show was hard to keep up, but the rivals did their best. They had to wait until 1 March 1998, when Schröder faced an election in Lower Saxony. Although only a state poll, the vote became a kind of primary; if Schröder did well, he would have the nomination. During their waiting game, Lafontaine used his post to best advantage, scheduling himself for prominent speeches at party meetings and putting Schröder low down on the speakers' list. Schröder polished his image as a dynamic manager. As the Lower Saxony vote drew near, he veered off his centrist path to have his state buy a local steel mill rather than let it be sold to an Austrian firm amid wide-scale layoffs. The unions applauded his determination to save jobs, while business frowned on the sudden switch to state intervention.[1]

Around 4 pm on 1 March, just after pollsters delivered their projections on the Lower Saxony election to the SPD, Schröder answered the telephone at his Hanover apartment. Lafontaine greeted him with "Hello, candidate!" The exit polls, due to be broadcast when voting ended in two hours, estimated over 47 per cent for Schröder. The final result was even better – 47.9 per cent, the biggest victory the SPD had ever scored in Lower Saxony. Schröder came right to the point in his victory speech: "The Kohl era is over."[2]

THE NEW POLITICS

Schröder was finally alone in the spotlight. His rise to power, using the media and primary-style votes to go over the heads of the party hierarchy, was something new in German politics. The old pattern by which a politician rose up the ranks of his party, won its support, shaped its programme and then led it into battle was fading. In its place, an "Americanised" campaign, short on politics and long on personality, was coming.

66 Schröder was relaxed on television with his three-piece suits and fat Cuban cigars 99

Thanks to years of practice on the talk-show circuit, Schröder was relaxed on television. With his three-piece suits and fat Cuban cigars, he seemed more at ease with captains of industry than with the SPD rank and file. To define his quest, he made un-SPD-like statements such as, "The board of directors of Germany Inc. needs a new chairman." He liked to praise

Kohl's achievements and then declare, "Thank you, Helmut, that's enough now." He promised he would "not do everything different, but some things better."

Kohl's camp was near panic. Even though he had spotted Schröder as the SPD's most formidable candidate early in the decade, the chancellor seemed convinced that Lafontaine would not stand aside to let him run.[3] His campaign team was ready to pounce on Lafontaine, not Schröder. Its soundbites about red socks or the SPD's Bundesrat blockade were aimed at the "Saar Napoleon". Schäuble hurriedly drew up a new list of reform pledges to present as a serious party platform in contrast to the media campaign Schröder would wage. All that this did was lead to a feud with the CSU, which acted as if the election were already lost.

The Schröder steamroller also upset the party that hoped for an SPD victory most. The Greens' only real hope for power was in a coalition with the Social Democrats. They had slowly built up their electorate and were regularly scoring 12 per cent or higher in the opinion polls. Instead of getting a tailwind from Lower Saxony, though, the Greens got a rude wake-up call. Schröder had successfully poached votes from them. The more realistic Greens discovered to their horror that the *Zeitgeist* party of the 1980s was no longer in the vanguard when unemployment and tax reform dominated the political agenda. Instead of shaping up, though, the Greens lurched back to their roots with a call to triple petrol prices to 5 marks per litre. When the inevitable criticism came, the leftist Green Jürgen Trittin shrugged it off as a problem only for macho males who like to drive high-powered cars. Not surprisingly in car-crazy Germany, their popularity plummeted.

KOHL'S EUROPEAN DREAM SOURS

Kohl placed his campaign bets squarely on the euro. An EU summit in Brussels on 2 May was due to name the countries qualifying for the new currency. The chancellor was sure his work for European unity would boost his campaign just as German unity had done in the past. The build-up started according to plan, with statistics published in March showing that 14 of the 15 EU states met the Maastricht criteria. With Greece missing the cut and Britain, Denmark and Sweden opting out, the monetary union would go ahead on 1 January 1999 with 11 members. The European Commission and the European Monetary Institute also gave all 11 EMU candidates the nod.

All the actors on the German side played their part. The Bundestag approved the Amsterdam Treaty by a large majority. On 27 March, the Bundesbank issued its long-awaited report on EMU. It criticised the high overall debt ratios in Italy and Belgium, but stopped short of calling for a delay or disqualifying any of the 11 candidates. After going to the brink with its warnings, the report described the euro as "justifiable in terms of stability policy". The final sentence read, "The selection of participants ultimately remains a political decision." So even Tietmeyer, the high priest of central bank independence, deferred to the government in the end.[4]

On 2 April, the supreme court threw out a suit claiming that EMU was inherently shaky and therefore violated the economic stability that, according to the plantiff, the German constitution guaranteed. Even Schröder, who only a month earlier had warned that the euro would be a "sickly premature birth" liable to kill jobs, lined up in the pro-euro camp for the final Bundestag vote on EMU on 23 April. In the vote that followed, all but the PDS supported the resolution empowering Kohl to sign Germany up for EMU. That was the death warrant for the deutschemark. It also spelled the end of EMU as an effective campaign issue.

Only one partner didn't play his part. Jacques Chirac had been grumbling for months about the European Central Bank. He did not like Wim Duisenberg, the Dutch "Tietmeyer clone" at the head of the European Monetary Institute. He did not like the way the central bankers and the other EU states had lined up behind Duisenberg as the only candidate to become ECB president. So in November 1997, he and Prime Minister Lionel Jospin publicly backed the head of the Bank of France, Jean-Claude Trichet, as candidate for ECB president. It was a classic Chirac bombshell, dropped without any prior warning to Bonn, and it angered Kohl intensely.

Haggling over the ECB president started months before the May EU summit. Chirac insisted that Duisenberg retire at 65, after only two years in office, to make way for Trichet. The Dutchman agreed to go after four years, but refused to put this in writing because it would weaken his authority on the job. When the EU leaders sat down for lunch at their Brussels summit to decide the issue, Chirac was still insisting that Duisenberg put his pledge in writing. The "lunch" dragged on until past midnight. Duisenberg wrote a statement saying he would not serve the full term but stay at least until euro banknotes and coins were introduced, i.e. the first half of 2002. The shabby compromise put a cloud over the ECB in Germany. How independent could it be if its first chief had to kow-tow to France to get the job?

Exhausted and fed up, Kohl tried his spinmeister best to defend the compromise at a late-night briefing. According to his campaign script, he should have been on the evening news hours earlier leading the EU into a new era. But Chirac had ruined it. The euro was now tarnished and the weakened chancellor was no longer the undisputed Mr Europe. After several hostile questions, Kohl lost his cool and petulantly berated the reporters for their critical questions. When that failed to convince the press, he plugged for sympathy. "This was a real fight, a tough struggle, these were some of the most difficult hours I've ever experienced," he confessed. "There were many moments when I was not sure if we could reach an agreement." As he left the summit, Kohl was heard to say, "It was different with Mitterrand." Back in Bonn, as he feared, the feud overshadowed the historic launch of the euro. Business leaders, the SPD and the media all said the Duisenberg deal would only raise German voters' scepticism about the single currency.

> 66 Chirac had ruined it. The euro was now tarnished 99

All this was clearly on Kohl's mind the following week when he met Chirac again for a Franco-German summit in the southern French city of Avignon. At the closing news conference, he launched into a monologue that sounded like a farewell address. "Governments come and go, but the peoples remain," he mused. Anyone like himself who had worked for half a century to promote understanding between the former enemies knew how difficult this could be. "But it has opened up a horizon for the future that seemed impossible back then," the chancellor said. "It is good to recall in moments like this that visionaries are the true realists in history."

THE NEW CENTRE

At the official kick-off to his campaign in April, Schröder entered the Leipzig Fair hall as if he were arriving to claim a Hollywood Oscar. Once on the stage, he and Lafontaine grinned and waved for the television cameras until the music faded, just as the script dictated. "We want to be the party of the New Centre," Schröder told the crowd. "I want to take away from the CDU the bastions they think they have in the business community ... The days are past when it seemed as if social democratic policies were not feasible and feasible policies were not social democratic." It was all so smooth and glitzy that it hardly seemed like an SPD rally at all. But the scent of success was too strong to want to ruin it by debating the issues. To critics of his "Americanised" game plan, campaign manager Müntefering responded, "I have never met anyone who said, 'I've read your platform and think it's great, so I'll vote for you.'"

The concerns of the New Centre (*Neue Mitte*) were more practical than ideological. Many middle class people were educated white collar workers in two-income families who still had a hard time making ends meet. They paid more and more taxes while the rich used the loopholes politicians always complained about. The baby boomers expected the welfare state they had grown up with to remain essentially the same. Jobs and pensions should stay as secure as before, even while other things changed. The next chancellor, they said, should be as modern as the new British and American leaders without the phase of Thatcherism and Reaganomics that preceded them. These voters warmed to the SPD not out of solidarity with the working class, but to save themselves from slipping back and joining it.

To personify this New Centre, Schröder brought two success stories from the business world into his leadership team. The first was Jost Stollmann, a German Bill Gates who had launched his own software company at the age of 29 after studying at Harvard Business School. Now 43 and a multimillionaire, he embodied the can-do dynamism of the post-Kohl era. The second symbol of change was such a '90s man that he no longer even lived in Germany. Publisher Michael Naumann, 56, had been working in New York for three years. Named as Schröder's culture czar in mid-July, he jetted over for a whirlwind week of campaigning. With disarming candour, he opposed the huge Holocaust memorial that Kohl wanted to be built near the Brandenburg Gate in Berlin. It looked as if Nazi architect Albert Speer had designed it, he remarked. He pledged to make his first official trip abroad to Hollywood to promote German films. It wasn't exactly "Cool Germany", but it was certainly a gust of fresh air.

Schröder skilfully played chancellor-in-waiting. "It sometimes seems to me as if we are already in government and the others in the opposition," he remarked with studied nonchalance in July. "I experience reactions to my decisions. I barely need to react to their decisions. They hardly make any." Visiting Bonn's main foreign partners, he promised continuity while hinting at interesting little breaks from the Kohl era. Russia was important, he remarked in Moscow, but Germany shouldn't lend it money blindly. Franco-German ties were a cornerstone of Bonn's foreign policy, he ventured in Paris, but how about expanding the duo into a triangle with Blair's Britain? With a discipline few thought he had, Lafontaine loyally played second fiddle and worked to ensure the SPD won.

Most reassuring of all was the way Schröder seemed to aim for a grand coalition with the CDU. He was careful not to get too close to the Greens. He teased voters with speculation about working with the CDU, going so far as to express his preference for Volker Rühe as vice chancellor rather than Wolfgang Schäuble. Thanks to these winks and nods, the New Centre voter could imagine a dream team of Schröder and Rühe at the helm and lateral entrants such as Stollmann ready to push reforms ahead. The polls were so close that it seemed a grand coalition was likely. Instead of upsetting the voters, as the CDU hoped, it seemed to reassure them. This could be a way of combining "time for a change" with the legendary CDU campaign slogan "No Experiments!"

THE ELECTION

At the election night party outside the SPD headquarters in Bonn, the celebrations were well under way by the time Schröder climbed on to the outdoor stage. The results were still coming in, but the Social Democrats were clearly in the lead. With Lafontaine shadowing him, Schröder strode up to the microphone to announce a new era. "Ladies and gentlemen, dear friends, after 16 years, the era of Helmut Kohl is over," he declared. "The New Centre has triumphed and the SPD has won it back."

Within earshot of the SPD party, the CDU was holding its political wake. But when Kohl entered, they broke into a round of "Helmut! Helmut!" cheers, just as they had in their hero's glory days. Flanked by his wife Hannelore and his aides, the loser looked relieved as he got straight to the point. "The election result is clear, the Social Democrats have won. The voters have clearly opted for red–green ... It's also a personal victory for state premier Gerhard Schröder and I wish him success," declared Kohl. The chancellor announced he would step down as CDU chairman, a post he had held for 25 years. The only touch of wistfulness came at the end of his short speech as he looked back over 16 years in office. "It was a great time. We achieved a lot," he told the crowd. "But, as democrats, we accept the decision of the voters. The voters have decided and we respect this decision. Life goes on."

> 66 Schröder strode up to the microphone to announce a new era 99

The voters' decision could not have been clearer. The SPD advanced by four points to 40.9 per cent, becoming the largest faction in the Bundestag for the first time since 1972. The unpredictable element of

Überhangmandate, the extra seats that assured Kohl his majority in 1994, swung this time to the SPD's benefit. They won 12 in the east and one in the west. With the Greens, who won 6.7 per cent of the vote, Schröder would have a 21-seat majority. The CDU/CSU plummeted six points to 35.1 per cent, its worst result since Adenauer's first election in 1949. The FDP dropped slightly to 6.2 per cent.

The eastern vote turned against the CDU with a vengeance. Kohl's "unity effect" was gone and his party's vote dropped to just over a quarter. The PDS advanced from 4.4 per cent to 5.1 per cent, clearing the cut-off point to become a fully-fledged faction in the Bundestag. The ex-communists won four direct mandates in east Berlin and more than 20 per cent in all eastern states. The far right once again failed to live up to pre-poll fears. The DVU's surprise 12.9 per cent in the Saxony-Anhalt state election in April had spawned worried predictions about a new turn to the extremist fringe.[5] When the votes were counted, though, it ended up with only 1.2 per cent nation-wide. The Republicans hardly fared any better, winning 1.8 per cent, which came mainly from their support in the south.

The election threw overboard two political rules of thumb lingering from old West Germany. The first was that chancellors were not voted out of office but unseated by shifts in coalitions. Voters were traditionally too cautious and parties too powerful to allow strong swings to the left or right. Germans saw their readiness to vote out a chancellor as a step towards a more normal democracy. The election of a red–green coalition also meant a departure from the habit of governing from the centre. In 49 years, Bonn had known centre–right, centre–left and grand coalitions.[6] For the first time, a government was built on the left side of the parliamentary spectrum. Red–green, the reformers' dream in the last years of old West Germany, had finally come to pass as Germany was getting ready to say goodbye to Bonn.

❝ To emphasise the message of continuity, Schröder spared no praise for the man he had beaten ❞

Schröder went out of his way to reassure everybody that his alliance with the once-radical Greens would not mean a lurch to the left. This was especially true at the foreign ministry, where Fischer would soon be the new boss. "No one needs to have any worries, we will ensure continuity in foreign policy," the chancellor-elect told journalists a day after the election. "Germany is a member of NATO and will stay so, and has supported the process of NATO expansion to the east. This will stay that way, no ifs, ands or buts about it." He also buried any lingering remnants of euroscepticism, saying, "The euro must be a success." Schröder copied Kohl's example by flying to Paris soon after the election to reassure the French they were still Germany's preferred ally. He even found a way of encouraging a more active British role in Europe without making it sound as if he would play off London against Paris.

To emphasise the message of continuity, Schröder spared no praise for the man he had beaten. By chance, he was the host for the 1998 German Unity Day celebrations one week after the election, because Lower Saxony currently chaired the Bundesrat. At the main ceremony in Hanover's Market Square church, he interrupted his speech to turn to the front row where Kohl sat. "Mr Chancellor, I'd like once again to express my respect for the part you played in winning back our country's unity and constructing a united Europe," Schröder announced. "I am sure people in Germany will never forget this."

Kohl furtively wiped away a tear or two.

NOTES

1   Schröder had the last laugh. The company was privatised in June for a profit.

2   For more on Schröder, see Anda, Béla and Kleine, Rolf (1998) *Gerhard Schröder: Eine Biographie*. Berlin: Ullstein; and Herres, Volker and Waller, Klaus (1998) *Der Weg nach Oben: Gerhard Schröder, eine politische Biographie*. Munich: Econ.

3   In an off-the-record conversation with foreign correspondents that I attended in St Martin in the Palatinate on 9 June 1992, Kohl described Schröder as the best candidate the SPD had.

4   When Tietmeyer presented the Bundesbank report to the cabinet that day, the ministers were astonished to hear he was more concerned about overall debt ratios than the famous 3.0 per cent deficit hurdle. "Environment Minister Angela Merkel and Transport Minister Matthias Wissman looked at each other in amazement. The dispute about budget deficits of no more than 3.0 per cent had been nothing but an endless phantom debate." See *Die Zeit*, 29 April 1998.

5   For example, a *Sunday Times* (13 September 1998) headline on the German election read, "Neo-Nazi on brink of first seats in Bonn."

6   The only exception was Konrad Adenauer's third government, from 1957 to 1961, when the CDU had 50.2 per cent of the vote and didn't need the FDP to complete a majority.

17

THE PAST THAT WILL NOT PASS AWAY

WITH THE ELECTION OVER, GERMANY COULD LOOK FORWARD to more new starts than ever – a new chancellor, a new government, soon a new capital and a new century. The Kohl years had lasted so long that the change to a new generation was long overdue. Yet with all this future ahead of him, two of the first issues Gerhard Schröder tackled dealt with the past. He got to work promptly on arranging compensation for Nazi slave labourers, and his cultural aide Michael Naumann set out to redesign the planned Holocaust memorial in Berlin. It was ironic to see a chancellor with so little interest in history being confronted with it so soon. But this went with the job. Even more than half a century after the war, the past refused to pass away.[1]

Germany might now be a quite normal country, but it still had a very abnormal past. Over the decades, the Germans (especially in the west) had accepted responsibility for the Third Reich and the Holocaust and used them as constructive negative examples for their post-war democracy. The past eventually became, as French political scientist Dominique Moïsi put it, a "transcended tragedy". But it was still there, like a prominent scar that remained long after the original wound had healed. In its own way, the Holocaust became as much a part of the Germans' collective memory as it did the Jews'.

In the years after 1995, the deeper symbolism of the *Wrapped Reichstag* emerged. After the lightness and confidence represented by the covered edifice, history returned in the form of the grey old Reichstag. But it could be seen with a liberating distance that had not been possible before. It could be amplified and brought up to date, literally with a glass cupola, or figuratively with a new interpretation of old facts.

At the same time, the multimedia generation brought a fresh new perspective to the practice of remembering the past. By now so far removed from the Nazi era that they could hardly imagine what their country had been like back then, student-age Germans often turned out to be harsh and emotional judges of their grandparents' and great-grandparents' behaviour. They responded with interest to photographs and videos, including films set in the Third Reich that were often meant more as box office entertainment than as civics lessons. They turned away from the detailed analyses preferred by German historians, and welcomed simplified theories with a strong moral message. The speechless monument of shame that Helmut Kohl wanted as a Holocaust memorial said little to them; they wanted a memorial that would portray in direct and even shocking terms the true nature of the Nazi genocide. Instead of forgetting the past, younger Germans challenged their elders to find new ways of explaining it.

> 66 Student-age Germans wanted a memorial that would portray in direct and shocking terms the true nature of the Nazi genocide 99

SLAVE LABOUR, NAZI GOLD, FASCIST PRAYERBOOKS

No sector of German society was as fast and flexible as the business élite. As globalisation gathered pace, the country's leading manufacturers, carmakers, banks and publishers moved production abroad or merged with foreign counterparts. This trend reached new heights in 1998 when German firms went on a stunning buying spree around Europe and the United States. Daimler took over Chrysler Corporation, the third-largest carmaker in the USA. Volkswagen bought Britain's Rolls-Royce, adding that luxury line to a stable that already included Lamborghini and Bugatti. Bertelsmann, the media giant from little Gütersloh, became the world's largest English-language book publisher by buying Random House in the United States. Deutsche Bank, Germany's biggest, swallowed up Bankers Trust in New York to create the world's largest bank.

As German diplomats could have told these firms higher profiles bring higher stakes. Some could be harmless. When Daimler merged with Chrysler in May 1998, one American television station began its report on the megadeal by saying, "They were the company that built the staff cars Hitler drove – Chrysler is the company that builds the Jeeps that defeated him."[2] The mood turned serious a few months later, though, when Holocaust survivors in the United States filed several class action lawsuits charging German companies with using slave labourers during the war. The Nazi war economy would probably have collapsed as early as 1942 without the slave labourers, numbers of which were variously estimated to have been between 6 million and 12 million in all. About a million were believed to be still alive. The list of companies being called to task half a century later included some of Germany's best-known firms – carmakers Volkswagen, Daimler and BMW, electronics giant Siemens, the Krupp-Hoesch steel conglomerate, MAN engineering group, Leica camera company and the metals and chemicals group Degussa. Suddenly, the past threatened to do serious damage to German companies' sales and expansion abroad.

Bonn paid more than 104 billion marks in compensation to Nazi victims between 1953 and 1999, but the complex payments rules meant that thousands of elderly Jewish victims in Eastern Europe were still uncompensated. As international pressure to settle the issue mounted, German companies looked to Bonn, arguing that the state should help because the Nazis had ordered them to take on slave labour. "If you think I'm going to open up the state budget again, the answer is no," Kohl told them just before the 1998 election.[3] Schröder, who sat on Volkswagen's supervisory board because Lower Saxony owned 20 per cent of the company, took a different approach. Threatened with a lawsuit on behalf of Hungarian Jewish labourers, Volkswagen set up a 20 million mark compensation fund in mid-1998. The state supported the deal.

66 **Suddenly, the past threatened to do serious damage to German companies** 99

In late October, Schröder brought eight captains of corporate Germany together to consider a fund for the former slave labourers.[4] He wanted to shield German firms from endless lawsuits stemming from the past. Under his plan, companies would meet all outstanding claims by the year 2000 while Bonn would work out a deal for immunity from any further claims. After months of bitter negotiations among Jewish groups, victims' lawyers, German industry and government, a 10 billion mark fund was agreed in December 1999. Bonn had to contribute half the sum when firms balked at paying too much.

German corporations sometimes ended up shedding light on the darker chapters of their past themselves. Like tycoons commissioning oil portraits, many rich firms began in the mid-1980s commissioning corporate histories tracing their path to greatness. Deutsche Bank produced a 1,012-page tome in 1995 that overlooked its handling of Nazi gold.[5] During the war, the bank had traded in gold ingots smelted down from jewellery, wedding rings and teeth fillings plundered from concentration camp victims. As pressure rose on Swiss banks to reveal their dealings with the Nazis, Deutsche Bank chose five leading historians in December 1997 to take a second look. The review detailed the gold sales and concluded, "The Deutsche Bank dealt in victim gold and thus became implicated in the harvest of the Holocaust."[6] New York officials held up the Bankers Trust merger over this issue but approved it in May 1999, after determining that the bank was dealing properly with its past.

Volkswagen took a more critical look back with its 1,055-page official history *Volkswagen and its Workers in the Third Reich*, which recounted how it employed about 15,000 slave labourers who lived in dismal conditions while they built jeeps, tanks and rockets.[7] Bertelsmann, which began by printing prayer books and hymnals in 1835, found it hadn't done enough homework after buying Random House. Executives proudly told American audiences that Bertelsmann had been shut down by the Nazis. But research into its past showed it had stayed open and published pro-Nazi titles such as *Dr. Martin Luther's Little Catechism for the Man in Brown* and *With Bombs and Machine Guns over Poland*. The company promptly hired a leading Holocaust expert, Israeli historian Saul Friedländer, to prepare a fuller version of its past.

THE HOLOCAUST MEMORIAL

On taking office, Schröder also inherited a decade-long dispute over a planned Holocaust memorial in Berlin. A group of prominent Germans, including Willy Brandt and Daimler chairman Edzard Reuter, began a campaign in 1988 for a memorial to the murdered Jews of Europe. The project got a decisive boost in 1993 when Helmut Kohl picked the *Neue Wache* ("New Guard House") as the official memorial for the war dead in Berlin. The squat neo-classical building had been the Weimar Republic's memorial for dead of World War I, and East Germany's "Memorial to the Victims of Fascism and Militarism".

The chancellor wanted to install a copy of *Mother with Dead Son*, a touching 1937 pietà-style sculpture by the anti-war expressionist Käthe Kollwitz. There would be a dedication "To the Victims of War and

Tyranny" and a separate plaque to list Jews, gypsies, homosexuals and other groups that had been persecuted by the Nazis. But when these groups were approached for their approval, Jewish leader Ignatz Bubis asked the chancellor to back the Holocaust project in return. The memorial's dedication, an ambiguous 1950s western formula that could apply both to Auschwitz victims and their SS guards, would not be enough to commemorate the six million dead Jews. Kohl agreed to the deal ensuring the controversial memorial would be built. He even offered the organisers a large plot that before the fall of the Wall had been a no-man's-land near the Brandenburg Gate.

> 66 Kohl's choice was seen as a daunting edifice, meaningless in the media age 99

The design competition to find ideas for the plot was flooded with 528 entries. It opened several years of debate on whether it was even possible for art to communicate the enormity of the crime it was supposed to commemorate. Kohl rejected the winner, a vast overturned concrete gravestone, as "gigantomaniac", and eventually opted for a project to cover the lot with 2,700 symbolic gravestones. This attempt to build a silent memorial as big as the crime was his generation's way of dealing with the shame. Naumann saw Kohl's plan as "a suspension of guilt in art", a daunting edifice that would be meaningless in the media age. Audiovisual generations born decades after the building of the memorial would want pictures and sound to help them understand the issue. When the new government came in, he began redesigning the project to add a Holocaust documentation centre to the field of gravestones.

WEHRMACHT CRIMES

A tortured dispute running parallel to the Holocaust memorial debate underlined the power of the visual over the monumental. A chilling exhibition entitled "War of Extermination – Crimes of the Wehrmacht 1941–1944" challenged the widespread assumption that the average German soldier played no part in the Holocaust. The SS were usually blamed for the atrocities in the east. Once Russian archives opened after the fall of communism, however, a less flattering picture emerged. Photographs and letters that the Red Army confiscated from German POWs showed the Wehrmacht was often a willing accomplice to the Holocaust. It was clearly too involved to be absolved any more.

The findings might have gone unnoticed if the Hamburg-based Institute for Social Research had not put together the exhibition that began touring around major German cities in 1995. Panel after panel of grainy photographs showed soldiers rounding up Jews and partisans and organising their massacre. Soviet POWs were shown dead or dying. One series showed young soldiers laughing as they snipped off the beard of an old Orthodox Jew. Letters taken from captured soldiers left no doubt about the way the troops had thought. "Yesterday, we and the SS were generous. Every Jew we caught was shot. Today, it's different ... they're being beaten to death with clubs and spades," one soldier wrote home. The Institute estimated that the Wehrmacht systematically killed 1.5 million Jews – about as many as died in Auschwitz – in its campaigns through Serbia and the Soviet Union.

The exhibition caused an uproar that grew with each new opening. Conservative politicians often tried to ban the exhibition from public buildings in their cities. Two elderly men were arrested in Erfurt in mid-1996 for spray-painting the word "Lies" over the pictures. When it opened in Munich's City Hall in February 1997, about 6,000 protesters turned out to support or oppose it. Kept apart by steel barriers, left-wingers jeered, booed and threw eggs at neo-Nazis who paraded outside in protest, brandishing placards reading "We are proud of our grandfathers!" and waving the red-white-black flags of the far-right National Democratic Party. Once the opening protests were over, long lines gathered to see the exhibition.

The Institute's founder, Jan Philipp Reemtsma, said that younger visitors were especially interested in examining the past. "They are much more ready to get personally involved and to ask what actually happened ... I think more and more people realise that they can live better with the truth, even if it is distasteful or horrible, than with only a vague notion of what happened," he said.

THE WILLING LISTENERS

The stage at Hamburg's Kammerspiele theatre was set out as if for a wake. The backdrop was pitch black. The tables for the discussion round were draped in black. In the midst of five older men, Daniel Jonah Goldhagen, a young assistant professor from Harvard University, tried to explain the Holocaust to the Germans. His best-selling book *Hitler's Willing Executioners* claimed to have found the answer that five decades of scholarship had missed. Pre-1945 Germans, he argued, were gripped by a bloodthirsty "eliminationist anti-Semitism" that drove them to slaughter Jews. This essentially applied to all Germans of the period; the ones who did not kill Jews would have if given the chance. The racist Jew-hating normally ascribed to rabid Nazis was "integral to German political culture", Goldhagen wrote in his book. It was a "national project". Explaining his approach, he said, "The study of Germans and their anti-Semitism before and during the Nazi period must be approached as an anthropologist would a previously unencountered preliterate people and their beliefs."[8]

The Hamburg debate in September 1996 launched a promotion tour around Germany just as a translation of his book went on sale. German historians had torn apart his argument when it was published that spring in the United States. Goldhagen had sent back savage responses that were printed in the German press. But when Daniel entered the lions' den, he seemed like a different person. He was polite, even deferential to the older men brought out to criticise him. Looking younger than his 37 years, he had a wholesome charm that stood out among the panellists. His critics hesitated to attack this Holocaust surviver's son in person as they had on paper. When they made specific objections, he often conceded the point. Goldhagen spoke in relaxed English, sometimes breaking into halting German with a strong American accent. Despite his devastating portrait of Germans' past, he reassured his audience that today's citizens were nothing like those in the Third Reich.[9]

> 'I missed a clear explanation of how German anti-Semitism was unique,' said Oskar Shapiro

Many in the Hamburg audience were baffled. "I missed a clear explanation of how German anti-Semitism was supposed to be unique," said Oskar Shapiro, a retired local Jewish businessman who fled Germany in 1937 and fought in the British army against the Nazis. Goldhagen's subsequent appearances did little to shore up the sweeping statements meant to prove his single-factor thesis. No reasonable person doubted that anti-Semitism was rife in the Third Reich. But it was a daring logical leap to then say that *all* ordinary Germans would have killed Jews. Critics found it astonishing that what claimed to be a thorough academic study did not compare anti-Semitism in pre-Hitler Germany with prejudice against Jews elsewhere in Europe at the time. Major factors in the rise of Nazism, such as the defeat in World War I, were also passed over quickly. When critics tried to pin this down, Goldhagen chided them for misunderstanding his argument or overlooking an obscure footnote.[10]

Despite all that, the ten-day book tour turned out to be what *Die Zeit* called a "triumphal procession". For his last stop in Munich, organisers had to hire a symphony hall with 2,500 seats to meet the unexpected demand. Sales of his book soared. Several discussions were broadcast in full on German television. Why were Germans giving so much attention to a 461-page book that *The Economist* called "a painfully bad read"?[11] Why, as columnist Josef Joffe asked, were there so many "willing listeners?"

Guido Knopp, the ZDF television historian who moderated two of the public debates, said the young Germans who predominated in the audiences appreciated the moral indignation Goldhagen brought to the subject. "I had the impression that individual points and criticisms didn't really interest them," he said. "They saw a young American come along and give his opinion to these old guys who had been trying to fool them all along about how it had been ... The younger part of the audience was quite ready to be unfair, to simplify things and say, 'Well, you old guys, you didn't stop that. You're to blame that we have to carry this legacy (of the Holocaust) around with us. How are we supposed to deal with this? We have to find out.'

> 66 My God, a bit of morality in dealing with our history is not such a bad thing, after all 99

"It is almost a kind of new generational conflict that threatens to break out over an issue like this. The more the older generation dies off and younger people step into their shoes, the stronger this moralistic impulse will be. It *is* unfair. But, my God, a bit of morality in dealing with our history is not such a bad thing after all."[12]

As if to counter Goldhagen's contested thesis, a posthumously published diary of one German Jew's life under the swastika competed with *Hitler's Willing Executioners* on the bestseller list. Victor Klemperer was a pensioned professor of Romance languages who stayed in Dresden with his Christian wife until it was too late to leave. His two-volume, 1,700-page diary *I Will Bear Witness To The End*, published without much fanfare in late 1995, turned out to be a treasure chest of insight into what it was like to be a Jew during the Third Reich. Reviewers hailed it as a unique historical document, comparable to *The Diary of Anne Frank*. The impression Klemperer gives of the majority of Germans during the Third Reich is one of fear, indifference and cold-heartedness. "The most unsolvable but decisive puzzle is the popular mood. What do they think?" he wrote in February 1940. "*Vox populi* collapses into countless *voces populi* ... I often ask myself where the wild anti-Semitism is hiding. For myself,

I often meet with a lot of sympathy, people help me, but of course fearfully."[13] While anyone in power tormented Jews, many other people simply looked away or did not see what was happening. The diary offers no neat theory about the Holocaust, but a rich tapestry of everyday episodes that defy a single explanation. After its publishing success, the diary was made into a 13-part German television series and was translated into English.

Other films set in the Third Reich helped show aspects of life that had not been highlighted before. The 1998 box-office musical hit *Comedian Harmonists* told the story of the six-man singing group that became the "supergroup" of the late 1920s and early 1930s. Like the Fred Astaire and Ginger Rogers movies, their concerts – always flawless performances with dinner jackets and perfect harmonies – helped Germans forget for a moment the grim Depression years. But three of the group were Jews and the Nazis finally drove them apart in 1935. In its own breezy way, the film put a face and a story on one of the tragedies of the Third Reich. *Aimée and Jaguar* told the story of two German lesbians, one the wife of a soldier and the other a Jew, in wartime Berlin. It opened the 1999 Berlin film festival, which showed markedly more films about the Nazi era than ever before.

Knopp said the more emotional and visually-oriented approach to the past could be a reaction to the ponderous documentaries on the Third Reich and war period that were used to teach earlier generations. He was not sure whether the more emotional tone that younger people preferred did justice to the facts. "But we will have to deal with this new interest," he said. "There is a new virulence in discussions about the Nazi period and issues stemming from it. This discussion will not go away. It won't be like in 1995, when we thought it would fade away. On the contrary. That's probably one of the most important lessons we can learn from this discussion."[14]

NOTES

1 This is not to say the new leaders with no personal memory of the war were untouched by it. Schröder grew up without a father because his was killed in battle in 1944 just before his birth. Fischer's family were ethnic Germans living near Budapest who were expelled after the war. Joschka is the Hungarian diminutive for his first name, Joseph.

2 NBC evening news reporting the Daimler–Chrysler merger, as quoted in the *Daily Telegraph*, 23 May 1998.

3 *Süddeutsche Zeitung*, 11 September 1998.

4   Board chairmen or leading managers of Siemens, VW, Daimler-Benz, BMW, Thyssen-Krupp, BASF, Deutsche Bank and Dresdner Bank attended the closed-door meeting. See *Süddeutsche Zeitung*, 22 October 1998.

5   *Die Deutsche Bank 1870–1995* (Munich: Verlag C.H. Beck, 1995), written by historians Lother Gall, Gerald D. Feldman, Harold James, Carl-Ludwig Holtfrerich and Hans E. Büschgen.

6   This follow-up report was prepared by historians Avraham Barkai (Jerusalem), Gerald D. Feldman (Berkeley), Professor Lothar Gall (Frankfurt am Main), Professor Harold James (Princeton) and Dr Jonathan Steinberg (Cambridge). See *Die Deutsche Bank und ihre Goldtransaktionen während des Zweiten Weltkrieges*. Munich: Verlag C.H. Beck, 1999.

7   Mommsen, Hans and Grieger, Manfred (1996) *Das Volkswagenwerk und seine Arbeiter im Dritten Reich*. Düsseldorf: Econ Verlag.

8   Goldhagen, Daniel Jonah (1996) *Hitler's Willing Executioners: Ordinary Germans and the Holocaust*. New York: Alfred A. Knopf, page 45.

9   He stated this in the introduction to the German edition of the book. In the original US edition, this argument appears in footnote 53 on page 593. For the German introduction, see *Hitlers willige Vollstrecker: Ganz normale Deutsche und der Holocaust*. Berlin: Siedler Verlag, 1996, page 12.

10   For a detailed critique of his thesis, see Finkelstein, Norman G. and Birn Bettina, Ruth Bettina (1998) *A Nation on Trial: The Goldhagen Thesis and Historical Truth*. New York: Metropolitan Books.

11   See its review in the 20 July 1996 edition.

12   Conversation with the author, 21 November 1996.

13   Klemperer, Victor (1995) *Ich will Zeugnis ablegen bis zum letzten*. Berlin: Aufbau-Verlag, Volume II, pages 512–13.

14   Conversation with the author, 21 November 1996.

18

RED–GREEN IN POWER

CHANCELLOR OF BUSINESS ... CHANCELLOR OF BROKEN PROMISES ...
Comrade of the Bosses ... Boss of the Comrades ... Cashmere Chancellor ...
War Chancellor ... In his first 12 months in office, Gerhard Schröder had
more titles than the year had seasons. He began as the fresh new face,
presided over chaos, led the country in war, flirted with the "Third Way"
and rescued jobs with good old-fashioned state intervention. He out-
foxed the darling of the SPD and became the most unlikely chairman his
party had ever seen. He looked towards Britain and aligned with France.
After a year of this, he was in a stronger position than ever, a success not
wholly of his own making.

The first year of Schröder's "red–green" government was a roller coaster
ride into the new political landscape of the Berlin Republic. On the main
foreign policy issue – Germany's continued commitment to the
European Union and NATO – the new chancellor followed in Helmut
Kohl's footsteps. Foreign Minister Joschka Fischer stressed continuity so
much that he took to speaking in the bland communiqué language
known in Bonn as "Genscherese". On the economic front, Schröder
bounced back and forth between traditional Social Democratic policies
and programmes that only business could applaud. His political management was so uneven that the SPD lost in every big election it contested.

As the government settled into its new quarters in the autumn of 1999, Schröder was being written off as a lame duck who might not make it until the next election in 2002. By the time he reached New Year, he was sitting firmly in the saddle. Just where he stood was not exactly clear, but he showed he deserved another title that might outlive all the others – *Comeback Kid*.

WHERE'S SCHRÖDER?

The new government spent its first few months trying to sort out who had actually won the election. Schröder quickly slipped into the role of Chancellor, speaking reassuringly about his plans and travelling to foreign capitals for his introductory visits. Although he was supposed to be finance minister, Lafontaine acted from the start as a "shadow chancellor" who would actually run the show. He had played loyal second fiddle to Schröder all year, channelling his enormous ambition towards the goal of an SPD victory. Now it was payback time.

The Napoleon from the Saar wasted no time in clearing his path of potential rivals. His first target was Rudolf Scharping, whom he pushed out of his post as SPD parliamentary leader and shunted over to the defence ministry. Lafontaine then neatly outmanoeuvred Jost Stollmann, the symbol of Schröder's "New Centre," by switching key departments from the economics ministry to the finance ministry. When Stollmann was told his ministry was being asset-stripped, he refused to take up the post. Left without an economics minister on the day he was supposed to announce his cabinet, Schröder quickly called another advisor to offer him the job. Werner Müller was still in his bathrobe at home when the telephone rang. He agreed at once, got dressed and rushed off to Bonn to meet the press.

> ❝ Lafontaine had played loyal second fiddle to Schröder all year ... Now it was payback time ❞

While he was shaping Schröder's cabinet, Lafontaine also began his assault on economic orthodoxy. The Jesuit-educated chairman was a staunch neo-Keynesian convinced that the state had to spend more to stimulate demand in the economy, even if that meant going further into dept. He thought the conventional economic approach of the 1990s, which focused on cutting state spending, deficits and taxes to free up capital for investment, was a mistaken right-wing policy to help the rich. Although both Schröder and the Greens wanted to slash the heavy tax burden stifling job creation in Germany, Lafontaine made sure the tax cut package was modest. At the same time, the Government would raise child benefits and tax breaks for families, and roll back the pension reform that Kohl's government had ordered.

The day after the election, Lafontaine began exhorting the Bundesbank to cut interest rates to boost domestic demand. Decrying international currency markets as a "global casino", he also advocated target zones for the world's major currencies. The Bundesbank flatly opposed both ideas, and Washington quickly rejected the currency idea out of hand. When France's Socialist Finance Minister Dominique Strauss-Kahn – a presumed ally – also demurred, Lafontaine had to quietly back down. By contrast, his campaign to harmonise taxes in Europe – the policy that earned him the title "the most dangerous man in Europe" from the London tabloid, the *Sun* – enjoyed wide support in Germany and among some EU partners.

The coalition broke new ground by agreeing to start shutting down Germany's 19 nuclear plants, which provided about a third of Germany's power. Schröder made sure, however, that Bonn would first hold round table talks with the energy utilities to seek consensus on a phase-out. Although the Green left-winger Jürgen Trittin would be environment minister, he would have to share responsibility for the issue with the economics minister. Müller was a former power utility executive who knew the nuclear issue as well if not better than Trittin himself.

This was no *Neue Mitte* but a "New Muddle". This "New Centre" looked more like an updated version of the old SPD, a blueprint for the Bonn Republic Lafontaine would have run if he had won in 1990. "I didn't fail," the sidelined Stollmann said after the negotiations. "The failures were the ones in the SPD who wanted to move towards the New Centre." The press was merciless. *Der Spiegel* printed a cover showing Schröder's piercing blue eyes gazing out from the clouds over the headline "Where is Schröder?"[1]

Schröder's inaugural speech in the Bundestag on 10 November was tellingly vague on the economic issues he had made the centrepiece of his campaign. Once Lafontaine had tied his hands, the best he had to say for the disappointing tax reform reached in the coalition talks was that it was a "first step". The chancellor made employment his top priority and pledged to reverse Kohl's cuts in pensions, sick pay and job protection laws. He announced a new "Alliance for Jobs" as "a permanent instrument to fight unemployment", but gave few details.

More striking was Schröder's stress on the new generation of Germans in power. "More and more, our country is being led by a generation that had no direct experience of World War II ... Many of us were in the protest movements of the 1970s and 1980s. The former civil rights groups in East Germany, which with the East German Social Democrats led the peaceful revolution, are part of this government. This generation stands in the tradition of civic responsibility and civil courage.

"Our democracy is no longer a tender plant, but a strong tree. With the help of friends and allies, the Germans have been able to achieve unification in peace and self-determination ... Today we are democrats and Europeans not because we have to be, but because we want to be."

The same self-confidence shone through in the one real reform that Schröder announced. In a few sentences, the chancellor brushed aside years of embarrassing hair-splitting about the so-called foreigners in Germany. "Reality shows us that Germany has seen an irreversible immigration in the past few decades. We invited the people who came here in the 1950s. And we say today to these fellow citizens living among us that they are not strangers. In fact, the strangers are the ones who preach racial hatred. We don't want that. We will respond to these deluded minorities with an active policy of integration. Immigrants who work here, pay their taxes and respect the law have been told far too long that they are only 'guests'. They have long since become fellow citizens in Germany. So this government will develop a modern citizenship law. It will ensure that those who live here permanently, and their children who are born here, can have full citizenship. Nobody who wants to become a German citizen will have to give up or deny his foreign roots. So we will also allow dual citizenship."

> 66 Germany would finally send a convincing signal to its racists and neo-Nazis 99

That one passage made up for the rest of the speech. A chancellor had finally admitted that decades of immigration had changed Germany. The state would finally stop labelling as "foreign" the tens of thousands who were born in the country, educated in its schools and who worked in its factories and offices. Germany would finally send a convincing signal to its racists and neo-Nazis that these people were not second-class citizens. No amount of well-meaning speeches praising "our foreign compatriots" could erase this as long as the law did not recognise them as equals. More than anything else, the new citisenship law would be the emblematic reform of the red–green government.

LIFE AFTER HELMUT

The CDU had a hard time weaning itself from the father figure of Helmut Kohl. After 25 years under his leadership, the party had become a well-oiled *Kanzlerwahlverein* ("elect-the-chancellor club"). It had focused its energy on supporting the chancellor and accepted the discipline and taboos that went with that. The party stood for the pragmatic centre-right and, as Kohl liked to say, "The centre is where I am." For Kohl, the party was not an organisation but an extended family. His protégés were favourite nephews and nieces who were expected to show respect to the *pater familias*. Ingrates were sidelined, sometimes disinherited. Journalists searching for the CDU soul only had to attend the members' dinner at each annual congress: here, Kohl held court, greeted delegate after delegate by name and ended the evening by telling the organist which of his favourite Glen Miller hits to play.

The old order began to collapse on election night with Kohl's resignation as party chairman. His CSU sidekick Theo Waigel stepped down the next day and the heads of several veteran regional barons rolled. The forty-something generation of "wild youngsters" began speaking up more openly than ever before. "We need a dramatic change of generation," said Hamburg CDU leader Ole von Beust. But that did not happen. Schäuble was duly elected party chairman in November with Angela Merkel, the unassuming Protestant pastor's daughter who had quietly become the CDU's leading *Ossi*, chosen as CDU general secretary. After his misty-eyed farewell to a party congress in Bonn, delegates crowded around Kohl to have him autograph books, photographs and coffee cups.

With a state election looming in Hesse in February, Schäuble promptly went on the offensive against the SPD. The plan to allow dual citizenship, he argued, was a Trojan horse that "makes people envious of these special Germans with a discount price". The party launched its petition campaign against the government's reform. It was an immediate hit, gathering 35,000 signatures on the first weekend. Over the next few months, about a million citizens signed the appeal. At the same time, the government revealed that fewer than 100,000 asylum-seekers had come to Germany in 1998, a third of them ethnic Albanians fleeing Serbian repression in Kosovo. The 1993 tightening of the asylum law had slowly brought the mass influx under control.[2]

With disappointment at Schröder's government spreading, the petition was just what the opposition needed to carry it to victory. Hesse's red–green coalition fell in the February election, and the CDU came back to power with the FDP. Losing a key state election so soon after taking office was doubly disastrous for Schröder. He failed the first test of Red–Green's popularity. On top of that, the change in Hesse robbed the SPD of its majority in the Bundesrat. The CDU could now delay or block SPD tax and social reform bills, just as the SPD did to Kohl for years.

The Hesse setback also meant the government had to water down its main reform. The law that was finally passed dropped the idea of unconditional dual citizenship, which would have allowed about 4 million resident foreigners to become German citizens with little difficulty or delay. Foreigners could become citizens after living in Germany for eight years, rather than 15 as before, but had to give up their earlier passport. Children born in Germany of resident foreign parents would enjoy dual citizenship from birth, but had to choose one by the age of 23. The reform lost its sharp edge, but it was still a major step forward in breaking down the ethnic definition of German citizenship.

> 66 It was a departure worthy of a diva. Without warning, the second most powerful man in Bonn was gone 99

OSKAR QUITS

Fischer was jogging along the Rhine on 11 March when a bodyguard handed him a portable telephone. Schröder was on the line, asking him to come to his office immediately. Minutes later, still sweating in his shorts and baseball cap, Fischer sat down in the chancellery for the shock. "Oskar has resigned from all his offices," the chancellor said. "All of them?" Fischer asked. "Yes."[3]

As they met, Lafontaine was speeding down the autobahn on his way home to Saarbrücken. He refused to take Schröder's call to his car phone. There was nothing left to discuss, Lafontaine told the chancellor's secretary. It was a departure worthy of a diva. Without warning, the second most powerful man in Bonn was gone.

It is hard to recall any democratically elected politician whose resignation was so well received at home and abroad. Apart from some stunned SPD left-wingers and Greens, few in Bonn stood up to defend him. Financial markets were euphoric. Within minutes of the news hitting dealers' screens, the ailing euro, which had been steadily sliding since its launch in January, jumped in value by two cents to $1.10. When the

Frankfurt stock exchange opened the next morning, the index surged by six per cent in giddy trading. Shares in insurance and utility companies, the main targets for Lafontaine's tax plans, soared by over 10 per cent. The euro's jump showed just how much his policies had weighed on the new currency. The *Financial Times* called his resignation "a seismic event in the birth of the single European currency".[4]

Lafontaine's patience had snapped after a dressing down from Schröder in the cabinet the previous day. The chancellor had told him and the Greens to stop harassing the business sector with new taxes and plans to shut down nuclear power plants. "What's happening here is unique in the world – the whole business sector is wary of investing and creating jobs," he said. "There is a point at which I won't take responsibility for policies like this any more."[5] When he finally spoke, after three silent days at home, Lafontaine betrayed his bitterness at the failure of his shadow chancellor plan. "The reason for my resignation was the poor teamwork we have shown in the past few months. We can't work successfully without good teamwork," he complained. His parting words for the SPD were classic Oskar: "There's one thing it must not forget. The heart is not yet traded on the stock market. It has a home. It beats on the left."[6]

Ironically, Lafontaine's departure paved the way for the lower interest rate he had so loudly demanded. The European Central Bank, concerned about proving its independence, could hardly cut rates without seeming to be caving in to his browbeating. A month after he quit, the bank surprised the markets by cutting interest rates by 0.5 per cent to 2.5 per cent. It was a telling end to the Lafontaine drama, showing how central a role the twists and turns of German domestic politics could influence the international value of the euro.

GERMANS AS LIBERATORS

The next few weeks showed just how timely Lafontaine's departure was. The looming war in Kosovo overshadowed all other concerns in Bonn. The red–green government had pledged from the start to join its NATO allies if they needed to use force to stop Slobodan Milošević. With Germany holding the EU presidency in the first half of 1999, Schröder and Fischer were on the front line of the Western response to the ethnic cleansing in Kosovo. Public opinion was torn; polls showed that 60 per cent opposed the bombing and 60 per cent wanted Germany to act with its allies. Only Lafontaine, who had expressed grave doubts about the

Kosovo mission, had the anti-war credentials, political clout and rhetorical gifts to rally the doubters against the war. But he was gone.

By contrast, Schröder and Fischer never left any doubt about their support for a Kosovo mission. As the countdown to war dragged on, Schröder kept up a square-jawed determination oddly missing in other policies. In the whirlwind of NATO, EU and bilateral consultations lasting until June, he acted every bit the resolute *Kriegskanzler* ("War Chancellor"). It was a new role for the man the press called the "Chaos Chancellor" or the "Cashmere Chancellor" (when he had posed in expensive suits for a men's fashion magazine). "We received solidarity from our partners in difficult times, and we are duty-bound to show solidarity at other times," Schröder told the delegates at an emergency congress in April. "The response, especially from us Germans, must be clear – deportations, murder and expulsion must never be allowed again." When the delegates elected Schröder as their new chairman, the man who never cared much for his own party was in control. He could finally step out of Lafontaine's shadow.

> 66 Protest posters depicted Fischer and Schröder as modern-day Hitlers 99

Fischer had more trouble getting his party to accept olive green. "This is the first time in this century that Germany is on the right side," he repeatedly told his critics. "Kosovo is the first war in which the united Europe stands up against the nationalist Europe of the past." In their frequent briefings, he and Defence Minister Rudolf Scharping portrayed the Serbs as latter-day Nazis repeating the atrocities of the SS. The more mistakes NATO raids made, such as bombing the Chinese embassy in Belgrade, the stronger their statements became.

The Bielefeld sports hall where the Greens met in May looked more like a nuclear plant picketed by ecologists than a place for a party congress. Coils of barbed wire and hundreds of riot police surrounded the building. Protest posters depicted Fischer and Schröder as modern-day Hitlers. At the speakers' podium, delegates hooted "war mongers!" at the party leadership. Suddenly Fischer, sitting awaiting his turn to speak, bent over clutching his right ear in pain. A paint bomb had hit him on the head, perforating his ear drum. With red paint splattered on his hair and face and down his grey suit, he sat stunned for minutes. "Joschka Goebbels! Joschka Goebbels!" echoed from the back of the hall.

"I'm not going to stop, I won't do you that favour!" Fischer bellowed when he finally began his speech. He recalled the party's rage at neo-Nazi attacks on Turks in Germany and asked why racist killings in another European country were any different. "No more war, no more Auschwitz, no more genocide, no more fascism. All that goes together for me," he declared. The delegates ended by urging him to seek a cease-fire and resume negotiations for peace.

The rapturous welcome the anxious troops got in Prizren was the last thing they expected. Rumbling into the western Kosovo city on 13 June after Belgrade had capitulated to the NATO bombs, the first German soldiers in the region since Hitler's Wehrmacht army were hailed as liberators. Delirious crowds threw flowers as the olive-green columns arrived, and onlookers chanted *"Deutschland! Deutschland!"* Soon, smiling sergeants sported flowers that women had stuffed into their flak jackets. Soldiers hoisted children up on to their tanks or posed with teenagers. "I didn't expect this at all," a bewildered young captain muttered as he surveyed the celebrations in the crowded square. "We thought they would be afraid, maybe a bit reserved, even though they know we are coming to bring peace." Eset Mati, a Kosovar Albanian whose furniture store was burned down by Serbs when the NATO bombing began, was not reserved at all. "Fifty years ago, the Germans were the occupiers here," he said amid the celebrations. "It's good they come here fifty years later as the liberators."

The party didn't last long. When they ventured beyond Prizren, the soldiers saw at first hand what "ethnic cleansing" meant. They found charred corpses littering burned-out farmhouses and lifeless bodies scattered in the fields. Struggling to express their feelings, several soldiers muttered, "just like the Nazis."

The Bundeswehr's debut at the front was a success, but it felt odd saying so. The media searched for parallels from the past, even noting that the troops" local radio played the World War II hit, "Lili Marlene". On a visit in July, Schröder reminded the troops that their mission could still not erase what the Nazis had done in the Balkans. "But it can help to give the people a picture of a peaceful Germany," he said. "German soldiers here are showing a Germany always hoped for in this region but not seen until now."

EUROPE AGAIN

The Kosovo campaign was such a success that it overshadowed Schröder's difficult debut on the diplomatic scene. The new chancellor had started off by frightening the neighbours with thick dollops of "German assertiveness". In a campaign-style speech in December, he said one of his goals for the six months was to end Bonn's "chequebook diplomacy" in Brussels. Bonn paid 22 billion marks more to the EU than it got back in subsidies, far more than any other member. "The Germans pay more than half the money that's squandered in Europe," he thundered. "Crises are solved by getting the Germans to pay the bill – this is now going to stop." Schröder blamed Kohl for raising Bonn's EU bill at the Edinburgh summit in 1992. "I have to see how I can reduce this sum that made Kohl into the great European," he said.

Schröder emerged from the usual EU horse-trading with a barely disguised defeat. His drive to slash through the EU budget jungle got caught in a thicket of other countries' interests. France, the main beneficiary of the extensive Common Agricultural Policy subsidies, stonewalled until he dropped his idea to have member states pay more for farm support. The "poor four" – Spain, Portugal, Ireland and Greece – rejected Bonn's idea of cutting the "cohesion funds" they got. Britain opposed any tampering with the budget rebate it got under Margaret Thatcher. As the late-March EU summit to approve the "Agenda 2000" budget drew near, Schröder began to give in. With the defeat in Hesse, Lafontaine's departure and the looming war in Kosovo, he could not afford a failure at the Berlin summit.

> 66 'The Germans pay more than half the money that's squandered in Europe,' Schröder thundered 99

When agreement was reached on 26 March after a night of bargaining, Germany emerged as the main loser. Its contributions would be reduced only slightly over time. This was the best it could get if it wanted to reach a compromise and have the budget approved. Defending the compromise, a bleary-eyed Fischer told the Bundestag only hours later, "Last night, it became clear to me for the first time – and I'm saying this as a convinced European, maybe Dr Kohl can confirm this from his wide experience – that this Europe will fall apart if our country does not live up to its leadership duty in Europe."

"That was what we told you for 16 years!" Kohl called out from the opposition benches.

THE THIRD WAY

With Lafontaine gone and the war won, Schröder turned his attention to the "New Centre". Unemployment was still over 10 per cent and growth was stuck at 1.5 per cent, while other European economies were picking up. Economists were blaming the euro's continued slide on Germany's stagnation. To underline his will to reform, he joined Tony Blair in early

June to unveil a joint "Third Way" manifesto that advocated "a new supply-side agenda for the left". It championed deregulation and corporate tax cuts. Social security systems had to be streamlined and "workfare" programmes launched to get the unemployed off the dole. The blueprint for a brave new world of deregulation reflected post-Thatcherite Britain more than the softer German welfare state. Trying to apply this to Germany was a bold step, but Schröder seemed determined to take the lead.

Voters did not want to follow. Five days after the manifesto, the red–green government took a drubbing at the European Parliament election. Undeterred, the new finance minister, Hans Eichel, presented a budget that cut spending and trimmed pensions to allow the 30 billion marks of tax cuts that Lafontaine had refused to accept. "It would have been right to pursue Eichel's financial policies from the start," Schröder admitted in July.

The electoral calendar came up with another of its occasional steeplechase courses – five state elections in as many weeks – and the SPD stumbled at all the hurdles. The CDU won the state election in Saarland on 5 September, ending 14 years of SPD rule there. The CDU stole so many votes from Brandenburg's SPD premier Manfred Stolpe that the same day he had to take them into the state government on Potsdam. The next weekend, the CDU swept to an absolute majority in Thuringia, where the SPD ended third behind the PDS. CDU premier "King Kurt" Biedenkopf trounced the SPD the next weekend in Saxony, where the PDS again came in second. The final humiliation came in Berlin on 10 October, where the SPD plunged to 22 per cent, its worst result since the war. "Sometimes during the autumn, we didn't know whether we'd make it to the end of the legislative period," Eichel later remarked. "We were not far away from losing power. We had already admitted that to ourselves privately."[7]

Unable to turn his party around as quickly as he hoped, a chastened Schröder drifted back to more orthodox Social Democratic positions. The flirt with Blair's Third Way cooled markedly and the chancellor set to work on repairing his brittle relations with the more traditional socialist Lionel Jospin. The two met in Strasbourg in mid-October to announce the merger of the aerospace companies Dasa and Aerospatiale in a huge Franco-German deal. He spoke out for traditional German consensus management in mid-November when the British mobile phone company Vodafone AirTouch made a hostile takeover bid for Mannesmann.

His real chance came soon afterwards when hundreds of construction workers marched through Frankfurt to demand their bankrupt company be bailed out. The 150-year-old firm Philipp Holzmann AG was the country's largest builder, an industrial landmark that had played a key role in rebuilding West Germany after the war and Berlin after the Wall fell. When its creditor banks refused to rescue it, 28,000 jobs seemed doomed. Schröder dashed to Frankfurt and threw enough state money into the rescue package to secure the banks' support. "Dear friends, we've made it!" he announced to a cheering crowd of workers in hard hats and fluorescent jackets. "We're all fighting for jobs and can't afford to lose a single one without a struggle." The euro slipped on the news of the deal, prompting a rare criticism from ECB head Wim Duisenberg himself, but this was now music to Schröder's ears.

> ❝ The 'comrade of the bosses' made way for the 'boss of the comrades' ❞

The "comrade of the bosses" made way for the "boss of the comrades". The SPD's annual congress in December greeted him like a prodigal son. Amid the Lafontaine-style rhetoric he now used, he slipped in the news that the austerity programme would still go ahead. But this was a detail now. The chameleon had finally found the reddish tinge the party liked.

Schröder's last surprise of the year was a time bomb that could reform Germany more quickly and deeply than anything discussed to date. On 21 December, he and Eichel unveiled a plan to accelerate corporate and personal tax cuts. The chancellor presented this as a boost for low and medium income families.

Two days later, when economists had read the fine print, the Frankfurt stock exchange erupted; financial stocks soared by up to 17 per cent. Among the proposals was one to eliminate a tax of up to 50 per cent on profits from sales of the cross-holdings that form the backbone of corporate Germany. Banks and insurance companies traditionally have large holdings in a wide variety of companies. Faced with such high taxes if they sold them off, most preferred to keep even underperforming stakes on their books. Tearing away that hurdle would free German companies to streamline, modernize and merge with unimagined speed. The entrepreneur culture Schröder praised in his "Third Way" manifesto with Blair would hit Germany faster than anyone expected. "That would be the death of Germany Inc.," an official at one insurance company said. "We're in shock because we didn't ask for a change of this magnitude."

NOTES

1   *Der Spiegel*, 9 November 1998.

2   Although opposed to dual citizenship for non-Germans, the Christian Democrats supported it for ethnic Germans abroad. About 500,000 ethnic Germans still live in the Polish region of Silesia and tens of thousands of them now have two passports.

3   *Der Spiegel*, 4 October 1999.

4   *Financial Times*, 12 March 1999.

5   The leaked reports appeared on 11 March in pro-Schröder papers of the Springer chain – *Bild*, *Die Welt* and *Berliner Morgenpost*.

6   For Lafontaine's version of events, see his book *Das Herz schlägt links*. Munich: Econ Verlag, 1999.

7   *Stern*, 30 December 1999.

19

THE BERLIN REPUBLIC

NOVEMBER 1999. IT WAS TIME TO LOOK BACK, it was time to look forward. Surveying the ten years just passed, Germans had to pinch themselves to make sure it was not all a dream. The Wall was gone. Communism was finished. Their homeland was united. There had been times during the rough passage when it looked like it could all go wrong. But as the months and years passed, the Germans and their neighbours saw that their worst fears had not come true. Germany had respected and even strengthened the interlocking partnerships that anchored it in a democratic Europe. The sirens of nationalism and hatred had called but remarkably few had responded. Unlike the Reich with enemies all around, the reunited state was now "encircled by friends". The unification process had gone through shocks and strains, especially in the east, but the Federal Republic had proved it was up to the challenge. There had been a change of government, a change of generation and an historic move back to the old capital. By the time the tenth anniversary of the Wall's fall came around, Berlin stood out more as a window on Germany's dynamic future than a reflection of its brooding past.

There was so much reassuring continuity amid the change that it seemed only natural that Helmut Kohl stole centre stage at the anniversary ceremonies. After keeping a low profile following his defeat, the former chancellor suddenly appeared daily in newspaper interviews and on television. His moving address at the Reichstag ceremony on 9 November upstaged fellow speakers Gerhard Schröder, Joachim Gauck, George Bush and Mikhail Gorbachev. As he strolled by the Brandenburg Gate that evening, shouts of *"Helmut! Helmut!"* rose up from the crowd. Opinion polls rated him more popular than his hapless successor and put the CDU far ahead of the SPD. With the 1998 vote looking like a fluke, interviewers began asking if he would run again in 2002. Kohl chuckled and ducked the question, but always made sure to drop remarks such as: "Wherever I go, I'm approached on the street and people tell me: 'We're so sorry that you left office.'"

Three weeks later, Kohl's star went into an eclipse that turned darker with every week that passed. When a campaign finance scandal exposed the sleazy side of the CDU, the former chancellor had to admit he had kept a secret slush fund for years. After that shock, the petty and vindictive side to the long-admired chancellor of German unity was suddenly on full public view. Kohl brazenly denied he had broken any law, even though he himself had brought in the tough party financing rules he flouted. He refused to name his donors, as the law required, despite desperate pleas from CDU leaders. Even worse, he defiantly held rallies with his hard-core fans to show he still had support within the party. The effect of Kohl's scorched earth defence on the CDU was disastrous and the party went into a tailspin.

Kohl's finance scandal was the final nail in the coffin of the Bonn Republic. While the move to Berlin had changed much of the atmospherics of German politics, many of the reflexes of the old *Parteienstaat* ("party state") were still clinging to life within the CDU. The undisputed leader, the concentration of power, the back-room deals and shady finances –

> 66 Kohl's star went into an eclipse that turned darker with every week that passed 99

much of the Bonn style had survived even after Kohl had nominally gone. But the once-solid electoral blocs were already wobbling and undecided voters were on the rise. The growing influence of globalised markets was undermining the close ties between government, business and trade unions. The print and broadcast media, once rich with a heavy diet of grey political news, were turning more to scandal and "infotainment". By toppling the old-style CDU, the last bastion of the Bonn era, the Kohl scandal actually accelerated the trends that would characterise the Berlin Republic. Finally emerging from Kohl's shadow, the united Germany of the twenty-first century turned out to be more open, lively and confident than any of the united or divided states it saw in the century before.

BURYING THE BONN REPUBLIC

After 25 years as chairman, Kohl was so much a part of the CDU that neither he nor many of its members could really imagine it without him.
Even out of office, the former chancellor was such a towering figure that
younger leaders still laboured under his shadow. Wolfgang Schäuble and
his new general secretary Angela Merkel could hardly establish their own
authority while Kohl the *Überkanzler* (super-chancellor) kept pulling the
strings behind the scenes. To his contacts at home and abroad, the
former chancellor made it clear he thought the new CDU chief was not
up to the job. Officials in the party headquarters, especially the few dealing with his slush funds, kept wheeling and dealing behind the new
leaders' backs. The fresh start that the "wild youngsters" had proclaimed
so loudly after the 1998 defeat never really came about.

This success at preserving power finally led to his downfall. Kohl's return
to centre stage in November 1999 looked so well organised that many
suspected it was a trial balloon for a comeback. TV interviewers were not
the only ones asking the question that the ex-chancellor liked to duck.
Even former senior aides speculated privately that *der Dicke* ("the fat
man") might run again. At the same time, news of a mysterious 1 million
mark contribution kept in a secret CDU bank account was beginning to
seriously embarrass the party. Investigators suspected the money was a
bribe, either as part of a tank deal for Saudi Arabia or from the French oil
company Elf Aquitaine after it bought the east German chemical plant at
Leuna. Rumour had it that the ex-chancellor was somehow involved.

As all this speculation mounted, one of Kohl's most prominent victims
stepped forward to sabotage him. Heiner Geissler, the man Kohl had fired
as CDU general secretary ten years earlier, revealed in late November that
the boss had long kept a war chest separate
from official party accounts. "I always believed
this was wrong and it must be cleared up
now", he proclaimed without saying why he
had waited so long to put it right. Geissler
repeated his belated whistle-blowing in so many interviews that his
revenge seemed as well planned as Kohl's rumoured return. In fact, it was
not clear what Kohl was really up to, but everybody noticed that Geissler
made sure he did not succeed.

> 66 Nobody who knew Kohl could believe he had lined his own pockets 99

Nobody who knew Kohl could believe he had lined his own pockets.
Money didn't make Kohl tick, power did. But he had held sway over the
CDU for so long that he no longer differentiated between the party's good

and his own. Money was there to use as he saw fit. "I regret if the result of this procedure was a lack of transparency and control and possibly a violation of the party financing law," he said on 30 November when he admitted taking the cash. 'This is not what I wanted, I wanted to serve my party", he declared with carefully dosed remorse. When he broke his silence two weeks later to reveal a few details about the slush fund, he justified it with the need to finance CDU work in eastern Germany. "Most of the money entrusted to me – it totalled 1.5 to 2 million marks between 1993 and 1998 – was passed on to the CDU social committees for work in factories", he said.[1] This had a ring of plausibility. Kohl knew he would win or lose re-election in the east and that a strange eastern hybrid – the working class CDU voter – was a crucial factor.

But what was plausible anymore? Kohl had broken a law his own government had written, by failing to name donators for any gift over 20,000 marks. He made it worse by refusing to name them now, smugly declaring the "word of honour" he gave to keep their names secret mattered more than legal formalities. Since he did not take a personal bribe, he argued, his apology for this "mistake" should suffice. This outrageous stand convinced some of his supporters, who ignored the sin because they idolised the sinner, but the majority were not fooled. The press dubbed him "Don Kohleone" and gleefully wrote about all the "kohl-lateral damage" he was causing. Schäuble begged him to come clean for the sake of the party, but all Kohl would do was give up his title as honorary chairman of the CDU.

> 66 It's as if the head of Greenpeace were caught as part of a Mafia-like cartel that illegally disposed of toxic chemicals 99

The part was paralysed, unable to break free from Kohl even as he threatened to bring it down with him. Merkel broke the taboo in December in an open letter blasting him for breaking the law and damaging the party. With a refreshing *Ossi* directness, she wrote: "The party has to learn to walk by itself, to trust itself to take up the struggle without its old war horse and go its own way."[2] While Merkel began going her own way, Schäuble got entangled in his own scandal over an undeclared donation of 100,000 marks from the same arms dealer whose largesse in the Saudi tank deal had started the Kohl scandal rolling.

Even more shocking was what came to light in Hesse. In mid-January, the state CDU admitted it had over 7 million marks hidden in Swiss bank accounts and drew on it secretly to finance its operations. The head of this scam was the law-and-order hard-liner Manfred Kanther, who as Kohl's interior minister from 1993 to 1998 had repeatedly thundered on about the need to fight organised crime and illegal immigration. Now it turned out that, as head of the Hesse state CDU, he was running a major money laundering scheme on the side. "It's as if the head of Greenpeace were caught as part of a Mafia-like cartel that illegally disposed of toxic chemicals", Joschka Fischer fumed.[3] After Kanther quit in disgrace, it emerged that the real sum stashed away in the Alps was more like 18 million marks.

Some details of the money laundering were also stranger than fiction. Whenever he drew on these accounts, the state CDU treasurer – clearly hoping to ward off too many questions – said the new funds had been bequested by German Jewish exiles who had just died abroad. The trick seemed to have worked. Before the Kohl scandal, nobody openly questioned why exiled Jews conveniently passed away before German elections and left behind so much money to a party that called itself Christian.

By early February, the national CDU finally admitted it had run a system of slush funds and Swiss bank accounts for decades. It could trace the flow back as far as 1971 but it clearly started under Bonn's first chancellor, Konrad Adenauer, who collected secret donations from West German industry to shore up the CDU in the fight against communism. Slowly the CDU's Cold War past was exposed, revealing a party whose leaders were ready to break the law to keep the left from power. Climbing up the career ladder in that tense period, future CDU leaders such as Kohl and Kanther saw this shady financing as a justified means to the party's ends. It was such an integral part of the CDU system that the party continued using it even after the so-called Flick affair in the mid-1980s. Kohl barely wriggled out of that scandal, which exposed sham associations in his own state that laundered money from the Flick industrial empire to the CDU and FDP, and tightened party financing laws twice subsequently.

The average voter, who thought the Flick affair had finally cleaned up German politics, was stunned to see the CDU carried on as if nothing had happened. When the press speculated that former French President François Mitterrand helped finance Kohl's 1994 re-election campaign through a kickback from Elf's Leuna refinery deal, the public was ready to believe it. After all, crucial documents concerning the deal were missing from the chancellery files. Kohl vehemently denied this. It did seem strange that the French would pay a bribe to buy a rusting refinery the Germans could hardly give away. But where nothing could be proven, anything could be imagined.

The fallout from the scandal was devastating. Wolfgang Thierse, who as speaker of the Bundestag oversaw the way parties complied with the financing rules, followed the law to the letter and fined the CDU a staggering 41 million marks for omitting the slush funds from its official accounts. His credibility shattered, Schäuble quit the next day as the CDU chairman and parliamentary leader. CDU deputies soon chose, as their new leader, Friedrich Merz, 44, a conservative tax expert so distant from Kohl that he once rebuffed the chancellor for calling him by his first name. The party chairman's post was more difficult. The party's old guard preferred Volker Rühe over the grass roots favourite Merkel. But in late February, Rühe lost the Schleswig-Holstein election that had seemed a sure win for him before the scandal broke.

Merkel's election as party chairwoman on 10 April amounted to a cultural revolution for the CDU. Only 45, she was the first woman and first easterner to head a major party. A Protestant divorcee in a mostly Catholic party, she was once criticised by a Catholic bishop for living for years with a Berlin professor without marrying him (she finally did in late 1998). She spoke fluent Russian and had been in the East German communist youth movement FDJ. With her schoolmarm looks and plain speaking style, she was hardly the charismatic figure to lead the CDU out of its crisis. But she was a fresh face, untouched by scandal despite eight years in Kohl's cabinet, and the best chance the party had to win back its credibility and confidence. Kohl skipped the CDU congress in Essen, the first one he had missed since 1951, and his name was hardly mentioned in the speeches and debates there.

WINDS OF ECONOMIC CHANGE

Along with these changes on the political scene, "Germany Inc." was being shaken up in ways hardly imaginable under the old Federal Republic. The increased competition brought by globalisation and the euro was quickly making many of the old links between government and business look out-of-date if not completely irrelevant. The German business world had hardly digested the news of Schröder's tax cuts in December when another earthquake of equal magnitude struck. In early February 2000, the British telecommunications company Vodafone AirTouch bought Mannesmann in the first cross-border hostile take-over ever to take place in Germany. With a price tag of 180 billion euros, it was the world's biggest company merger to date. Significantly, Mannesmann, which had evolved from producing steel pipes to running telecommunications networks, was not an ailing dinosaur but one of Germany's healthiest companies. If even the quick and nimble could be gobbled up on the new world market, what did that say for other German companies?

The Mannesmann merger brought home the reality that globalisation was a two-way street. The future would not just consist of rich German companies snapping up firms abroad. German companies were vulnerable at home too, especially from British or American firms with the investing clout of private pension funds behind them. The concept of "shareholder value" could be more powerful in introducing change than all the traditional supervisory boards, cross-holdings and labour laws typical of "Rhineland capitalism" had been in fending it off. The old German-centred system had been inherently conservative, favouring established industries over innovative new firms. But if the banks favoured the present, the new international stock market culture would favour the future. The German economy, until now heavily weighted towards smokestack industries, would have to follow world trends more closely.

> 66 Along with these changes on the political scene, 'Germany Inc.' was being shaken up in ways hardly imaginable under the old Federal Republic 99

It would also have to follow them more quickly. And, it did. Only a month after the Mannesmann take-over, Deutsche Bank and Dresdner Bank – Germany's number one and two – announced they would merge to form the world's largest bank with $1.2 trillion in assets. They planned to sell off their costly retail banking networks in Germany and concentrate on being a global player in more lucrative activities such as asset management and wholesale banking. The two giants had held on-off talks in the past, but the Mannesmann take-over convinced them to move before some foreign competitor did. Thanks to Schröder's surprise tax reform, they and a major mutual shareholder – the Allianz AG insurance company – could also shed their cross-holdings without paying prohibitive capital gains taxes. It was the beginning of the end for Germany Inc. The thick network of industrial cross-holdings and interlocking directorships that created the Economic Miracle in the 1950s but proved too costly in the 1990s was starting to unravel.

The deal, which would have cut 16,000 jobs, broke down in April in a dispute over Deutsche's plan to sell off all or part of Dresdner's London-based investment banking unit Dresdner Kleinwort Brenson. But the die was cast. Takeovers, layoffs or bankruptcies would become more common, as would the recurring question of whether the government should help save jobs. In the medium term, the restructuring of the economy should help boost growth. But growth was only 1.4 per cent in 1999, the second-slowest rate in the European Union ahead of Italy, and unemployment at the start of the new year was still above 10 per cent.

The new Internet economy also led to new options unimaginable and probably impossible only a short while earlier. With German high-tech firms clamouring for computer experts to fill new jobs, Schröder unveiled a plan in February 2000 to invite 20,000 skilled foreigners to become a new kind of cyber-age *Gastarbeiter*. Many of them would inevitably be from India, the Third World's leading software centre. Trade unions criticised the plan, saying the unemployed should be trained first. The CDU in North Rhine-Westphalia, modelling its state election campaign on Hesse's, launched an anti-foreigner campaign with the moto *Kinder statte Inder* (i.e. Germany should train its children rather than import Indians). But even within the CDU, more and more voices spoke out for modern immigration policies based on present-day realities rather than yesterday's prejudices.

The Berlin Republic got started only months after the launch of the euro. After only one year of operation, the single currency's full effects were still far from being felt, but the major mergers pointed the way. The euro would surely act as a time bomb deeper down in the economy when it finally took over completely from national currencies in 2002. With all prices in the Eurozone denominated in euros, the inevitable comparisons would unleash downward pressure on prices, fees and taxes (seen to be too high in Germany). It was not clear exactly which direction these changes would take, but they had to move away from the regulated and anti-consumerist pattern of the past.

The dominant role the German economy played in the overall value of the euro could also open Berlin to more pressure for reform from its partners. In its first year, the euro proved quite sensitive to developments in Germany. Its value responded most strongly both to economic indicators and major news from Germany; it rose when Oskar Lafontaine quit, for example, and fell when Gerhard Schröder stepped in to rescue Holzmann. Although this caused no major problems in 1999, Berlin could expect pressure from its partners in the future if the euro's value continued to slide because Germany could not get its economy growing as strongly as its partners did.

THE EAST, TEN YEARS LATER

Ten years after the Wall's fall, eastern Germany still lagged behind the west economically. Despite all the new construction and bright city centres, the unemployment rate, at 17 per cent, was still twice as high as that in the west. The average household's purchasing power was still only 70 per cent of that in the west. *Ossis* still moved West; 182,000 left the region in 1998, 30,000 more than those (*Wessis* and transplanted easterners) who moved in the opposite direction. Most easterners were pragmatic about the region's outlook and felt no real desire to turn the clock back. But the pay differences certainly rankled.

Another problem that flared up at unification, far-right violence, continued to tarnish the east. Although nothing like the wave of xenophobic attacks in 1992–93, there were still all-too-frequent attacks on foreigners in states such as Brandenburg or Saxony. The rate of the violence there was twice as high as in the west. The culprits were still mostly drunken teenagers, still with aggressively racist views and still not organised as a political threat. The biggest difference was in the public reaction to them. Many of the same schools, churches, trade unions and political parties that were almost speechless earlier in the decade were by its end running campaigns for integration and tolerance. Courts got tougher on hate crimes. In April 2000, a judge in the eastern Baltic port of Stralsund sentenced five extremists to between four and six years in jail for the attempted murder of two Vietnamese men they had attacked the previous summer.

> 66 Ten years after the Wall's fall, eastern Germany still lagged behind the west economically 99

One of the country's most prominent *Ossis*, Joachim Gauck, struck a defensive note as he addressed the Reichstag ceremony on the tenth anniversary of the Wall's opening. Chosen to represent the East German protest movement, the man who controlled the Stasi files recalled how confused the easterners had been once they were reunited with the west. "Many felt like strangers in their own country," he reminded his mostly western audience. "Their bitterness arose from their new helplessness and disappointment. They had dreamed of paradise and woken up in North Rhine-Westphalia". But the *Ossis* had made history with their peaceful revolution and no *Wessi* could take that away from them. "We can look you in the west straight in the eye," Gauck said. "We may be poorer, but we're not broken people and certainly not beggars".

The focus on east–west differences sometimes blinded Germans from recognising how much progress had been made. During the Kohl scandal, there was so much emphasis on the lurid details that few noticed the fact that two *Ossis* – Merkel and Thierse – played central roles in trying to resolve a *Wessi* crisis. When Stasi records of tapped telephone calls emerged quoting CDU officials talking about the party's slush funds, panicked western politicians realised some skeletons in their closets could be exposed too. Like many easterners before him, Kohl fought to have his dossier kept under wraps and demanded to see his files before any publication. But *Ossis*, finally seeing some poetic justice in the Stasi saga, insisted there could not be a different standard for *Wessis*. Saxony-Anhalt premier Reinhard Höppner said Kohl could not "benefit from a west German zip code while in east everyone who ever snooped on a fellow student 20 years ago is barred from the civil service."[4]

Ironically, just as other *Ossis* were making their mark, Gregor Gysi announced he would quit as PDS parliamentary leader. A brilliant orator and tireless spokesman for the losers of reunification, Gysi gave up after hard-line leftists in the party rejected his reform policies including support for German participation in UN peacekeeping missions. The party could end up paying a heavy price for its ideological purity. Thanks to his energetic campaigning, sharp Berlin wit and frequent talk show appearances, Gysi has established the PDS as a force to be reckoned with in the east. Just as significantly, he helped integrate some of unity's staunchest opponents into the new Germany. Without his leadership, the party risked losing its way among its sectarian debates.

Almost ten years to the day after the Wall fell, Egon Krenz and Günter Schabowski learned they had to serve time in jail, after all, for the deaths along the former German–German border. On 8 November, they lost their appeals against earlier convictions for manslaughter linked to the shoot-to-kill orders East Berlin gave its border guards. The news brought back all the ambiguity of the post-unity trials. Schabowski, who had won respect in the west by being the only top former East German leader to say he had been wrong, quietly accepted the court's right to put him behind bars for three and a half years. The unpopular Krenz protested even as he began his six-year sentence, arguing he hadn't built the Wall and shouldn't be made to pay for it. Once again, the clear answer proved elusive.

WELCOME TO THE BERLIN REPUBLIC

So, like the Bundestag sitting in the renovated Reichstag building, the Berlin Republic preserved the solid fundamentals of its predecessor in Bonn but added some modern and even innovative touches. The main lines of government policy, as Gerhard Schröder, Joschka Fischer and Hans Eichel showed, amounted to a pragmatic updating of patterns set along the Rhine. The breaks in continuity, such as the new citizenship law or the support for a more competitive economy, served to bring Germany more in step with its western partners than draw it away from them. But something new was emerging from the crucial decade since the Wall was breached. After all the worrying and wondering about Germany's future, the contours of the new political landscape were visible.

The Berlin Republic was here and it promised to be:

A more open republic – the Kohl scandal did more than just discredit him and undermine his party. It ended a political machine that had influenced German politics for a quarter of a century and ensured that another would not easily spring up in its place. The scandal shook the CDU badly, prompting officials and rank-and-file members to ask why they accepted Kohl's domineering style for so long. The more honest among them admitted they had grown lazy riding along on the coat-tails of the country's best campaigner. Some even asked whether this showed the Germans had slipped back into their old-style discipline.

This fresh breeze of introspection brought more debate and competition into the main conservative party. Schäuble may have exaggerated in his farewell speech at the CDU congress in Essen when he announced "The time of backroom deals and pulling strings is over," but the thunderous applause that followed showed what the delegates thought. The renewal of the CDU in many ways mirrored the gradual transformation the SPD had already made in the 1990s from an inward-looking opposition movement to a media-age party.

The CDU's weakness threatened to open the political spectrum for some possible new formations on the right. Until the Kohl scandal, the decline of the two main parties (which by themselves had commanded up to 90 per cent of the vote until the early 1980s) had hurt the Social Democrats the most. The SPD first lost voters to the Greens in the 1980s and found the PDS poaching potential voters in the east in the 1990s. It could now be the CDU's time to face new competition. A far-right party would seem the obvious option, a German version of Austria's Freedom Party (FPÖ), but Germany has no charismatic figure such as Jörg Haider to lead one. A small group in the FDP tried in the mid-1990s to copy the FPÖ and steer the liberal party towards more right-wing policies, but it failed. The only recent far-right leader with a wider appeal, Franz Schönhuber, was too boisterously Bavarian to win nationwide support and eventually fell victim to the vicious infighting typical of extremist sectarian groups. The CSU, while closely tied to the CDU in national politics, could also step up the pressure for more right-wing policies from its bigger partner. The CDU would certainly not give up its position as the dominant party on the centre-right, but it would have to campaign and argue more openly to defend it.

A more unpredictable republic – the decline of the Kohl-style party machine gave another boost to the "media democracy" already embraced by Schröder's SPD. Image and communications played an increasingly important role in German politics in the 1990s as private and cable television boomed. In contrast to the respectful state television channels, the popular private stations set the trend for more sensation, stars and "infotainment". The proliferation of talk shows on late night television created a new chattering class of younger politicians ready to discuss any and all issues before the camera. All-news "info radios" increased the demand for fresh sound bites. Older politicians such as Kohl and Genscher were caught unprepared when television images of war in Iraq and Yugoslavia unleashed a groundswell of popular revulsion in Germany. Schröder was far more skilful riding on popular waves, but that meant he often signalled left and then turned right in a confusing policy slalom.

The move to Berlin also brought a major change to the cosy relationships that politicians used to have with the press. During the Bonn years, lines were clearly drawn. The local press was decidedly local. Investigative journalism was mostly left up to *Der Spiegel*, *Stern* and *Bild*, all from Hamburg. The national newspapers – the conservative *Frankfurter Allgemeine Zeitung* and *Die Welt* and the liberal *Süddeutsche Zeitung* and *Frankfurter Rundschau* – had clear political stands and their reporting could be partisan. Leading politicians regularly met small "circles" of like-minded reporters in Bonn to disclose the latest off-the-record news that would then turn up unsourced in the press. The real masters of this game, such as Hans-Dietrich Genscher, were quite adept at using the media to their own advantage. Working so closely with their sources, many journalists also saw themselves as part of the government process rather than as critical observers of it.

> ❝ The move to Berlin also brought a major change to the cosy relationships that politicians used to have with the press ❞

In the Berlin Republic, the government sits in the middle of the most competitive newspaper market on the continent. Berlin has three dailies of a national standard – *Der Tagesspiegel* and *Die Welt* in the west and the *Berliner Zeitung* in the east – and six smaller papers ranging from conservative to communist. Quality newspapers from the west all boosted their Berlin coverage to compete for upmarket readers there. The launch in

February 2000 of *Financial Times Deutschland*, a German-language version of London's business daily, shook up the press landscape even more. With all this new competition, the polite old rules no longer applied. Politicians soon complained that journalists were more aggressive than in Bonn. The coverage of the CDU funding scandal highlighted the changes underway. Newspapers did not line up in the usual pro- and anti-Kohl camps. All of them, from left to right, were digging away for scoops.

A more competitive republic – the dismantling of "Germany Inc." promised to shake up the consensual post-war economic system like no other change before it. The two pillars of business in the Bonn Republic – the high stakes that banks and insurance companies held in major companies and the extensive *Mittelstand* network of family-owned small and medium-sized firms – came under mounting pressure to reform. The high costs and social stability this system produced were a competitive disadvantage in a global economy where shareholder value came first. The big companies had to streamline while many *Mittelstand* firms faced the prospect of being gobbled up by nimbler competitors in the mergers and acquisitions wave rolling across Europe. The flip side of this trend was the boom in start-up companies listed on the *Neuer Markt* (New Market), Frankfurt's answer to the Nasdaq in New York. Soaring stock prices broke down investors' traditional aversion to risk while the lure of stock options – something unknown when the market started up in 1997 – radically changed the way young German managers thought about their careers. Suddenly, flexibility and fast thinking were at a premium.

The widening gap between rich and poor looked certain to bring new political challenges with it. Business was scrambling to catch up with the "Anglo-Saxon" free market model but there was no German equivalent of Ronald Reagan or Margaret Thatcher calling for a radical rollback of the welfare state. With a Social Democratic government in power, trade unions could be expected to step up pressure for protection against the layoffs that were bound to come.

A more European republic – Thomas Mann would have been pleased to see how European his Germany had turned out to be by the end of the tumultuous century. The Kosovo peace mission marked the final step in Germany's transformation from Europe's adversary to a fully integrated military partner. The public acceptance of the euro showed that Germans were willing to integrate their economy with their partners as well. The remarkable lack of a nationalist reaction to Vodafone's take-over of Mannesmann was another sign that Germans increasingly saw economic issues through the same "post-national" prism they applied to foreign policy. Dealing with semi-sovereignty was one of the most important lessons the west Germans learned. In an ever more integrated European Union, the ability to balance national interests and multilateral compromises would become increasingly crucial. Here was where the "European Germany" could enjoy an important advantage over states that still thought in narrowly national terms.

Reunification has not meant Germany automatically became the dominating power in Europe. Apart from its victory on EMU, Germany has tended to melt into the majority on many European issues. Its economic problems meant it had to cut its defence budget after the Kosovo war, limiting its options in shaping the defence union that looked set to become the next big integrating step forward for the European Union. With "chequebook diplomacy" ruled out for budgetary reasons, Berlin has actually narrowed its options to play an independent leadership role in foreign affairs. Even the much-discussed role of mediator between the European Union and prospective new members in eastern Europe dissolved during the decade. Once their EU entry negotiations began, Poland, Hungary and the Czech Republic had no more reason to take a detour through Germany to make a point in Brussels.

In fact, the role of Brussels has grown so much in recent years that the Berlin Republic often has less room to manoeuvre than Bonn did. The main issues in relations with non-EU states were handled through Brussels. German officials estimated that 70 per cent of all economic legislation came from Brussels rather than the Bundestag. In many ways, reunited Germany in fact slipped back in its partners' perceptions into the role that West Germany used to play. It was big, rich and influential, a good ally to have on one's side, but not so powerful that other states were dependent on it. Despite all the publicity and attention paid to the Berlin Republic, one could actually ask whether it was not more appropriate to speak of an emerging "Brussels Republic".

The EU's coordinated sanctions against Austria, after Jörg Haider's far-right Freedom Party joined the Vienna government in February 2000, showed this Europeanisation could be a two-way street. The past of a country like Germany (or a German-speaking one like Austria) no longer belonged to Germany alone. The vast scale of World War II and the Holocaust made it part of Europe's history as well. And Europe, as illustrated by the Haider case and a major conference on remembering the Holocaust that was held in Stockholm in January, would stand up and interfere if the Germans started to forget history's lesson. This focus on the twentieth century's horrors, sometimes described as "the politics of memory", has been growing steadily in the western world since the great ideological challenge of communism died. There is no reason to think it would ware soon.

A more lively republic – during the Bonn–Berlin debate in 1991, the flimsiest arguments the pro-Bonn lobby used were the ones recalling the ghosts of the city's past. But Berlin itself, one of the youngest of the world's great capitals, has always looked much more towards Germany's future. Twenty-first-century Germany found a microcosm of its problems within the borders of greater Berlin. The daily tensions between east and west Germans, the challenge of integrating the country's largest Turkish population, the difficulties of rebuilding the eastern economy and the enormous opportunities of a city and country at the crossroads of eastern and western Europe were all part of everyday life in Berlin. So was the pioneering spirit that all the change in the city has spawned.

Added to that was the irreverent nature of Berlin itself, the very opposite of the provincial fog that enveloped the politicians in Bonn. Where else would the biggest annual public gathering not be a civil servants' rally or anti-war protest, but the world's premier techno music festival, the Love Parade? Where else would streakers dash out in front of the Pope (as they did in 1996) or new Bundeswehr recruits hold their swearing-in ceremony (as in July 1999)? Where else could the Jewish community be revived and attract waves of Jewish immigrants from the former Soviet bloc?

> 66 The older it gets, the younger and brighter it looks 99

Before the government moved, party whips tried to avoid holding important parliamentary votes in the Reichstag because some deputies might skip the session to seek out (or recover from) Berlin's other attractions. They used to wait to get back to Bonn before trying anything uncertain. They did not have that luxury anymore.

"There is a strange phenomenon in this country," the Turkish-German Bundestag deputy Cem Özdemir, 33, said approvingly when the Federal Republic celebrated its 50th birthday in 1999.[5] "The older it gets, the younger and brighter it looks."

A more reliable republic – although it faced more uncertainty in everyday politics, the reunited state would be the most reliable Germany that its neighbours have seen for generations. Once the test of reunification was successfully passed, it became clear that the events of 1989–90 not only overcame Germany's division and ended the Cold War. The way the country reunited – in coordination with its partners and in step with further European integration – left no major unfinished business behind to fan the flames of future tensions. The new Germany was finally at peace with itself and its neighbours. The nagging "German question" was finally answered.

Germany's predicament, as a late developer among nation-states with no stable borders to define it, had haunted Europe for the better part of two centuries. Bismarck's attempt to resolve the issue created a "restless Reich" that stretched out far to the east and threatened neighbours all around. Imperial Germany tried but failed to establish a dominant position in Europe in World War I, only to see its territory shrink and large ethnic German populations get left behind as minorities in eastern Europe. Undaunted, Hitler tried only 20 years later to impose his murderous rule over all of Europe and ended in total disaster. Even the radical solution the wartime Allies used – dividing the country and imposing competing political systems – only put the issue on hold. The recurrent Western concerns about Bonn cutting a neutrality deal with Moscow to achieve reunification testified to the uncertainty the "German question" contained.

All that now belongs to a closed chapter of history. The country that emerged from reunification is the smallest united German state that ever existed. But it is also the first one with clearly marked frontiers that everyone accepts. It belongs unequivocally to the democratic West. It operated according to accepted rules rather than trying to impose itself by force on its neighbours. The onward march of European integration and globalisation means Berlin's real scope to go it alone has shrunk even though its power to do so seems to have grown. Germany remains an important country and will not hesitate to defend its interests. But it will be acting in the same category as, say, France or Britain, not as a frustrated power with a hidden agenda that its neighbours have good reason to fear.

Against such a backdrop, Kohl's scandal was a sorry end to an illustrious career. Images often mellow with time and history should be kinder to him than the headlines. The great achievements of reunification, though, remain valid no matter what. When history offered Germany a second chance, Kohl seized it. The German eagle was freed of its post-war chains, but did not simply soar away as others had done in the past. By the time the chancellor had finally ran out of steam, he had brought Germany into line with its European neighbours many times over. The Berlin Republic could start off on a solid footing. It was finally a normal country.

NOTES

1   "Was nun, Herr Kohl?" in ZDF, 16 December 1999 and *Bild*, 18 December 1999.

2   For text, see *Frankfurter Allegmeine Zeitung*, 22 December 1999.

3   *Stern*, 27 January 2000.

4   According to *Der Tagesspiegel* (10 April 2000), the Stasi began intercepting Kohl's calls as far back as 1975. It quoted former Stasi agents as saying this monitoring produced 25 to 30 pages of transcripts per week, or at least 9,000 pages from the time he became chancellor in 1982 until the end of the operation in 1989. About 30 Kohl aides were also monitored.

5   *Die Woche*, 21 May 1999.

INDEX